MICHELIN
GUIDE

TOKYO
YOKOHAMA
KAMAKURA
2011

RESTAURANTS
& HOTELS

DEAR READER

We are delighted to present our fourth edition of the MICHELIN Guide Tokyo and, with it, our first guide to Yokohama and Kamakura.

The success of our guide made quite an impact. The quality of the restaurants in Tokyo is constantly improving and we have continued to seek out those establishments offering the finest cooking.

We are pleased to announce the inclusion of Yokohama and Kamakura for the first time. In doing so, we have created a comprehensive guide to the Kanto region, now one of the most exciting gastronomic areas in the world.

You will also see that new symbols have been created to highlight those restaurants that are new to the guide as well as those that have been newly promoted. Our inspectors have also taken budgetary factors into account and, to this end, we have added a ⬢⬢ symbol, to point out establishments where one can eat for 5,000yen or less.

As part of our meticulous and confidential evaluation process, Michelin inspectors made many anonymous visits in order to fully reflect the richness and diversity of the hotel and restaurant scene. The inspectors are the eyes and ears of our readers and thus their anonymity is key to ensuring that they receive the same treatment as any other guest.

This guide is renewed and revised each year and we are committed to providing the most up to date information to ensure the success of your dining experience. This is why only this year's edition of the guide to Tokyo, Yokohama and Kamakura is worthy of your complete trust.

The decision to award a star is a collective one, based on the consensus of all the inspectors who have visited that establishment. When awarding stars, we consider a number of factors, including the quality of the ingredients, the technical skill and flair that has gone into their preparation, the clarity of flavours and the balance of the menu. Just as important is the ability to produce excellent cooking time and again. We make as many visits as we need to be sure of the quality and consistency of each establishment.

Our company's founders, Édouard and André Michelin, published the first MICHELIN Guide in France in 1900, to provide motorists with practical information about where to service and repair their cars, find accommodation or enjoy a good meal.
The star rating system for outstanding cooking was introduced in 1926. Today, these awards are the benchmark of reliability and excellence in over twenty European countries, the USA, Japan, Hong Kong and Macau.

We are always very interested to hear what you, our readers, think. Your opinions and suggestions matter greatly to us and help shape the guide, so please get in touch.
Email us at nmt.michelinguide@jp.michelin.com

We wish you the very best in your hotel and dining experiences in Tokyo, Yokohama and Kamakura.

Bon appétit!

THE MICHELIN GUIDE'S COMMITMENTS

"This volume was created at the turn of the century and will last at least as long".

This foreword to the very first edition of the MICHELIN Guide, written in 1900, has become famous over the years and the Guide has lived up to the prediction. It is read across the world and the key to its popularity is the consistency of its commitment to its readers, which is based on the following promises.

Anonymous inspections:

Our inspectors make regular and anonymous visits to restaurants and hotels to gauge the quality of products and services offered to an ordinary customer. They settle their own bill and may then introduce themselves and ask for more information about the establishment. Our readers' comments are also a valuable source of information, which we can then follow up with another visit of our own.

Independence:

Our choice of establishments is a completely independent one, made for the benefit of our readers alone. The decisions to be taken are discussed around the table by the inspectors and the editor. Inclusion in the Guide is completely free of charge.

Selection and choice:

The Guide offers a selection of the best restaurants and hotels.

This is only possible because all the inspectors rigorously apply the same methods.

Annual updates:

All the practical information, the classifications and awards are revised and updated every single year to give the most reliable information possible. Consistency: The criteria for the classifications are the same in every country covered by the Michelin Guide.

...And our aim:

To do everything possible to make travel, holidays and eating out a pleasure, as part of Michelin's ongoing commitment to improving travel and mobility.

CONTENTS

THE MICHELIN GUIDE OVER THE YEARS

Today the MICHELIN Guide and its famous red cover are known around the world. But who really knows the story behind this «travellers' bible» that has served people in many countries for many years? After winning over Europe and the United States, Bibendum – «The Michelin Man» – is now in Japan, and will relate the fantastic adventure that started in France, a long time ago...

The first steps

Everything began one fine day in 1900, when André and Édouard Michelin published a guide to be offered free of charge to motorists. It included information to help these pioneers (barely 3,500 automobiles were on the road) to travel around France: garages, town plans, sights to see, lodgings and restaurants, and so forth. The guide was an instant success and became the indispensable companion of all drivers and travellers, bar none.

On the strength of this success and driven on by the development of the motor car, the *Manufacture française* extended the scope of «the little book

with the red cover» to other European countries beginning in 1904, and a few years later (1908) published an adaptation of the *Guide France* in English.

A star is born

As of 1920, the guide was no longer free, but marketed for sale. Little by little, the practical information gave way to a wider selection of hotels and restaurants. The mysterious, daunting «Michelin inspector» was not in the picture at first. Rather, it was touring clubs and readers that contributed to the discerning selection of establishments.

The goal of officially identifying places «where one dines well» was materialized in 1926 by the *Étoile de Bonne Table* – the first Michelin star – soon to be followed by two and three-star establishments (1931 for the provinces and 1933 for Paris). The guide thus clearly focused on gastronomy and the quest for good restaurants became its real driving force.

In step with the times

During the Second World War, the guide did not appear. The post-war edition of 1945 did not use star ratings, which were applied again as of 1951, when conditions were more settled. Ever more successful, the Guide was to cover all of Western Europe as of the 1960s. In 1982, *Main Cities of Europe* was published in English, marking Michelin's decidedly European dimension.

100 years young...

2000 was a winning year for Michelin: the Guide celebrated its 100th anniversary and The Michelin Man was voted best corporate logo of the century!

More dynamic than ever, the «little red guide» took on new challenges and set off for the United States. The guide New York not only lived up to expectations, but the first edition was awarded the prize for «Best Restaurant Guide in the World». Next off the presses: San Francisco in 2006, Los Angeles and Las Vegas in 2007.

The newest challenge: discovering the best restaurants in Asia. In autumn 2007, Michelin Tokyo guide was published with a great response. Tokyo is well known as one of the world's famous capitals of fine cuisine.

Twenty countries covered in Europe, two guides to US cities, one guide to Hong Kong and Macau, two guides to Japan: as the third millennium begins, the MICHELIN Guide confirms its international dimension. Just a gleam in the eyes of the founders more than a century ago, The Michelin Man is now an international star to be proud of, carrying the Michelin tradition into the 21st century.

HOW TO USE THIS GUIDE – RESTAURANT

New entry in the guide ———

Type of cuisine ———

Name of restaurant ———

Stars for good food ———

✿ to ✿✿✿

Map references ———

Restaurant
classification
according to comfort
(more pleasant if in red)

❉   Quite comfortable

❉❉   Comfortable

❉❉❉   Very comfortable

❉❉❉❉   Top class comfort

❉❉❉❉❉   Luxury

Lowest / highest prices
for a complete meal, set
or à la carte

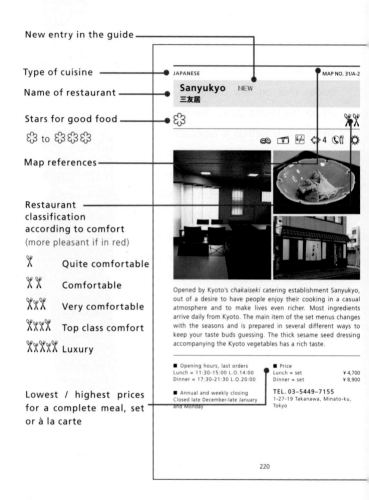

JAPANESE   MAP NO. 31/A-2

Sanyukyo   NEW
三友居

Opened by Kyoto's *chakaiseki* catering establishment Sanyukyo, out of a desire to have people enjoy their cooking in a casual atmosphere and to make lives even richer. Most ingredients arrive daily from Kyoto. The main item of the set menus changes with the seasons and is prepared in several different ways to keep your taste buds guessing. The thick sesame seed dressing accompanying the Kyoto vegetables has a rich taste.

■ Opening hours, last orders
Lunch = 11:30-15:00 L.O.14:00
Dinner = 17:30-21:30 L.O.20:00

■ Annual and weekly closing
Closed late December-late January
and Monday

■ Price
Lunch = set   ¥ 4,700
Dinner = set   ¥ 8,900

TEL. 03-5449-7155
1-27-19 Takanawa, Minato-ku,
Tokyo

220

Restaurant promoted from 1 to 2 stars or 2 to 3 stars

JAPANESE   MAP NO. 21/C-1

Sasada 🐝
笹田

✿✿   ✗

☒ 🚃 ⓒ♨

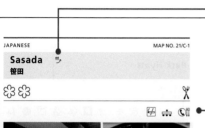

Run by Hidenobu Sasada and his wife, this small restaurant has an intimacy that guarantees individual care and attention. Try the *oden* in winter - this dish balances flavours such as Shamo gamecock skin and fried fish cakes with seasonal vegetables such as Shogoin turnip, yam and *kyo-ninjin* carrot containing generous amount of Kansai-style soup stock. The *omakase* menu ends with a serving of fragrant rice cooked in a clay pot.

■ Opening hours, last orders
Dinner = 18:00-21:00 (L.O.)

■ Annual and weekly closing
Closed mid-August, late December-
early January, Sunday and Public
Holidays

■ Price
Dinner = set   ¥ 12,600-31,500

TEL. 03-3507-5501
1-18-8 Nishishinbashi, Minato-ku,
Tokyo

221

Restaurant symbols

🕸	lunch and/or dinner for ¥ 5,000 and less
¥	Cash only
¥ LUNCH	Cash only at lunch
♿	Wheelchair access
🎋	Garden
👞	Shoes must be removed
🍴	Terrace dining
⇸	No smoking area
☒	Completely no smoking restaurant
≼	Interesting view
☞	Valet parking
🅿	Car park
🚪25	Private room with maximum capacity
🚃	Counter restaurant
ⓒ♨	Reservations required
ⓧ♨	Reservations not accepted
☼	Open Sunday
🕐	Late dining
🍇	Interesting wine list
🍶	Interesting sake list

HOW TO USE THIS GUIDE – HOTEL

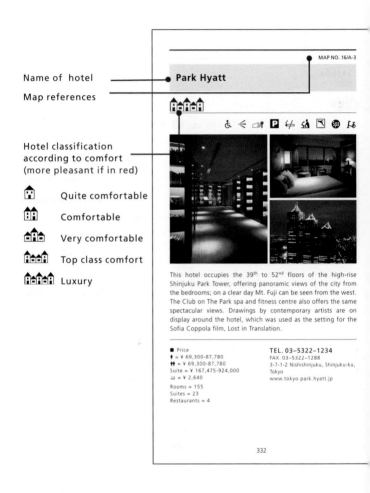

Name of hotel

Map references

Hotel classification
according to comfort
(more pleasant if in red)

Quite comfortable

Comfortable

Very comfortable

Top class comfort

Luxury

MAP NO. 16/A-3

Park Hyatt

This hotel occupies the 39th to 52nd floors of the high-rise Shinjuku Park Tower, offering panoramic views of the city from the bedrooms; on a clear day Mt. Fuji can be seen from the west. The Club on The Park spa and fitness centre also offers the same spectacular views. Drawings by contemporary artists are on display around the hotel, which was used as the setting for the Sofia Coppola film, Lost in Translation.

■ Price
† = ¥ 69,300-87,780
†† = ¥ 69,300-87,780
Suite = ¥ 167,475-924,000
⇌ = ¥ 2,640
Rooms = 155
Suites = 23
Restaurants = 4

TEL. 03–5322–1234
FAX. 03–5322–1288
3-7-1-2 Nishishinjuku, Shinjuku-ku, Tokyo
www.tokyo.park.hyatt.jp

332

Royal Park

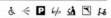

This hotel is close to Tokyo City Air Terminal and offers regular services to and from Narita and Haneda airports. Bedrooms are on the 6th to 18th floors and have bright walls and chic modern interiors. They have panoramic views and modern extras such as a computer. The private salon, swimming pool, fitness club and meeting rooms are free of charge for those on the Executive Floors. Stroll in the beautiful 5th-floor garden.

■ Price
♦ = ¥ 27,300-53,550
♦♦ = ¥ 35,700-57,750
Suite = ¥ 89,250-262,500
⇌ = ¥ 1,365
Service charge = 10%

Rooms = 395
Suites = 11
Restaurants = 6

TEL. 03-3667-1111
FAX. 03-3667-1115
2-1-1 Nihonbashikakigaracho,
Chuo-ku, Tokyo
www.rph.co.jp

Hotel symbols

  Wheelchair access

  Garden

  Interesting view from bedrooms

  Valet parking

  Car park

  No smoking bedrooms

  Conference rooms

  Indoor swimming pool

  Outdoor swimming pool

  Spa

  Fitness

TOKYO

RESTAURANTS
& HOTELS

RESTAURANTS

STARRED RESTAURANTS

All the restaurants within the Tokyo Yokohama Kamakura Guide have one, two or three Michelin Stars and are our way of highlighting restaurants that offer particularly good food.

When awarding stars there are a number of factors we consider: the quality and freshness of the ingredients, the technical skill and flair that goes into their preparation, the clarity of the flavours, the value for money and, ultimately, the taste. Of equal importance is the ability to produce excellent food not once but time and time again. Our inspectors make as many visits as necessary so that you can be sure of this quality and consistency.

A two or three star restaurant has to offer something very special in its cooking that separates it from the rest. Three stars – our highest award – are given to the very best. Cuisines in any style of restaurant and of any nationality are eligible for a star. The decoration, service and comfort levels have no bearing on the award.

Exceptional cuisine, worth a special journey.

One always eats here extremely well, sometimes superbly. Distinctive dishes are precisely executed, using superlative ingredients.

Araki	NEW	XX	Japanese Sushi	71
Esaki		XX	Japanese contemporary	96
Hamadaya	♨	XxxX	Japanese	106
Ishikawa		XX	Japanese	130
Joël Robuchon		XxXxX	French contemporary	133
Kanda		XX	Japanese	137
Koju		X	Japanese	147
Quintessence		XxX	French contemporary	200
7chome Kyoboshi	♨	X	Japanese Tempura	228
Sukiyabashi Jiro Honten		X	Japanese Sushi	237
Sushi Mizutani		X	Japanese Sushi	251
Sushi Saito		X	Japanese Sushi	255
Usukifugu Yamadaya	♨	XxX	Japanese Fugu	284
Yukimura		XX	Japanese	303

Excellent cuisine, worth a detour.
Skillfully and carefully crafted dishes of outstanding quality.

A very good restaurant in its category.
A place offering cuisine prepared to a consistently high standard.

Émun	NEW	XX	French contemporary	95
Faro		XXX	Italian	97
Florilège		XX	French contemporary	98
Fukamachi		X	Japanese Tempura	100
Gordon Ramsay		XX	French	103
Goriot	NEW	XX	Steakhouse	104
Grill Ukai	NEW	XX	European	105
Hatanaka		X	Japanese Tempura	108
Hei Fung Terrace		XX	Chinese	110
Hifumian		XX	Japanese	111
Higuchi		X	Japanese	112
Hiramatsu		XXXX	French	113
Hiromichi	NEW	XX	French	114
Hirosaku		X	Japanese	115
Hiyama	NEW	XX	Japanese Sukiyaki	117
Hosokawa		X	Japanese Soba	119
Hosokawa	NEW	X	Japanese	120
Icaro	NEW	X	Italian	121
Ichie		X	Japanese	122
Ichigo	NEW	XX	Japanese Oden	123
Ichirin		XX	Japanese	125
Iconic		XXXX	Italian contemporary	126
Ise	NEW	X	Japanese Tempura	127
Ishibashi		XX	Japanese Sukiyaki	128
Ishibashi		XX	Japanese Unagi	129
Itosho		XX	Japanese Shojin	131
Izumi	NEW	XX	Japanese Fugu	132
Kagura	NEW	XX	Japanese	135
Kamiya Nogizaka		XX	Japanese	136

Mitsuta		✗✗	Japanese Tempura	179
Momonoki		✗	Chinese	180
Monnalisa Ebisu		✗✗✗	French	181
Monnalisa Marunouchi		✗✗✗	French	182
Motoyoshi	NEW	✗	Japanese Tempura	183
Muroi		✗	Japanese	184
Muto	NEW	✗	Japanese Soba	185
Nabeya	NEW	✗✗	Japanese	186
Nagazumi	NEW	✗	Japanese	188
Nakajima		✗	Japanese	189
Nico	NEW	✗	Japanese	190
Nodaiwa		✗✗	Japanese Unagi	191
Obana	NEW	✗	Japanese Unagi	192
Ogasawara Hakushaku-tei		✗✗✗	Spanish contemporary	193
Ohara's		✗✗	French	194
Okina		✗✗	Japanese Soba	195
Ozaki		✗	Japanese	196
Pachon		✗✗	French	197
Piatto Suzuki		✗✗	Italian	198
Ranjatai	NEW	✗	Japanese Yakitori	202
Restaurant-I	NEW	✗✗	French	205
Ristorante Honda		✗✗	Italian contemporary	207
Ristorante La Primula		✗✗	Italian contemporary	208
Rokkaku		✗	Japanese Izakaya	209
Rokukaku-tei		✗	Japanese Kushiage	210
Ryuan		✗✗	Chinese	211
Ryutenmon		✗✗	Chinese	213
Sakuragaoka		✗✗	Japanese	214
Sakuragawa		✗✗	Japanese	215
Sanda	NEW	✗	Japanese Beef Specialities	216
Sangoan		✗	Japanese Soba	217

Tapas Molecular Bar	XX	Fusion	263
Tateru Yoshino Ginza	XXX	French contemporary	264
Tateru Yoshino Shiodome	XX	French contemporary	266
Tatsumura	X	Japanese	267
Tenmo	X	Japanese Tempura	268
Tetsuan	X	Japanese	269
Toriki	X	Japanese Yakitori	271
Torishiki　　NEW	X	Japanese Yakitori	272
Totoya Uoshin	XX	Japanese	273
Tsukasa	X	Japanese Fugu	276
Uchitsu	X	Japanese Tempura	277
Uchiyama	XX	Japanese	278
Uemura Honten	XX	Japanese	279
Ukai-tei Ginza	XX	Japanese Teppanyaki	280
Ukai-tei Omotesando	XXX	Japanese Teppanyaki	281
Uotoku	XX	Japanese	283
Yamaji	X	Japanese	287
Yamane	XX	Japanese Fugu	289
Yamanochaya	XX	Japanese Unagi	290
Yamasaki	X	Japanese	291
Yokota	X	Japanese Tempura	292
Yokoyama	X	Japanese Tempura	293
Yonemura	XX	Fusion	294
Yoneyama	X	Japanese	295
Yorozuya Okagesan　　NEW	X	Japanese Izakaya	296
Yoshicho	X	Japanese Yakitori	297
Yoshifuku	X	Japanese	298
Yoshihashi	XX	Japanese Sukiyaki	299
Yotaro	X	Japanese Tempura	300
Yotsuha	X	Japanese	301
Yukicho	XX	Japanese	302

RESTAURANTS BY AREA

Adachi-ku

Bird Court	NEW ❀	✗	Japanese Yakitori	80

Arakawa-ku

Obana	NEW ❀	✗	Japanese Unagi	192

Bunkyo-ku

Echikatsu	NEW ❀	✗✗✗	Japanese Sukiyaki	93
Hifumian	❀	✗✗	Japanese	111
Ishibashi	❀	✗✗	Japanese Unagi	129
Kurogi	NEW ❀	✗	Japanese	151
Shinsuke	NEW ❀	✗	Japanese Izakaya	233

Chiyoda-ku

Aimée Vibert	❀❀	✗✗✗	French	65
Akimoto	NEW ❀	✗	Japanese Unagi	68
Au Goût du Jour Nouvelle Ère	❀	✗✗	French contemporary	75
Den	NEW ❀	✗✗	Japanese contemporary	91
Fukudaya	❀❀	✗✗✗✗	Japanese	101
Grill Ukai	NEW ❀	✗✗✗	European	105
Hei Fung Terrace	❀	✗✗✗	Chinese	110
Ishibashi	❀	✗✗✗	Japanese Sukiyaki	128
La Tour d'Argent	❀	✗✗✗✗	French	159
Les Saisons	❀	✗✗✗✗	French	169
Monnalisa Marunouchi	❀	✗✗✗	French	182
Nadaman Honten Sazanka-so ❧ ❀❀		✗✗✗✗	Japanese	187
Ranjatai	NEW ❀	✗	Japanese Yakitori	202
Shofukuro	NEW ❀	✗✗	Japanese	234
Sushi Hashiguchi	NEW ❀	✗	Japanese Sushi	242
Yamanochaya	❀	✗✗	Japanese Unagi	290

NEW : new entry in the guide
❧ : restaurant promoted from 1 to 2 stars or 2 to 3 stars

Chuo-ku

Joël Robuchon		✿✿✿ ✗✗✗✗	French contemporary	133
La Table de Joël Robuchon		✿✿ ✗✗✗	French contemporary	156
Ryutenmon		✿ ✗✗✗	Chinese	213
Suzuki		✿ ✗	Japanese	257

Minato-ku

Ajiman		✿✿ ✗	Japanese Fugu	66
Aragawa		✿ ✗✗✗	Steakhouse	70
Ayumasa		✿ ✗✗	Japanese	76
Banrekiryukodo		✿ ✗✗✗	Japanese contemporary	77
Basara	NEW ✿	✗✗	Japanese	78
Casa Vinitalia	NEW ✿	✗✗✗	Italian	82
China Blue		✿ ✗✗✗	Chinese	85
Chugoku Hanten Fureika 🍃		✿✿ ✗✗	Chinese	87
Crescent		✿✿ ✗✗✗✗	French	88
Daigo		✿✿ ✗✗✗✗	Japanese Shojin	90
Florilège		✿ ✗✗	French contemporary	98
Gordon Ramsay		✿ ✗✗✗	French	103
Hatanaka		✿ ✗	Japanese Tempura	108
Hiramatsu		✿ ✗✗✗✗	French	113
Hirosaku		✿ ✗	Japanese	115
Hishinuma		✿✿ ✗✗	Japanese	116
Horikane		✿✿ ✗	Japanese	118
Hosokawa	NEW ✿	✗	Japanese	120
Ichigo	NEW ✿	✗✗	Japanese Oden	123
Itosho		✿ ✗✗	Japanese Shojin	131
Izumi	NEW ✿	✗✗✗	Japanese Fugu	132
Kadowaki		✿✿ ✗	Japanese	134
Kagura	NEW ✿	✗✗	Japanese	135
Kamiya Nogizaka		✿ ✗✗	Japanese	136
Kanda		✿✿✿ ✗✗	Japanese	137
Kanesada	NEW ✿	✗	Japanese Sushi	138
Karin	NEW ✿	✗✗✗	Chinese	139
Kien		✿ ✗	Japanese	141

Sushi Kazui	NEW ✿✿	✗✗	Japanese Sushi	249
Yoshifuku	✿	✗	Japanese	298

Shibuya-ku

Abasque	NEW ✿	✗	French	64
Ànu retrouvez-vous	NEW ✿	✗✗	French contemporary	69
Chez Matsuo	✿	✗✗✗	French	83
Émun	NEW ✿	✗✗	French contemporary	95
Esaki	✿✿✿ ✗✗		Japanese contemporary	96
Higuchi	✿	✗	Japanese	112
Ichie	✿	✗	Japanese	122
Ichirin	✿	✗✗	Japanese	125
Kogetsu	✿✿	✗	Japanese	146
Le Jeu de l'Assiette	NEW ✿	✗✗	French contemporary	162
Les Enfants Gâtés	✿	✗✗✗	French	167
Maison Paul Bocuse	✿	✗✗✗	French	172
Masa's Kitchen 47	✿	✗✗	Chinese	174
Monnalisa Ebisu	✿	✗✗✗	French	181
Okina	✿	✗✗	Japanese Soba	195
Pachon	✿	✗✗✗	French	197
Restaurant-I	NEW ✿	✗✗✗	French	205
Ristorante Aso	✿✿	✗✗✗	Italian contemporary	206
Sekiho-tei	✿✿	✗✗	Japanese	226
Shigeyoshi	✿✿	✗	Japanese	230
Uchitsu	✿	✗	Japanese Tempura	277
Ukai-tei Omotesando	✿	✗✗✗	Japanese Teppanyaki	281

Shinagawa-ku

Ise	NEW ✿	✗	Japanese Tempura	127
Makimura	🍃 ✿✿	✗✗	Japanese	173
Ohara's	✿	✗✗✗	French	194
Takahashi	✿	✗	Japanese Yakitori	259
Torishiki	NEW ✿	✗	Japanese Yakitori	272
Yoshicho	✿	✗	Japanese Yakitori	297

Shinjuku-ku

RESTAURANTS BY CUISINE TYPE

JAPANESE

Ayumasa		✿	✗✗	Shinbashi	76
Basara	NEW	✿	✗✗	Shiba	78
Chiso Sottaku		✿	✗	Ginza	86
Emori		✿	✗	Asakusa	94
Fukudaya		✿✿	✗✗✗✗	Kioicho	101
Fukuju	❀	✿✿	✗	Ginza	102
Hamadaya	❀	✿✿✿	✗✗✗	Nihonbashiningyocho	106
Hifumian		✿	✗✗	Sendagi	111
Higuchi		✿	✗	Jingumae	112
Hirosaku		✿	✗	Shinbashi	115
Hishinuma		✿✿	✗✗	Roppongi	116
Horikane		✿✿	✗	Shirokanedai	118
Hosokawa	NEW	✿	✗	Shinbashi	120
Ichie		✿	✗	Hiroo	122
Ichimonji		✿✿	✗✗	Kagurazaka	124
Ichirin		✿	✗✗	Jingumae	125
Ishikawa		✿✿✿	✗✗	Kagurazaka	130
Kadowaki		✿✿	✗	Azabujuban	134
Kagura	NEW	✿	✗✗	Akasaka	135
Kamiya Nogizaka		✿	✗✗	Akasaka	136
Kanda		✿✿✿	✗✗	Motoazabu	137
Kien		✿	✗	Akasaka	141
Kikuchi	❀	✿✿	✗	Nishiazabu	142
Kikunoi		✿✿	✗✗✗	Akasaka	143
Kisaku	NEW	✿	✗	Azabujuban	144
Kogetsu		✿✿	✗	Jingumae	146
Koju		✿✿✿	✗	Ginza	147

NEW : new entry in the guide
❀ : restaurant promoted from 1 to 2 stars or 2 to 3 stars

JAPANESE BEEF SPECIALITIES

JAPANESE CONTEMPORARY

JAPANESE FUGU

JAPANESE IZAKAYA

JAPANESE KUSHIAGE

JAPANESE ODEN

JAPANESE SHOJIN

JAPANESE SOBA

JAPANESE SUKIYAKI

JAPANESE SUSHI

Name		Awards	Utensils	Area	Page
Hatsunezushi		❀❀	XX	Nishikamata	109
Kanesada	NEW	❀	X	Roppongi	138
Kuwano		❀	X	Ginza	152
Sawada		❀❀	X	Ginza	222
Shimizu	NEW	❀	X	Shinbashi	231
Shin		❀	X	Nishiazabu	232
Sukiyabashi Jiro Honten		❀❀❀	X	Ginza	237
Sukiyabashi Jiro Roppongi	🍃	❀❀	X	Roppongi	238
Sushi Aoki Ginza		❀	X	Ginza	239
Sushi Aoki Nishiazabu		❀	X	Nishiazabu	240
Sushi Fukumoto		❀	X	Daizawa	241
Sushi Hashiguchi	NEW	❀	X	Kojimachi	242
Sushiichi	NEW	❀	XX	Ginza	243
Sushi Imamura	NEW	❀	X	Shirokane	244
Sushi Isshin Asakusa		❀	X	Asakusa	245
Sushi Isshin Ginza	NEW	❀	X	Ginza	246
Sushi Iwa		❀	X	Ginza	247
Sushi Kanesaka		❀❀	X	Ginza	248
Sushi Kazui	NEW	❀❀	XX	Nakamachi	249
Sushiko Honten		❀	X	Ginza	250
Sushi Mizutani		❀❀❀	X	Ginza	251
Sushi Musashi		❀	X	Minamiaoyama	252
Sushi Nakamura		❀	X	Roppongi	253
Sushi Ohno		❀	X	Ginza	254
Sushi Saito		❀❀❀	X	Akasaka	255
Sushiya Mao		❀	X	Ginza	256
Taku		❀❀	XX	Nishiazabu	261
Umi		❀❀	X	Minamiaoyama	282

JAPANESE TEMPURA

Name	Awards	Utensils	Area	Page
Asagi	❀	X	Ginza	74
Fukamachi	❀	X	Kyobashi	100
Hatanaka	❀	X	Azabujuban	108

JAPANESE TEPPANYAKI

JAPANESE TONKATSU

JAPANESE UNAGI

JAPANESE YAKITORI

FRENCH CONTEMPORARY

FUSION

Tapas Molecular Bar	✿	❌❌	Nihonbashimuromachi	263
Yonemura	✿	❌❌	Ginza	294

ITALIAN

Casa Vinitalia	NEW ✿	❌❌❌	Minamiazabu	82
Faro	✿	❌❌❌	Ginza	97
Icaro	NEW ✿	❌	Kamimeguro	121
Piatto Suzuki	✿	❌❌	Azabujuban	198

ITALIAN CONTEMPORARY

Argento Aso	✿✿	❌❌❌	Ginza	72
Aroma-Fresca	✿	❌❌	Ginza	73
Iconic	✿	❌❌❌	Ginza	126
Ristorante Aso	✿✿	❌❌❌	Sarugakucho	206
Ristorante Honda	✿	❌❌	Kitaaoyama	207
Ristorante La Primula	✿	❌❌	Azabujuban	208

SPANISH CONTEMPORARY

Ogasawara Hakushaku-tei	✿	❌❌❌	Kawadacho	193
Sant Pau	✿✿	❌❌❌	Nihonbashi	219

STEAKHOUSE

Aragawa	✿	❌❌	Nishishinbashi	70
Dons de la Nature	✿	❌❌	Ginza	92
Goriot	NEW ✿	❌❌	Ginza	104

RESTAURANTS SERVING LUNCH AND/ OR DINNER FOR ¥ 5,000 AND LESS

Abasque	NEW ✿	✗	lunch & dinner	64
Ajisen	NEW ✿	✗	dinner	67
Akimoto	NEW ✿	✗	lunch & dinner	68
Ànu retrouvez-vous	NEW ✿	✗✗	lunch	69
Au Goût du Jour Nouvelle Ère	✿	✗✗	lunch	75
Basara	NEW ✿	✗✗	lunch & dinner	78
Beige Alain Ducasse	✿	✗✗✗	lunch	79
Bird Court	NEW ✿	✗	dinner	80
China Blue	✿	✗✗	lunch	85
Chiso Sottaku	✿	✗	lunch	86
Chugoku Hanten Fureika ♨	✿✿	✗✗	lunch	87
Émun	NEW ✿	✗✗	lunch	95
Faro	✿	✗✗✗	lunch	97
Florilège	✿	✗✗	lunch	98
Grill Ukai	NEW ✿	✗✗✗	lunch	105
Hei Fung Terrace	✿	✗✗✗	lunch	110
Hiramatsu	✿	✗✗✗	lunch	113
Hiromichi	NEW ✿	✗✗	lunch	114
Hishinuma	✿✿	✗✗	Lunch	116
Hosokawa (Japanese Soba)	✿	✗	lunch & dinner	119
Ichie	✿	✗	lunch	122
Iconic	✿	✗✗✗	lunch	126
Ise	NEW ✿	✗	lunch & dinner	127
Ishibashi (Japanese Unagi)	✿	✗✗	lunch & dinner	129
Karin	NEW ✿	✗✗✗	lunch	139
Katsuzen	NEW ✿	✗	lunch & dinner	140
Kisaku	NEW ✿	✗	lunch	144

NEW : new entry in the guide
♨ : restaurant promoted from 1 to 2 stars or 2 to 3 stars

PARTICULARLY PLEASANT RESTAURANTS

Restaurant		Stars	Comfort	Cuisine	Page
Aimée Vibert		✿✿	XxX	French	65
Ànu retrouvez-vous	NEW	✿	XX	French contemporary	69
Araki	NEW	✿✿✿	XX	Japanese Sushi	71
Argento Aso		✿✿	XxX	Italian contemporary	72
Aroma-Fresca		✿	XxX	Italian contemporary	73
Beige Alain Ducasse		✿	XxX	French contemporary	79
Casa Vinitalia	NEW	✿	XX	Italian	82
Chez Matsuo		✿	XxX	French	83
China Blue		✿	XX	Chinese	85
Chugoku Hanten Fureika ⤴		✿✿	XX	Chinese	87
Cuisine[s] Michel Troisgros		✿✿	XxX	French contemporary	89
Daigo		✿✿	XxX	Japanese Shojin	90
Esaki		✿✿✿	XX	Japanese contemporary	96
Fukudaya		✿✿	XxXxX	Japanese	101
Grill Ukai	NEW	✿	XxX	European	105
Hamadaya ⤴		✿✿✿	XxX	Japanese	106
Hei Fung Terrace		✿	XxX	Chinese	110
Hiramatsu		✿	XxX	French	113
Ichimonji		✿✿	XX	Japanese	124
Ishikawa		✿✿✿	XX	Japanese	130
Joël Robuchon		✿✿✿	XxXxX	French contemporary	133
Kagura	NEW	✿	XX	Japanese	135
Kanda		✿✿✿	XX	Japanese	137
Kikunoi		✿✿	XxX	Japanese	143
Koju		✿✿✿	X	Japanese	147
La Bombance		✿	XX	Japanese contemporary	154
L'Atelier de Joël Robuchon		✿✿	XX	French contemporary	157
La Tour d'Argent		✿	XxXxX	French	159

NEW : new entry in the guide
⤴ : restaurant promoted from 1 to 2 stars or 2 to 3 stars

RESTAURANTS OPEN ON SUNDAY

Abasque	NEW ✿	𝕏	French	64
Aimée Vibert	✿✿	𝕏𝕏𝕏	French	65
Ànu retrouvez-vous	NEW ✿	𝕏𝕏	French contemporary	69
Araki	NEW ✿✿✿ 𝕏𝕏		Japanese Sushi	71
Argento Aso	✿✿	𝕏𝕏𝕏	Italian contemporary	72
Au Goût du Jour Nouvelle Ère	✿	𝕏𝕏	French contemporary	75
Beige Alain Ducasse	✿	𝕏𝕏𝕏	French contemporary	79
Casa Vinitalia	NEW ✿	𝕏𝕏	Italian	82
Chez Matsuo	✿	𝕏𝕏	French	83
China Blue	✿	𝕏𝕏	Chinese	85
Chugoku Hanten Fureika ❦	✿✿	𝕏𝕏	Chinese	87
Cuisine[s] Michel Troisgros	✿✿	𝕏𝕏𝕏	French contemporary	89
Daigo	✿✿	𝕏𝕏𝕏	Japanese Shojin	90
Emori	✿	𝕏	Japanese	94
Émun	NEW ✿	𝕏𝕏	French contemporary	95
Florilège	✿	𝕏𝕏	French contemporary	98
Grill Ukai	NEW ✿	𝕏𝕏	European	105
Hatanaka	✿	𝕏	Japanese Tempura	108
Hei Fung Terrace	✿	𝕏𝕏	Chinese	110
Hifumian	✿	𝕏𝕏	Japanese	111
Hiramatsu	✿	𝕏𝕏𝕏	French	113
Hiromichi	NEW ✿	𝕏𝕏	French	114
Hosokawa	✿	𝕏	Japanese Soba	119
Ichie	✿	𝕏	Japanese	122
Ichigo	NEW ✿	𝕏𝕏	Japanese Oden	123
Ichimonji	✿✿	𝕏𝕏	Japanese	124
Ichirin	✿	𝕏𝕏	Japanese	125
Iconic	✿	𝕏𝕏𝕏	Italian contemporary	126

NEW : new entry in the guide
❦ : restaurant promoted from 1 to 2 stars or 2 to 3 stars

LATE DINING

Abasque	NEW ❀	ɪ	L.O. 23:00	64
Ajiman	❀❀	ɪ	L.O. 22:00	66
Ajisen	NEW ❀	ɪ	L.O. 22:20	67
Aragawa	❀	ɪɪɪ	L.O. 22:00	70
Bird Court	NEW ❀	ɪ	L.O. 22:30	80
Casa Vinitalia	NEW ❀	ɪɪɪ	L.O. 1:00 (Sun. 20:30)	82
Chugoku Hanten Fureika ❧	❀❀	ɪɪ	L.O. 22:00	87
Den	NEW ❀	ɪɪ	L.O. 22:30	91
Emori	❀	ɪ	L.O. 23:00	94
Goriot	NEW ❀	ɪɪ	L.O. 22:00	104
Grill Ukai	NEW ❀	ɪɪɪ	L.O. 22:00	105
Harutaka ❧	❀❀	ɪ	Closing 24:00 (Sat. 22:30)	107
Hei Fung Terrace	❀	ɪɪɪ	L.O. 22:00	110
Hishinuma	❀❀	ɪɪ	L.O. 22:00	116
Hosokawa (Japanese)	NEW ❀	ɪ	Closing 23:00	120
Icaro	NEW ❀	ɪ	L.O. 1:00 (Sat. 24:00)	121
Ichigo	NEW ❀	ɪɪ	L.O. 1:00	123
Ishikawa	❀❀❀	ɪɪ	L.O. 22:00	130
Kadowaki	❀❀	ɪ	L.O. 23:00 (Sat. 22:00)	134
Kagura	NEW ❀	ɪɪ	Closing 23:00	135
Kanda	❀❀❀	ɪɪ	L.O. 22:00	137
Kisaku	NEW ❀	ɪ	L.O. 22:00	144
Koju	❀❀❀	ɪ	L.O. 23:30 (Sat. 21:30)	147
Kuikiri Eguchi	❀	ɪ	L.O. 22:00	150
Kurogi	NEW ❀	ɪ	L.O. 22:00	151

NEW : new entry in the guide
❧ : restaurant promoted from 1 to 2 stars or 2 to 3 stars

Kuwano		✿ ✗	L.O. 23:00	152
La Bombance		✿ ✗✗	L.O. 22:00	154
L'Atelier de Joël Robuchon		✿✿ ✗✗	L.O. 22:00	157
Lauburu	NEW	✿ ✗	L.O. 22:00	160
Les Saisons		✿ ✗✗✗✗	L.O. 22:00	169
Lugdunum Bouchon Lyonnais	NEW	✿ ✗	L.O. 22:00	170
Masa's Kitchen 47		✿ ✗✗	L.O. 22:30	174
Motoyoshi	NEW	✿ ✗	L.O. 23:00	183
Muroi		✿ ✗	L.O. 22:00	184
Nagazumi	NEW	✿ ✗	L.O. 22:30	188
Nico	NEW	✿ ✗	L.O. 22:00	190
Okina		✿ ✗✗	L.O. 22:30	195
Ozaki		✿ ✗	L.O. 22:00	196
Pachon		✿ ✗✗✗	L.O. 22:00 (Sun. & Public Holidays 21:00)	197
Piatto Suzuki		✿ ✗✗	L.O. 24:00	198
Ranjatai	NEW	✿ ✗	L.O. 1:00 (Sat. 21:00)	202
Ren	NEW	✿✿ ✗	L.O. 22:30	204
Ristorante Honda		✿ ✗✗	L.O. 22:00	207
Rokkaku		✿ ✗	L.O. 23:30	209
Rokukaku-tei		✿ ✗	L.O. 22:30	210
Ryugin		✿✿ ✗✗✗	L.O. 22:30	212
Sawada		✿✿ ✗	L.O. 22:00 (Sat. & Sun. 17:00)	222
Sense		✿ ✗✗✗	L.O. 22:00	227
Shigetsu	NEW	✿ ✗✗	L.O. 22:00	229
Shin		✿ ✗	Closing 23:00	232
Shunnoaji Ichi	NEW	✿ ✗	Closing 24:00	235
Signature		✿ ✗✗✗	L.O. 22:00	236
Sushi Aoki Nishiazabu		✿ ✗	Closing 23:00	240

Sushi Imamura	NEW ❄	✗	Closing 23:30 (Sat., Sun. & Public Holidays 22:00)	244
Sushi Isshin Asakusa	❄	✗	L.O. 22:00	245
Sushi Isshin Ginza	NEW ❄	✗	L.O. 23:00	246
Sushi Iwa	❄	✗	Closing 23:00 (Sun. 20:00)	247
Sushi Nakamura	❄	✗	L.O. 23:30	253
Sushi Ohno	❄	✗	L.O. 22:00	254
Sushi Saito	❄❄❄ ✗		L.O. 22:00	255
Sushiya Mao	❄	✗	L.O. 22:00	256
Taku	❄❄	✗✗	L.O. 1:00	261
Tamao	❄	✗	L.O. 23:00	262
Toriki	❄	✗	L.O. 22:00	271
Uchitsu	❄	✗	L.O. 22:00	277
Umi	❄❄	✗	L.O. 23:00	282
Usukifugu Yamadaya	☙	❄❄❄ ✗✗	L.O. 22:30	284
Yamaji	❄	✗	L.O. 22:00	287
Yorozuya Okagesan	NEW ❄	✗	L.O. 22:15	296
Yoshicho	❄	✗	L.O. 22:30	297
Yotaro	❄	✗	L.O. 22:00	300

RESTAURANTS WITH PRIVATE ROOMS

Aimée Vibert		✿✿	४४४	capacity 4	65
Ajiman		✿✿	४	capacity 12	66
Akimoto	NEW	✿	४	capacity 20	68
Ànu retrouvez-vous	NEW	✿	४४	capacity 8	69
Aragawa		✿	४४	capacity 6	70
Argento Aso		✿✿	४४४	capacity 10	72
Ayumasa		✿	४४	capacity 16	76
Banrekiryukodo		✿	४४	capacity 10	77
Basara	NEW	✿	४४	capacity 18	78
Bird Court	NEW	✿	४	capacity 8	80
Chez Matsuo		✿	४४	capacity 16	83
Chikuyo-tei Honten		✿	४४	capacity 25	84
China Blue		✿	४४	capacity 10	85
Chugoku Hanten Fureika 🍃		✿✿	४४	capacity 100	87
Crescent		✿✿	४४४	capacity 24	88
Cuisine[s] Michel Troisgros		✿✿	४४४	capacity 12	89
Daigo		✿✿	४४४	capacity 48	90
Den	NEW	✿	४४	capacity 6	91
Echikatsu	NEW	✿	४४	capacity 85	93
Esaki		✿✿✿	४४	capacity 10	96
Fugu Fukuji		✿✿	४	capacity 15	99
Fukudaya		✿✿	४४४४	capacity 40	101
Fukuju	🍃	✿✿	४	capacity 8	102
Grill Ukai	NEW	✿	४४	capacity 10	105
Hamadaya	🍃	✿✿✿	४४४	capacity 60	106
Harutaka	🍃	✿✿	४	capacity 4	107
Hei Fung Terrace		✿	४४	capacity 12	110

Name				Capacity	Page
Hifumian		❀	XX	capacity 6	111
Higuchi		❀	X	capacity 2	112
Hiramatsu		❀	XXX	capacity 14	113
Hirosaku		❀	X	capacity 4	115
Hiyama	NEW	❀	XX	capacity 50	117
Horikane		❀❀	X	capacity 16	118
Ichimonji		❀❀	XX	capacity 14	124
Ichirin		❀	XX	capacity 8	125
Iconic		❀	XXX	capacity 40	126
Ise	NEW	❀	X	capacity 8	127
Ishibashi (Japanese Sukiyaki)		❀	XX	capacity 30	128
Ishibashi (Japanese Unagi)		❀	XX	capacity 20	129
Ishikawa		❀❀❀	XX	capacity 6	130
Itosho		❀	XX	capacity 25	131
Izumi	NEW	❀	XX	capacity 12	132
Joël Robuchon		❀❀❀	XXXX	capacity 30	133
Kadowaki		❀❀	X	capacity 6	134
Kagura	NEW	❀	XX	capacity 8	135
Kamiya Nogizaka		❀	XX	capacity 12	136
Kanda		❀❀❀	XX	capacity 6	137
Karin	NEW	❀	XX	capacity 60	139
Katsuzen	NEW	❀	X	capacity 4	140
Kien		❀	X	capacity 8	141
Kikunoi		❀❀	XXX	capacity 10	143
Kisaku	NEW	❀	X	capacity 6	144
Kodama		❀❀	XX	capacity 8	145
Kogetsu		❀❀	X	capacity 6	146
Koju		❀❀❀	X	capacity 10	147
Komuro		❀❀	X	capacity 4	148
Kurogi	NEW	❀	X	capacity 15	151
La Bombance		❀	XX	capacity 8	154
La Tour		❀	XX	capacity 12	158
La Tour d'Argent		❀	XXXX	capacity 30	159

Sakuragawa		✿	✗✗	capacity 20	215
Sankame		✿	✗	capacity 6	218
Sant Pau		✿✿	✗✗✗	capacity 8	219
Sanyukyo	NEW	✿	✗✗	capacity 4	220
Seisoka		✿✿	✗✗✗	capacity 10	225
Sekiho-tei		✿✿	✗✗	capacity 10	226
Sense		✿	✗✗✗	capacity 18	227
Shigetsu	NEW	✿	✗✗	capacity 8	229
Shigeyoshi		✿✿	✗	capacity 10	230
Shofukuro	NEW	✿	✗✗	capacity 24	234
Signature		✿	✗✗✗	capacity 10	236
Sushi Aoki Ginza		✿	✗	capacity 10	239
Sushi Aoki Nishiazabu		✿	✗	capacity 6	240
Sushi Fukumoto		✿	✗	capacity 6	241
Sushiko Honten		✿	✗	capacity 10	250
Sushiya Mao		✿	✗	capacity 8	256
Takeyabu		✿	✗✗	capacity 10	260
Taku		✿✿	✗✗	capacity 6	261
Tamao		✿	✗	capacity 14	262
Tateru Yoshino Ginza		✿	✗✗✗	capacity 4	264
Tateru Yoshino Shiba	🥢	✿✿	✗✗✗	capacity 12	265
Tateru Yoshino Shiodome		✿	✗✗✗	capacity 28	266
Tatsumura		✿	✗	capacity 8	267
Tenmo		✿	✗	capacity 8	268
Tomura		✿✿	✗✗	capacity 14	270
Totoya Uoshin		✿	✗✗	capacity 6	273
Tsujitome		✿✿	✗✗✗	capacity 20	275
Tsukasa		✿	✗	capacity 8	276
Uchitsu		✿	✗	capacity 4	277
Uchiyama		✿	✗✗	capacity 16	278
Uemura Honten		✿	✗✗✗	capacity 12	279
Ukai-tei Ginza		✿	✗✗✗	capacity 9	280
Ukai-tei Omotesando		✿	✗✗✗	capacity 8	281

Abasque NEW

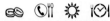

This is the place to enjoy Basque cuisine and wine presented by the owner-sommelier and his chef, who trained in France, working as a team. The menu, featuring dishes characteristic of the Basque region on the Spanish-French border, changes with each season. Choose a main dish after first trying some tapas or, as we recommend, order the *dégustation* menu which includes specialities like cod *pil pil* and Basque-style pork roast.

■ Opening hours, last orders
Lunch = Wed.- Fri. 11:30-13:30 (L.O.)
Sun. and Public Holidays
12:00-15:00 (L.O.)
Dinner = 18:00-23:00 (L.O.)

■ Annual and weekly closing
Closed mid-August, late December-
early January and Monday

■ Price
Lunch = set   ¥ 1,575-2,100
          set Sun.   ¥ 3,675-4,935
Dinner = set   ¥ 4,935-6,300
          à la carte ¥ 5,000-7,000
Seat charge = ¥525/person (dinner)

TEL. 03–5468–8908
2-12-11 Shibuya, Shibuya-ku,
Tokyo
www.esdesign.biz

Aimée Vibert

This restaurant near Kojimachi Station is housed in an Ile de France-style mansion and is named after the rose, also known as *Bouquet de la Mariée*. Traditional French cuisine is the draw: the hors d'oeuvre of crustacean gelée with sea urchin and cauliflower cream is an example. Dishes in which the meat is cooked in a cocotte provide wonderful balance as the accompanying vegetables become saturated with the flavour of the meat.

■ Opening hours, last orders
Lunch = 11:30-14:00 (L.O.)
Dinner = 18:00-21:00 (L.O.)

■ Annual and weekly closing
Closed mid-August, late December-early January and Tuesday

■ Price
Lunch = set   ¥ 5,250-8,400
        à la carte ¥ 10,000-19,000
Dinner = set   ¥ 10,500-21,000
        à la carte ¥ 10,000-19,000
Private room fee = ¥ 21,000
Service charge = 10%

TEL. 03–5216–8585
14-1 Nibancho, Chiyoda-ku, Tokyo
www.aimeevibert.com

Ajiman

味満ん

❀❀

This cosy restaurant is run by owner-chef Sadao Matsubara and four family members. He only uses firm, flavoursome wild *shiro tora-fugu* and most diners opt for *omakase*. Other *fugu* dishes include grilled *shirako* full of aroma, *shioyaki*, *kara-age*, *shabu-shabu* and rich *zosui* with *shirako* to end with. While *fugu* is considered a winter dish, here it can be enjoyed up to May. The name's literal translation is 'filled with taste'.

■ Opening hours, last orders
Dinner = 18:00-24:00 L.O.22:00

■ Annual and weekly closing
Closed July, August, 31 December-4 January and Sunday from April-June

■ Price
Dinner = set   ¥ 35,000-45,000
                à la carte¥ 30,000-40,000

TEL. 03-3408-2910
3-8-8 Roppongi, Minato-ku, Tokyo

Ajisen   NEW
味泉

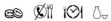

Shinichi Araki, who worked at the market in Tsukiji for 8 years, uses his trained eye to pick out quality seafood. Always packed in the evenings, the restaurant's specialities are homemade *satsuma age* and *nianago*. He is also proud of his sake selection, from prominent brands to obscure breweries. Dishes arrive quickly and in a random order so it's best to order as you go along. There is a 2½ hour limit on table usage.

■ Opening hours, last orders
Dinner = 17:30-23:00 L.O.22:20

■ Annual and weekly closing
Closed mid -August, late December-
early January,Sunday and Public
Holidays

■ Price
Dinner = set   ¥ 4,500-6,000
        à la carte   ¥ 3,500-7,000

TEL. 03–3534–8483
1-18-10 Tsukishima, Chuo-ku,
Tokyo

Akimoto   NEW
秋本

Taking Exit 3 from Kojimachi Station and look for the sign with the hiragana 'う'. The *shirayaki* is almost too soft to pick up with chopsticks, with the outside browned to seal in flavour; the *unaju* is served in a Wajima lacquered box separating the rice and the *kabayaki*. The *unagi-maki*, covered in stock, has a slightly sweet taste. It gets crowded at lunch, so arrive early. The *tatami* room is available by reservation only.

■ Opening hours, last orders
Lunch = 11:30-14:30 L.O.14:00
Dinner = 17:00-20:30 L.O.20:00

■ Annual and weekly closing
Closed mid-August, late December-
early January, Sunday, 2nd Saturday
of each month and Public Holidays

■ Prices
Lunch = à la carte ¥ 2,000-6,000
Dinner = set   ¥ 9,000-13,500
        à la carte ¥ 2,000-6,000
Private room fee = 15%
                  (lunch 10%)
Service charge = 10% (dinner)

TEL.03-3261-6762
3-4 Kojimachi, Chiyoda-ku, Tokyo

Ànu retrouvez-vous   NEW

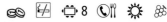

The owner-chef's philosophy is to pick the best ingredients and maximise their flavour. Vegetables are from farms in Nagano and Ishikawa; fish comes directly from his hometown of Hagi City, Yamaguchi. Placing importance on aroma and texture, the set menus consist of a large number of small plates. The speciality is duck *rôti*, and the champagne is reasonably priced. Make your reservations early as it is always crowded.

■ Opening hours, last orders
Lunch = 11:30-16:00 L.O.13:30
Dinner = 18:00-24:00 L.O.21:00

■ Annual and weekly closing
Closed late December-early January
and Tuesday

■ Prices
Lunch = set   ¥ 3,500-12,000
Dinner = set   ¥ 8,000-18,000
          à la carte ¥ 8,000-12,000
Service charge = 10%

TEL.03-5422-8851
5-19-4 Hiroo, Shibuya-ku, Tokyo
www.restaurant-anu.com

Aragawa

Emphasis is on unchanging values and creating the same feel as the original restaurant which opened in 1967 and moved here in 2009. There are no menus - the maître d' offers a verbal explanation. Tajima-Sanda beef from Hyogo is used exclusively. The meat is seasoned only with salt and pepper; the steaks are broiled on a brick stove using Bincho charcoal. Sirloin is the main choice; if you prefer tenderloin check availability.

■ Opening hours, last orders
12:00-22:00 (L.O.)

■ Annual and weekly closing
Closed late December-early January,
Sunday and Public Holidays

■ Price
Lunch = set   ¥ 52,500
           à la carte ¥ 40,000-80,000
Dinner = set   ¥ 52,500
           à la carte ¥ 40,000-80,000
Service charge = 12%

TEL. 03-3438-1867
3-23-11 Nishishinbashi, Minato-ku,
Tokyo

Araki  NEW
あら輝

✿ ✿ ✿   ✗✗

In 2010, this popular restaurant in Kaminoge opened a long-awaited branch in Ginza. Mitsuhiro Araki has an obsession with tuna. Letting the top quality tuna stand for a few days to bring out the flavour, he prepares five in a row of *akami*, *chu-toro* and *o-toro*; rice is salted and unsweetened to go with it. He is also a man of action, growing rice and going on fishing expeditions. His impulse for exploration knows no bounds.

■ Opening hours, last orders
Lunch = 12:00-14:00
Dinner = 18:00-20:30 (L.O.)

■ Annual and weekly closing
Closed early January, mid-August
and Wednesday

■ Price
Lunch = set   ¥ 21,000-26,250
Dinner = set   ¥ 21,000-26,250

TEL. 03-3545-0199
5-14-14 Ginza, Chuo-ku, Tokyo

Argento Aso

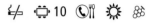

Bright and sunny by day, romantic and softly lit by night, the restaurant is elegant and graceful. Lobster with white balsamic vinegar jelly, served as an hors d'oeuvre, and spaghetti alla pescatora, with the seafood served separately, are house specialities. Dishes come on glass, adding a touch of fun to the experience. The extensive wine list is big on Italian and French regions, but it also has a wide selection of Armagnac.

■ Opening hours, last orders
Lunch = 11:30-15:30 L.O.13:30
Dinner = 18:00-23:00 L.O.20:30

■ Annual and weekly closing
Closed 1 January and Wednesday

■ Price
Lunch = set   ¥ 5,250-10,500
         à la carte ¥ 13,000-19,000
Dinner = set   ¥ 10,500-21,000
         à la carte ¥ 13,000-19,000
Service charge = 13%

TEL. 03-5524-1270
Zoe Ginza 8F,
3-3-1 Ginza, Chuo-ku, Tokyo
www.hiramatsu.co.jp/restaurants/
argento-aso

Aroma-Fresca

Relocated for a second time, the restaurant is now in Ginza making use of the luxurious top floor of a 12-storey building. The menu remains unchanged: dishes are light with delicate seasoning to fully bring out the freshness and natural flavours of the ingredients without overdoing the preparations. The service team also leave a favourable impression. After the meal, relax in the salon. The hard part is getting reservations.

■ Opening hours, last orders
Dinner = 17:30-23:00 L.O.20:30

■ Annual and weekly closing
Closed mid-August, late December-
early January, Sunday and Monday

■ Price
Dinner = set   ¥ 16,000-20,000

TEL. 03-3535-6667
Ginza Trecious 12F,
2-6-5 Ginza, Chuo-ku, Tokyo

Asagi
あさぎ

Owner-chef Hiroshi Asagi runs this modern tempura restaurant with his family. Using a large frying pot at the centre of the cooking counter, he delicately fries each ingredient using sesame oil. Bite into the shrimp *tempura* and it feels as if you are eating pure shrimp as his unique technique allows the seafood flavour to permeate the batter. He relocated from Sendagi district in 1999 and visits nearby Tsukiji market daily.

■ Opening hours, last orders
Lunch = Mon.-Fri. 12:00-13:00 (L.O.)
except Public Holidays
Dinner = 17:30-20:30 (L.O.)

■ Annual and weekly closing
Closed Golden week, mid-August,
late December-early January,
Sunday and Public Holiday
Mondays

■ Price
Lunch = set   ¥ 5,775-7,875
Dinner = set   ¥ 12,000-15,000

TEL. 03-3289-8188
6-4-13 Ginza, Chuo-ku, Tokyo

Au Goût du Jour Nouvelle Ère

The fresh, uncomplicated food is complemented here with light, fragrant sauces. It considers its cuisine to be of a 'new era,' as the name suggests. The flavour-laden pork back ribs and shoulder loin, cooked for two days and served with a port sauce, is one recommendation. The chef was a former pâtissier so dinner sees a variety of desserts. In winter, try apple chiboust with salted caramel ice cream. Irregular closing times.

■ Opening hours, last orders
Lunch = 11:00-13:30 (L.O.)
Dinner = 18:00-21:30 (L.O.)

■ Annual and weekly closing
Closed 1 January

■ Price
Lunch = set   ¥ 3,800-10,000
Dinner = set   ¥ 7,500-18,000
                 à la carte ¥ 9,000-10,000

TEL. 03-5224-8070
Shin-Marunouchi Building 5F,
1-5-1 Marunouchi, Chiyoda-ku,
Tokyo
www.augoutdujour-group.com/no

Ayumasa
鮎正

≠/ 🗂 16 🕐🍴

Welcome to the Shimane of Shinbashi restaurant where produce from the owner-chef's home prefecture is brought to life in its cuisine. The speciality is *ayu*; the most popular dish is roasted *ayu*, especially with the roe in October. The *ayu* is smoked with straw and timed to your reservation, so try not to be late. From late August to mid-September, crab from Takatsugawa is served and rare natural *suppon* from September.

■ Opening hours, last orders
Dinner = 17:00-22:00 L.O.21:30

■ Annual and weekly closing
Closed late December-early January,
Sunday and Public Holidays

■ Price
Dinner = set   ¥ 11,550-15,750
            à la carte ¥ 12,000-20,000
Private room fee = 10%

TEL. 03-3431-7448
4-21-14 Shinbashi, Minato-ku,
Tokyo

Banrekiryukodo
万歴龍呼堂

The restaurant features a simple, modern décor and its cavern-like basement has semi-private table seating. The menu changes monthly and features items like soup flavoured with the first tea of the season and smoke-scented broiled fish. Offering a new style of Japanese cuisine while respecting tradition, the set menus include meat dishes that go well with wine. Similar flair and individuality is reflected in the tableware.

■ Opening hours, last orders
Lunch = 11:30-13:30 (L.O.)
Dinner = 18:00-21:00 (L.O.)

■ Annual and weekly closing
Closed late December-early January
and Sunday

■ Price
Lunch = set   ¥ 6,300-12,600
Dinner = set   ¥ 8,400-31,500
Service charge = 10%

TEL. 03-3505-5686
2-33-5 Higashiazabu, Minato-ku,
Tokyo
www.banreki.com

Basara NEW
ばさら

We recommend the *tomato sukiyaki* speciality, a healthy choice that is available all year round, prepared and served by the waiting staff. First the tomatoes go in, followed by the onions and then the beef; the sweet *warishita* draws out the flavours. To end the meal, the remaining *warishita* is used to dress tomatoes and *tagliatelle* for some Japanese-style Italian. Prices are reasonable. Also popular is the *lettuce shabu-shabu*.

■ Opening hours, last orders
Lunch = 11:30-15:00 L.O.14:00
Dinner = 17:30-23:00 L.O.21:00

■ Annual and weekly closing
Closed mid-August, late December-early January, Sunday and Public Holidays

■ Price
Lunch = set   ¥ 900-10,000
         à la carte   ¥ 6,000-18,000
Dinner = set   ¥ 5,000-15,000
         à la carte   ¥ 6,000-18,000
Private room fee = ¥ 8,000-20,000
Service charge = 10% (dinner)

TEL. 03-5444-6700
DNI Mita Building B1F,
3-43-16 Shiba, Minato-ku, Tokyo

Beige Alain Ducasse

A collaboration between fashion brand Chanel and restaurateur Alain Ducasse. The cutting-edge French fare incorporates Japanese ingredients, such as vegetables from Kamakura, veal from Hokkaido and Meishan pork from Ibaraki. In spring 2010, a trusted Japanese chef became head chef. For dessert, try Carré Chanel, a concoction of chocolate, praline and hazelnut ice cream. Guests can also enjoy drinks on the rooftop terrace.

■ Opening hours, last orders
Lunch = 11:30-16:30 L.O.14:30
Dinner = 18:00-23:30 L.O.21:30

■ Annual and weekly closing
Closed late December-early January
and Monday

■ Price
Lunch = set　　　¥ 5,000-12,000
　　　à la carte ¥ 15,500-17,000
Dinner = set　　¥ 13,000-22,000
　　　à la carte ¥ 14,500-17,000
Service charge = 10%

TEL. 03-5159-5500
Chanel Building 10F,
3-5-3 Ginza, Chuo-ku, Tokyo
www.beige-tokyo.com

Bird Court   NEW

The owner-chef's face is a picture of seriousness as he arranges the charcoal in the grill of this *yakitori* restaurant, where you bump elbows with the person sitting beside you. He fans the charcoal, rotates the skewers and cuts off the burnt parts. The Okukuji *shamo* is juicy and firm and the chickens are cut into even pieces. If you like rare pieces like the *sot-l'y-laisse* (chicken oysters) then you should get here early.

■ Opening hours, last orders
Dinner = 17:30-23:00 L.O.22:30

■ Annual and weekly closing
Closed mid-August, late December-
early January, Sunday and Monday

■ Price
Dinner = set   ¥ 4,200-6,300
              à la carte ¥ 3,000-8,000
Seat charge = ¥ 300/person

TEL. 03–3881–8818,
3-68 Senju, Adachi-ku, Tokyo

Bird Land

 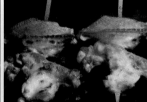

The chicken and eggs are from the okukuji breed, raised in Ibaraki. The menu includes *wasabi-yaki*, along with more original items like homemade patties and chicken breast with basil. The ingredients of the kebab vary but sometimes include chicken oysters - this was the first restaurant to serve them as part of the *yakitori*, at the suggestion of a customer. There are two starting times for dinner on Fridays and Saturdays.

■ Opening hours, last orders
Dinner = 17:00-22:00 L.O.21:30

■ Annual and weekly closing
Closed late December-early January,
Sunday, Monday and Public
Holidays

■ Price
Dinner = set   ¥ 6,300-8,400
            à la carte ¥ 6,000-10,000
Service charge = 10%

TEL. 03-5250-1081
Tsukamoto Sozan Building B1F,
4-2-15 Ginza, Chuo-ku, Tokyo
www.ginza-birdland.sakura.ne.jp

Casa Vinitalia   NEW

Sit on the terrace side for a feeling of spaciousness. Placing importance on freshness, the chef uses many domestically grown vegetables in dishes like vegetable *cocotte* and the colourful *bagna càuda* with about 20 different raw vegetables. We recommend the crab *riso pilaf*. There are also plenty of handmade pasta dishes. It is difficult to get reservations, but if you call at 2pm, there are sometimes openings for that evening.

■ Opening hours, last orders
Dinner = 17:30-1:00 (L.O.)
Sun. 14:30-20:30 (L.O.)

■ Annual and weekly closing
Closed mid-August, late December-early January and Monday

■ Price
Dinner = set   ¥ 7,500
            à la carte ¥ 6,000-10,500

TEL. 03-5439-4110
1-7-31 Minamiazabu, Minato-ku, Tokyo

FRENCH MAP NO. 27/A-1

Chez Matsuo

16

Chez Matsuo opened in 1980 as the city's first restaurant within a detached house. Just off the entrance is a salon bar with a fireplace and furniture from the early 1900s; private rooms past the bar have wooden flooring and panelling. The lobster mi-cuit flavoured with argan oil and paired with small turnips marinated in raspberry vinegar is particularly good; another recommendation is stewed baby boar with white bean purée.

■ Opening hours, last orders
Lunch = 12:00-15:00 L.O.13:00
Dinner = 18:00-23:00 L.O.20:30

■ Annual and weekly closing
Closed 31 December-4 January

■ Price
Lunch = set ¥ 8,400
Dinner = set ¥ 21,000-52,500
Private room fee = ¥ 31,500
Service charge = 10%

TEL. 03–3485–0566
1-23-15 Shoto, Shibuya-ku, Tokyo
www.chez-matsuo.co.jp

Chikuyo-tei Honten
竹葉亭 本店

🍴

✈ 🚐 25 ☎

This *unagi* restaurant has been in business since the late Edo Period and started out as an eatery for *samurai* in town to safeguard their lord's Edo mansion. *Unagi* is generally sent from Shizuoka and Aichi; for *kabayaki*, *unagi* fillets are broiled and basted with the house's special sauce simply made by combining soy sauce and *mirin*. *Shirayaki* is enjoyed with a little *wasabi* and soy sauce. A relaxed atmosphere prevails.

■ Opening hours, last orders
Lunch = 11:30-15:00 L.O.14:30
Dinner = 16:30-21:00 L.O.20:00

■ Annual and weekly closing
Closed late December-early January,
Sunday and Public Holidays

■ Price
Lunch = set   ¥ 7,350-10,500
Dinner = set   ¥ 12,600-14,700
Service charge = 10%

TEL. 03-3542-0789
8-14-7 Ginza, Chuo-ku, Tokyo

China Blue

Up on the 28th floor of the Conrad hotel, lights covered in blue cloth hang from the 8m high ceiling and the room provides views of Hamarikyu Onshi Teien Garden and the Tokyo Bay area. Of the three private rooms, the glass corner one is particularly popular. Dishes are served Western style and guests can enjoy not only traditional Cantonese cuisine but also contemporary creations accented with flavours of other Asian countries.

■ Opening hours, last orders
Lunch = 11:30-14:00 (L.O.)
Dinner = 17:30-21:00 (L.O.)

■ Price
Lunch = set ¥ 3,900-7,800
à la carte ¥ 6,000-13,500
Dinner = set ¥ 12,000-22,800
à la carte ¥ 6,000-13,500
Private room fee = ¥15,000-25,000

TEL. 03–6388–8000
Conrad Hotel 28F,
1-9-1 Higashishinbashi,
Minato-ku, Tokyo
www.conradtokyo.co.jp

Chiso Sottaku
馳走 啐啄

  LUNCH

This small restaurant is found in Ginza 6-chome in a building right in front of the parking lot of the Kojun Building. Shigemitsu Nishizuka takes delight in the tea ceremony and adheres to the philosophy of cherishing every encounter. Dishes are well-balanced, such as the jellied spiny lobster and the large, tenderised abalone. There are three *omakase* menus at dinner; the priciest one requires pre-ordering the day before.

■ Opening hours, last orders
Lunch = Mon.-Fri. 11:30-13:30 (L.O.)
Dinner = 18:00-22:00 L.O.20:00

■ Annual and weekly closing
Closed mid-August, late December-early January, Sunday and Public Holidays

■ Price
Lunch = set   ¥ 3,990-7,350
Dinner = set   ¥ 10,500-15,750
Service charge = 10%

TEL. 03–3289–8010
Urano Building 2F,
6-7-7 Ginza, Chuo-ku, Tokyo

Chugoku Hanten Fureika

中国飯店 富麗華

P 📺 100 ☎ ☀ 🕐

The menu offers a large variety of Cantonese and Shanghainese dishes, which come not only on large plates but are also served in individual portions. Recommended is the roasted pork dish prepared by the specialist Grill and Roast food chef. Shanghai soup dumplings bursting with juicy meat are prepared from scratch. Live performances featuring classical Chinese instruments showcase the subtlety and depth of Chinese culture.

■ Opening hours, last orders
Lunch = 11:30-14:00 (L.O.)
Dinner = 17:30-22:00 (L.O.)

■ Annual and weekly closing
Closed 31 December-1 January

■ Price
Lunch = set   ¥ 2,000-6,000
        à la carte ¥ 6,000-12,000
Dinner = set   ¥ 8,400-33,600
        à la carte ¥ 6,000-12,000
Service charge = 10% (dinner)

TEL. 03-5561-7788
3-7-5 Higashiazabu, Minato-ku, Tokyo
www.chuugokuhanten.com/
storefureika

Crescent

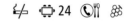

The house speciality, *compression de tomate*, consists of three layers: mousse, tartar and jelly. Lamb comes from Shiranuka in Hokkaido and various cuts are roasted on the bone and served on one plate with a typical seasonal sauce —salted lemon sauce in summer, for example, or truffle sauce in winter. Crescent offers three different *omakase* set menus. This restaurant is particularly suitable for those special occasions.

■ Opening hours, last orders
Dinner = 17:30-22:30 L.O.20:30

■ Annual and weekly closing
Closed mid-August, late December-early January, Sunday and Public Holidays

■ Price
Dinner = set   ¥ 18,900-31,500
Service charge = 10%

TEL. 03–3436–3211
1-8-20 Shibakoen, Minato-ku, Tokyo
www.restaurantcrescent.com

Cuisine[s] Michel Troisgros

❀ ❀   ✗✗✗✗

♿ 🚭 ☞ 🅿 📺12 ☎️🍴 ☀ ✿

Michel Troisgros is the third-generation owner-chef of Troisgros, a famed restaurant in Roanne, northwest of Lyons, and looks to Japanese cuisine as a source of inspiration. The chefs entrusted by him offer contemporary French cuisine with accents of citrus fruit, herbs and spices incorporating Japanese tastes. Aside from poultry, all ingredients are from Japan. Specialities include 'Cuisses de grenouilles sautées au tamarin'.

■ Opening hours, last orders
Lunch = 11:30-14:00 (L.O.)
Dinner = 18:00-21:30 (L.O.)

■ Annual and weekly closing
Closed Wednesday except
December

■ Price
Lunch = set   ¥ 5,300-10,500
        à la carte   ¥ 12,500-17,500
Dinner = set   ¥ 14,700-18,900
        à la carte   ¥ 12,500-17,500
Service charge = 10%

TEL. 03-5321-3915
Hyatt Regency Hotel 1F,
2-7-2 Nishishinjuku, Shinjuku-ku,
Tokyo
www.troisgros.com

Daigo
醍醐

Shojin ryori is meat-free and based on the concept of appreciating simple food. Various root vegetables are used as a starting point. Close attention is paid to seasonal ingredients and, in the *kaiseki* style, dishes come one at a time. Various flavoured broths are used: dried bonito, kelp and *shiitake* mushroom. The dining room exudes the refined *wabi-sabi* essence of Zen Buddhism, complemented by *ikebana* floral arrangements.

■ Opening hours, last orders
Lunch = 12:00-15:00 L.O.14:00
Dinner = 17:00-22:30 L.O.20:00

■ Annual and weekly closing
Closed early January

■ Price
Lunch = set   ¥ 10,000-19,000
Dinner = set   ¥ 15,000-19,000
Service charge = 15%

TEL. 03-3431-0811
Forest Tower 2F,
2-3-1 Atago, Minato-ku, Tokyo
www.atago-daigo.com

Den NEW
傳

The young owner-chef here uses only domestic ingredients and places importance on natural flavours. The salad is prepared with morning-fresh vegetables garnished with chopped *kombu*; cold *yuba chawanmushi* is topped with béchamel sauce made from soy milk. While Western-style techniques are incorporated, the basis is Japanese cuisine. The serving dishes, made by a friend, highlight the food. Recommended for the health-conscious.

■ Opening hours, last orders
Dinner = 17:00-23:30 L.O.22:30

■ Annual and weekly closing
Closed mid-August, late December-early January, Sunday and Public Holidays

■ Price
Dinner = set   ¥ 6,500-9,500
Private room fee = ¥ 4,000
Service charge = 10%

TEL. 03-3222-3978
2-2-32 Kandajinbocho,
Chiyoda-ku, Tokyo

Dons de la Nature

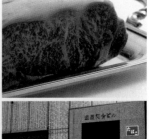

Yoshiji Otsuka is experienced in French cuisine and opened his restaurant after working at a steakhouse. Only Japanese black-haired heifers aged around 33 months are considered; the meat is aged and later smaller cuts are carved and swathed in cloth. Aged for another 7-10 days in a vacuum, an original salt blend and black pepper are then rubbed into it before grilling. Orders start at a minimum weight of 400 grams.

■ Opening hours, last orders
Dinner = 17:00-22:00 L.O.21:00

■ Annual and weekly closing
Closed mid-August, late December-early January, Sunday and Public Holidays

■ Price
Dinner = set   ¥ 21,000
            à la carte ¥ 21,000-34,000
Service charge = 10%

TEL. 03–3563–4129
Kawai Building B1F,
1-7-6 Ginza, Chuo-ku, Tokyo
www.dons-nature.jp

Echikatsu NEW
江知勝

Echigo native Katsujiro founded this restaurant in the early 1870s, and it was a favourite of great writers of the day. The hallway, its wood tanned by time, gives you a feel of its history. Carp swim in the garden pond, and there are old-style tatami rooms from which you can hear the murmuring water. Most meat is marbled, but there is also less fatty thigh meat available. The proprietress prepares spicy Edo style *warishita*.

■ Opening hours, last orders
Dinner = 17:00-21:30 L.O.19:30

■ Annual and weekly closing
Closed mid-August, late December-early January, Saturday in August, Sunday and Public Holidays

■ Price
Dinner = set   ¥ 7,350-11,550
Service charge = 10%

TEL. 03-3811-5293
2-31-23 Yushima, Bunkyo-ku, Tokyo

Emori
江森

The menu on the wall has typical Kyoto items like whole roasted
Kamo eggplant and marinated *tokishirazu* salmon. The simmered
Daitokuji wheat gluten and the *yuba* made from Tanba black
soybeans are rare items in the Kanto area. The *chawanmushi*
with no filling is especially recommended. The highlight of the
set menu is the hotpot made with freshwater clam stock. Owner-
chef Hiroyuki Emori handles all the cooking himself.

■ Opening hours, last orders
Dinner = 18:00-24:00 L.O.23:00

■ Annual and weekly closing
Closed mid-August, late December-
early January, Monday and 1st
Tuesday of each month

■ Price
Dinner = set   ¥ 10,500

TEL. 03–3875–5785
3-9-10 Asakusa, Taito-ku, Tokyo

Émun NEW

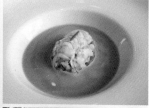

Although compact, this glass-enclosed restaurant has a high ceiling and feels more spacious than it is. Only set menus are available, but there is a wide selection; they are mainly comprised of vegetables and fish accented with olive oil or herbs. The speciality is the *exposition des légumes* featuring several dozen instantaneously chilled vegetables, each prepared differently. The proprietress provides memorable service.

■ Opening hours, last orders
Lunch = 12:00-15:00 L.O.14:00
Dinner = 18:00-22:30 L.O.21:00

■ Annual and weekly closing
Closed 31 December, 1 January
and Monday

■ Price
Lunch = set   ¥ 3,150-6,300
Dinner = set   ¥ 6,000-12,000
Service charge = 10% (dinner)

TEL. 03-6452-2525
Ebisu Hana Building 2F,
2-25-3 Ebisuminami, Shibuya-ku,
Tokyo
www.emu-francaise.jp

Esaki
えさき

❀ ❀ ❀

Shintaro Esaki's cuisine is inspiring and original; he conducts meticulous research on each product and his mastery of technique allows him to cross culinary boundaries. *Yurine manju senbei zutsumi* is a signature dish, which is replaced by *ayu* soup in summer. The same dishes are incorporated into both the lunch and dinner set menus, the prices of which differ according to the number of dishes but are both very appealing.

■ Opening hours, last orders
Lunch = Thu.-Sat. 12:00-14:00
L.O.13:30
Dinner = 18:00-23:00 L.O.21:30

■ Annual and weekly closing
Closed Golden week, mid-August,
late December-early January, Sunday
and Public Holidays

■ Price
Lunch = set   ¥ 5,250
Dinner = set   ¥ 8,400-13,650
Service charge = 10% (lunch 5%)

TEL. 03–3408–5056
Hills Aoyama B1F,
3-39-9 Jingumae, Shibuya-ku,
Tokyo
www.aoyamaesaki.net

Faro

Traditional Italian recipes are executed with the *esprit* of French cuisine. Homemade spaghetti with snow crab and a tomato reduction that goes well with the crab, is a highlight. In winter, one can enjoy carpaccio of marbled Wagyu beef served with truffle dressing or risotto with black truffles. As well as typical Italian desserts such as tiramisu and panna cotta, it offers *savarin*, *opéra* and other French favourites.

■ Opening hours, last orders
Lunch = 11:30-15:30 L.O.14:30
Dinner = 17:30-23:00 L.O.21:30

■ Annual and weekly closing
Closed late December-early January,
Sunday and Public Holidays

■ Price
Lunch = set	¥ 2,800-8,000
à la carte	¥ 7,000-21,000
Dinner = set	¥ 6,800-15,000
à la carte	¥ 7,000-21,000
Service charge = 10%

TEL. 03-3572-3911
Shiseido Building 10F,
8-8-3 Ginza, Chuo-ku, Tokyo
www.shiseido.co.jp/faro

Florilège

Owner-chef Hiroyasu Kawate's approach to cuisine involves fusing elaborate classical elements, achieved through techniques handed down by master chefs, with a contemporary style in which dishes are meticulously arranged. He innovatively pairs roasted foie gras with a lightly salted meringue, yielding a heavy-light contrast of textures and flavours. Meat consists of two dishes, prepared to complement each particular cut.

■ Opening hours, last orders
Lunch = 12:00-13:30 (L.O.)
Dinner = 18:30-21:00 (L.O.)

■ Annual and weekly closing
Closed late December-early January, Wednesday and 1st Tuesday of each month

■ Price
Lunch = set   ¥ 4,200
Dinner = set   ¥ 10,500
Service charge = 10%

TEL. 03-6440-0878
4-9-9 Minamiaoyama, Minato-ku, Tokyo
www.aoyama-florilege.jp

Fugu Fukuji
ふぐ 福治

✿ ✿   ✗

🛏 15   📞🍴

Takeshi Yasuge uses only wild tiger *fugu* from the Bungo Strait. For *sashimi*, the *fugu* is aged for several days to develop flavour and sliced thicker than usual. The *ponzu* sauce is made with *daidai* juice; the red chilli pepper used for the *momiji-oroshi* is ground with a stone mill to enhance its aroma. To finish, the chef or proprietress prepares *zosui* using eggs, *koto-negi* and soup from the hotpot with its bold *fugu* flavour.

■ Opening hours, last orders
Dinner = 17:00-23:00 L.O.21:30

■ Annual and weekly closing
Closed mid-August, late December-
early January, Saturday, Sunday and
Public Holidays from April-October

■ Price
Dinner = set   ¥ 27,300-34,650
Service charge = 10%

TEL. 03-5148-2922
Koda Building 3F,
5-11-13 Ginza, Chuo-ku, Tokyo
www.fukuji.jp

Fukamachi

深町

The owner-chef's *tempura* is thinly battered and lightly fried so as not to spoil the original taste of the ingredients. He uses two fryers set at two temperatures and high-quality white sesame oil for *tempura* soft on the palate. Vegetables are fried at a lower temperature to maintain their freshness and colour; seafood at a higher temperature to ensure a crisp tastiness. Enjoy *Edomae tempura* at this stylish restaurant.

■ Opening hours, last orders
Lunch = 11:30-14:00 L.O.13:30
Dinner = 17:00-22:00 L.O.21:00

■ Annual and weekly closing
Closed Golden week, mid-August,
late December-early January,
Monday, 1st and 3rd Sunday of
each month

■ Price
Lunch = set   ¥ 6,300-8,400
         à la carte ¥ 7,000-12,000
Dinner = set   ¥ 10,500-15,750
         à la carte ¥ 7,000-12,000

TEL. 03–5250–8777
2-5-2 Kyobashi, Chuo-ku, Tokyo

JAPANESE

MAP NO. 18/A-2

Fukudaya
福田家

 P 40

Fukudaya is well known for its close relationship with Rosanjin
Kitaoji, distinguished calligrapher, ceramicist and master chef.
Now run by the 3rd-generation owner, the restaurant has seven
bi-level dining rooms that are fine examples of traditional
architecture. Antiques and garden views behind the *shoji* screens
make you forget you're in the city. The traditionally prepared
kaiseki dishes will satisfy your five senses.

■ Opening hours, last orders
Lunch = 11:30-14:30 L.O.13:00
Dinner = 17:00-22:00 L.O.20:00

■ Annual and weekly closing
Closed late December-early January,
Sunday and Public Holidays

■ Price
Lunch = set   ¥ 21,000-26,250
Dinner = set   ¥ 26,250-36,750
Private room fee = ¥ 5,250/person
Service charge = 20%

TEL. 03-3261-8577
6-12 Kioicho, Chiyoda-ku, Tokyo

Fukuju
福樹

✿✿   ✄

¥ LUNCH 🍱 8 🚇 ☎️🍴 🍶

The private dining space is in the style of a tea ceremony room where, if reserved, guests enjoy a tea ceremony and meal put together by the chef, a certified instructor. Dishes are prepared to retain flavour and aroma; the disk abalone from the Sanriku coast served in a soup with a freshwater clam base is well worth trying. Beautiful serving vessels, including some from the Edo Period, add to the appeal of each dish.

■ Opening hours, last orders
Lunch = 12:00-15:00 L.O.13:00
Dinner = 18:00-22:30 L.O.20:30

■ Annual and weekly closing
Closed mid-August, late December-early January, Sunday and Public Holidays

■ Price
Lunch = set   ¥ 21,000-26,250
Dinner = set   ¥ 21,000-52,500
Service charge = 10%

TEL. 03–3571–8596
Iseyoshi Building 5F,
8-8-19 Ginza, Chuo-ku, Tokyo

Gordon Ramsay

Just past the chic entrance is an open kitchen; the chef's table here seats 6-8 people. The cooking style avoids placing too many ingredients on a single plate and accentuates them with side dishes and sauces. For example, *tortellini* of lobster features shellfish enveloped with thin pasta which is steamed and served with lemongrass sauce, basil and tomato chutney. The wine list includes well-known labels and a range of prices.

■ Opening hours, last orders
Dinner = 17:30-21:00 (L.O.)

■ Annual and weekly closing
Closed Sunday and Monday

■ Price
Dinner = set   ¥ 9,800-22,000

TEL. 03-6388-8000
Conrad Hotel 28F,
1-9-1 Higashishinbashi,
Minato-ku, Tokyo
www.conradtokyo.co.jp

Goriot NEW
哥利歐

This restaurant serves Tajima Sanda beef - choose from sirloin, filet, H-bone or rump, as the cut will determine the thickness. The only seasoning is salt and pepper. The meat is cooked on a skewer over a white charcoal grill, the dripping fat filling the air with a pleasant aroma. The name comes from *Le Père Goriot*, the novel by Balzac, a meat lover. A friendly veteran maître d' offers careful explanations of the meat.

■ Opening hours, last orders
12:00-23:00 L.O.22:00

■ Annual and weekly closing
Closed late December-early January
and 2nd Sunday of each month

■ Price
set   ¥ 23,100
à la carte   ¥ 30,000-50,000
Service charge = 10%

TEL. 03-3543-7214
8-18-3 Ginza, Chuo-ku, Tokyo

Grill Ukai NEW

The interior is an appealing cross between Japanese and Western sensibilities and the menu consists primarily of French cuisine, but the speciality is dishes grilled with infrared rays. As well as standard Ukai *kuroge wagyu* beef and Sanriku abalone, the wide range of items include Ezo pork, Kawamata Shamo chicken and *unagi*. To take in the atmosphere, a seat by the window is recommended; the courtyard is illuminated by night.

■ Opening hours, last orders
Lunch = 11:00-14:30 (L.O.)
Dinner = 17:30-22:00 (L.O.)

■ Annual and weekly closing
Closed 1 January

■ Price
Lunch = set   ¥ 3,680-6,300
            à la carte ¥ 6,500-21,000
Dinner = set   ¥ 7,350-15,750
            à la carte ¥ 6,500-21,000
Service charge = 10%

TEL. 03-5221-5252
Marunouchi Park Building 2F,
2-6-1 Marunouchi, Chiyoda-ku,
Tokyo
www.grill-ukai.jp

Hamadaya
濱田家

❀ ❀ ❀   ✕✕✕✕

    ✄ ☞ P ⬚ 60 ◕⟡

This prestigious restaurant is one of the few *sukiya*-style buildings remaining today. The head chef keeps to the traditions passed down from his predecessors: dishes are given subtle variations of flavour depending on the ingredients used and the order in which they are served. In *hamo* season, the *hamo* is covered with *kudzu* and rolled *yuba* is served in a soup using a light and tasty stock, while the hot pot of sliced Japanese beef and *sansho* are served *Edomae sukiyaki*.

■ Opening hours, last orders
Lunch = Wed., Thu. and Sat.
11:00-15:00 L.O.14:00
Dinner = 17:30-23:00 L.O.20:00

■ Annual and weekly closing
Closed mid-August, late December-
early January, Sunday and Public
Holidays

■ Price
Lunch = set   ¥ 15,750-24,150
Dinner = set   ¥ 26,250-52,500
Private room fee = ¥ 3,150/person
                            (dinner)
Service charge = 20% (lunch 15%)

TEL. 03-3661-5940
3-13-5 Nihonbashiningyocho,
Chuo-ku, Tokyo
www.hamadaya.info

Harutaka
青空

❀ ❀   ✕

⌁ ⬡4 ⛴ ☎🍴 ⏰

Harutaka Takahashi's day begins with a trip to Tsukiji market, where he selects only ingredients he judges to be good. *Hatsu gatsuo* is seared over a straw fire in May; there is wild *madaka* abalone between April and June; *shako* is purchased alive and quickly steamed to ensure freshness. The temperature ensures each topping is kept at its best. The rice is a special blend combining sweet-tasting rice with a less sticky variety.

■ Opening hours, last orders
Dinner = 17:00-24:00
Saturday 17:00-22:30

■ Annual and weekly closing
Closed Golden week, mid-August,
late December-early January,
Sunday and Public Holidays

■ Price
Dinner = set   ¥ 15,000-25,000

TEL. 03–3573–1144
Kawabata Building 3F,
8-5-8 Ginza, Chuo-ku, Tokyo

Hatanaka
畑中

Hiroyoshi Hatanaka set up his dream restaurant in Azabujuban in 1997, serving *tempura* using aromatic sesame oil. We recommend the combined seafood and vegetable set menu. The *makiebi* are cooked two different ways for contrasting sweetness and texture. The round aubergine slices, fried lightly golden and halved, are recommended with soy sauce. As the natural aroma of the ingredients is important, avoid wearing strong perfumes.

■ Opening hours, last orders
Dinner = 17:30-22:00 L.O.20:30

■ Annual and weekly closing
Closed mid-August, late December-early January and Wednesday

■ Price
Dinner = set   ¥ 8,400-10,500
          à la carte ¥ 8,000-12,000
Service charge = 5%

TEL. 03-3456-2406
2-21-10 Azabujuban, Minato-ku, Tokyo

Hatsunezushi
初音鮨

Owner-chef Katsu Nakaji serves only sushi - without appetisers. He prefers slightly firmer rice and flavours it with *akazu*; special care ensures the right temperature. In winter, yellowtail is sliced for a *shabu-shabu*-style dish; they are briefly dipped in boiling water to heat the surface and served with *ponzu* dipping sauce with grated radish and *yuzu* pepper. As Nakaji prepares all dishes himself, reservations are limited.

■ Opening hours, last orders
Dinner = 17:30-19:45 and
20:00-22:30

■ Annual and weekly closing
Closed Golden week, mid-August,
late December-early January,
Sunday and Public Holidays

■ Price
Dinner = set   ¥ 15,750

TEL. 03-3731-2403
5-20-2 Nishikamata, Ota-ku,
Tokyo

Hei Fung Terrace

This softly lit dining room is beautifully decorated with gently curving walls, a stone-paved floor and hanging birdcages. The three private rooms come with antique wooden accessories and furnishings from China. The menu features a number of dishes prepared in typical Cantonese style. Recommendations include 'superior bird's nest and bean curd in thick soup' and 'sautéed sliced abalone with lily bulbs and crab coral'.

■ Opening hours, last orders
Lunch = 11:30-14:30 (L.O.)
Dinner = 18:00-22:00 (L.O.)

■ Price
Lunch = set   ¥ 4,280-8,880
         à la carte ¥ 6,000-15,000
Dinner = set   ¥ 8,880-19,880
         à la carte ¥ 6,000-15,000

TEL. 03-6270-2738
The Peninsula Hotel 2F,
1-8-1 Yurakucho, Chiyoda-ku,
Tokyo
www.tokyo.jp.peninsula.com

Hifumian
一二三庵

The building dates from the late Taisho period and was home to a *Noh* performer. There are just two rooms: Western-style on the 1st floor, Japanese-style on the 2nd. Takamitsu Aihara opened Hifumian after training in Osaka, Kobe and Tokyo. The lightly roasted sea bass with *misansho* pepper and white *miso* is highly recommended. Only two groups are served each meal, both by reservation only and just two set courses are offered.

■ Opening hours, last orders
Lunch = 12:00-15:00 L.O.14:00
Dinner = 18:00-23:00 L.O.20:00

■ Annual and weekly closing
Closed Golden week, mid-August
and late December-early January

■ Price
Lunch = set   ¥ 8,400-15,750
Dinner = set   ¥ 15,750-21,000
Service charge = 10%

TEL. 03-5832-8677
4-2-18 Sendagi, Bunkyo-ku,
Tokyo
www.hifumi-an.com

Higuchi
樋口

 2

There is a counter, two tables and a private room for up to four.
Sea urchin jelly is a staple; for the *hamo shabu-shabu*, you dip
pieces of raw *hamo* into a stock made with *hamo* bones—a
pleasant summer dish. In winter, savoury egg custard with sea
cucumber gut and mackerel sushi are recommended. The last
course is either handmade buckwheat noodles or *tai meshi*. The
chef works alone, so sit back and enjoy the leisurely pace.

■ Opening hours, last orders
Dinner = 18:00-21:00 (L.O.)

■ Annual and weekly closing
Closed Golden week, mid-August,
late December-early January,
Sunday and Public Holidays

■ Price
Dinner = set   ¥ 12,600-18,900
Private room fee = ¥ 3,000
Service charge = 10%

TEL. 03–3402–7038
2-19-12 Jingumae, Shibuya-ku,
Tokyo

Hiramatsu

🥢 ⚡ 🍽 14 ☎🍴 ☀ 🍇

Hiroyuki Hiramatsu decided to pursue a culinary career after reading a book by 20C French chef Fernand Point. He now has several restaurants in Japan and has established a partnership with another French chef, Paul Bocuse. The dishes are a contemporary take on traditional French cuisine. Specialities include duck foie gras rolled in cabbage with truffle sauce and roast lamb slices and onion compote with truffle sauce.

■ Opening hours, last orders
Lunch = 12:00-13:30 (L.O.)
Dinner = 18:00-20:30 (L.O.)

■ Annual and weekly closing
Closed 1 January and Monday
except Public Holidays

■ Price
Lunch = set   ¥ 4,200-8,400
          à la carte ¥ 14,000-18,000
Dinner = set   ¥ 12,600-21,000
          à la carte ¥ 14,000-18,000
Service charge = 15%

TEL. 03–3444–3967
5-15-13 Minamiazabu, Minato-ku,
Tokyo
www.hiramatsu.co.jp/restaurants/
hiramatsu-hiroo

Hiromichi NEW

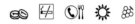

The signature dish at Hiromichi is *boudin noir* wrapped in potatoes and fried until crisp. Many of the dishes are traditionally French or from other countries and arranged according to the chef's sensibilities. The carrot mousse and young Ibaraki pigeon dishes is one speciality where modern presentation, classic techniques and skilful flavouring are brought together. Dinner changes every season; lunch every two months.

■ Opening hours, last orders
Lunch = 11:30-13:30 (L.O.)
Dinner = 18:00-21:30 (L.O.)

■ Annual and weekly closing
Closed late December-early January
and Monday

■ Price
Lunch = set   ¥ 2,600-11,000
          à la carte   ¥ 6,500-9,000
Dinner = set   ¥ 5,600-11,000
          à la carte   ¥ 6,500-9,000
Service charge = 10%

TEL. 03-5768-0722
1-12-24 Mita, Meguro-ku, Tokyo
www.restaurant-hiromichi.com

Hirosaku
ひろ作

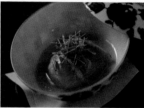

A friendly couple welcomes you to this simple dining room with a nostalgic Showa feel. The abalone is cooked salty-sweet; the *watari-gani* is dipped in a sauce made to a secret recipe. The light taste of the simmered Japanese branquillo is enhanced by the fine broth. As the last dish, enjoy glossy handmade soba noodles; they slide down smoothly and are in perfect harmony with the slightly sweet sauce. Good value lunch prices.

■ Opening hours, last orders
Lunch = 11:45-13:00 (L.O.)
Dinner = 18:00-20:00 (L.O.)

■ Annual and weekly closing
Closed mid-August, late December-early January, Saturday, Sunday and Public Holidays

■ Price
Lunch = set   ¥ 8,400-12,600
Dinner = set   ¥ 26,250-31,500

TEL. 03–3591–0901
3-6-13 Shinbashi, Minato-ku, Tokyo

Hishinuma
菱沼

Owner-chef Takayuki Hishinuma's goal is to 'serve society through food'. While Japanese cuisine is the base, he combines it with meat and creative Western-inspired dishes. A vegetarian menu is offered along with a *Hiyoko-san* menu for children to provide them with nutritional education. His love of wine allows him to suggest pairings. The tranquil, modern restaurant includes a wide counter, table seating and two private rooms.

■ Opening hours, last orders
Lunch = 11:30-13:30 (L.O.)
Dinner = 17:30-22:00 (L.O.)

■ Annual and weekly closing
Closed mid-August, late December-early January, Sunday and Public Holidays

■ Price
Lunch = set ¥ 3,570-7,350
Dinner = set ¥ 12,600-18,900
Service charge = 10%

TEL. 03-3568-6588
Axis Building B1F,
5-17-1 Roppongi, Minato-ku,
Tokyo

Hiyama NEW
日山

🛪 🍽 50 📞🍴

In 1935, a meat store opened a *sukiyaki kappo* restaurant on the 2nd floor of its building, built in the style of a tea-ceremony house. There are various sized rooms, and evidence of repeated extensions can be seen. The Hiyama *wagyu* is from the butcher's shop downstairs and its quality is constant; seasonal vegetables like *mitsuba* and mushrooms are used. There are dedicated cooking staff, allowing you to simply enjoy the food.

■ Opening hours, last orders
Lunch = 11:30-14:00
Dinner = 17:00-21:00

■ Annual and weekly closing
Closed mid-August, late December-early January, Sunday and Public Holidays

■ Price
Lunch = set   ¥ 6,825-9,975
Dinner = set   ¥ 8,400-18,900
Service charge = 10%

TEL. 03-3666-2901
2-5-1 Nihonbashiningyocho,
Chuo-ku, Tokyo
www.hiyama-nihonbashi.co.jp

Horikane
堀兼

🛋 16   🍽️   📞🍴

Owner-chef Hidehiro Horiuchi's kitchen is a place of focused concentration. Combining Chinese and Japanese styles, a spiced stew of Jinhua ham and vegetables is served on steamed papaya while *shirako* risotto is topped with white truffles from Alba; in winter, *shabu-shabu* of yellowtail and wild *nameko* mushrooms is delicious. The hotpot dish is served all year round. In Nittozakashita, near the entrance to the Shirogane Tunnel.

■ Opening hours, last orders
Dinner = 18:30-23:00 L.O.21:00

■ Annual and weekly closing
Closed Golden week, mid-August,
late December-early January,
Sunday and Public Holidays

■ Price
Dinner = set   ¥ 21,000-24,000

TEL. 03–3280–4629
5-10-13 Shirokanedai,
Minato-ku, Tokyo

Hosokawa
ほそ川

Owner chef Takashi Hosokawa not only buys good buckwheat but also grows his own on his farm in Ibaraki. The thin noodles are made from 100% buckwheat flour, ground daily. In winter, warm *kaki soba* is worth a try. The *anago tempura* is a popular appetiser. The interior is simple, with four shared tables and one semi-private room. Bookings are not accepted at weekends or holidays; guests are asked not to bring small children.

■ Opening hours, last orders
Lunch = 11:45-15:00
Dinner = 17:30-21:00

■ Annual and weekly closing
Closed mid-August, early January,
Monday and 3rd Tuesday of each
month

■ Price
Lunch = à la carte ¥ 3,000-6,000
Dinner = à la carte ¥ 3,000-6,000

TEL. 03-3626-1125
1-6-5 Kamezawa, Sumida-ku,
Tokyo
www.edosoba-hosokawa.jp

Hosokawa NEW
ほそ川

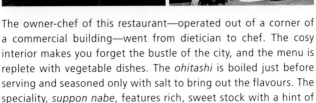

The owner-chef of this restaurant—operated out of a corner of a commercial building—went from dietician to chef. The cosy interior makes you forget the bustle of the city, and the menu is replete with vegetable dishes. The *ohitashi* is boiled just before serving and seasoned only with salt to bring out the flavours. The speciality, *suppon nabe*, features rich, sweet stock with a hint of ginger; order it when making reservations.

■ Opening hours, last orders
Dinner = 18:00-23:00

■ Annual and weekly closing
Closed late December-early January,
Sunday and Public Holidays

■ Price
Dinner = set   ¥ 6,300-10,500

TEL. 03-3581-8886
HK Shinbashi Building 5F,
2-12-2 Shinbashi, Minato-ku,
Tokyo

Icaro NEW

This small restaurant feels bigger than it is, thanks to the large window, and it has a casual, trattoria-style atmosphere. The chef uses his 7 years of experience in Italy, and his brother, a wine connoisseur, handles the service. The speciality is the braised Hokkaido deer *pappardelle* with sauce; the Japanese beef cheek goulash is northern Italian, a cuisine in which the chef excels. The wine is also reasonably priced.

■ Opening hours, last orders
Dinner = 18:00-1:00 (L.O.)
Saturday 18:00-24:00 (L.O.)

■ Annual and weekly closing
Closed late December-early January
and Sunday

■ Price
Dinner = set   ¥ 5,250
            à la carte ¥ 5,500-8,000
Seat charge=¥500/person

TEL. 03-5724-8085
Coms Nakameguro 4F,
2-44-24 Kamimeguro,
Meguro-ku, Tokyo
www.icaro-miyamoto.com

Ichie
一会

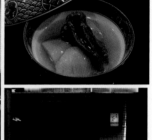

Junichi Watanabe became a chef at the age of 35, having previously pursued a different career path. Only set menus are offered. Giant abalone, a staple dish, steamed for over four hours in sake and very tender, fills your mouth with its flavour; served in a clay pot, Koshihikari rice from Aizu Kitakata region rounds off the meal. Chef prepares all the dishes himself but the wait is worth it as he puts his heart into them.

■ Opening hours, last orders
Lunch = 12:00-14:00 L.O.13:00
Dinner = 18:00-23:00 L.O.21:00

■ Annual and weekly closing
Closed mid-August and Tuesday

■ Price
Lunch = set   ¥ 4,800-10,500
Dinner = set   ¥ 10,500
Service charge = 10% (dinner)

TEL. 03-3280-1439
Excel Shirota Building B1F,
5-16-16 Hiroo, Shibuya-ku, Tokyo

Ichigo NEW
一期

Enjoy *oden* at this atmospheric restaurant that resembles a bar, with jazz in the background. The base stock is made from eight ingredients and no effort is spared in bringing out essential flavours, such as *yuba* – fried for a pleasant aroma – and the soft-boiled eggs marinated in stock. After *sashimi*, charbroiled *ichiyaboshi* and other dishes, have your favourite *oden* items. We recommend *chameshi* with *oden-dashi* to end with.

■ Opening hours, last orders
Dinner = 18:00-2:00 L.O.1:00

■ Annual and weekly closing
Closed Monday

■ Price
Dinner = set   ¥ 6,800
        à la carte ¥ 5,500-10,000
Service charge = 10%
Seat charge=¥ 800/person

TEL. 03–5772–2936
My-Corner Building B1F,
2-5-14 Azabujuban, Minato-ku,
Tokyo
www.azabu-ichigo.com

Ichimonji
一文字

❀ ❀   ✗✗

✂ ✄ 🖥 14 🚃 🕐🍴 ☼

Kazuhiko Hirose catered for tea ceremonies for 13 years (and continues to do so) before opening here in 2005. Each dish is in harmony with the colour and feel of the tableware on which it is served; soft, plump *hotate-shinjo* served with Kintoki carrot and *yuzu* is a colourful dish with the white, red and yellow standing out in the clear soup. There is sunken seating at the counter on the 1st floor and a tatami room on the 2nd.

■ Opening hours, last orders
Lunch = 12:00-14:00 (L.O.)
Dinner = 18:00-21:00 (L.O.)

■ Annual and weekly closing
Closed Golden week, mid-August
and late December-early January

■ Price
Lunch = set   ¥ 8,400-16,800
Dinner = set   ¥ 12,600-21,000
Private room fee = ¥5,250
Service charge = 10%

TEL. 03–5206–8223
3-6 Kagurazaka, Shinjuku-ku,
Tokyo

Ichirin
一凛

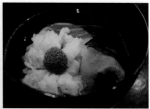

Mikizo Hashimoto serves Kyoto-style cuisine that reflects the season, as does his tableware and the arrangement of the dishes. Typical items in August include tofu of yams with green bamboo and potato leaves for a cooling sensation; or a Rikyu (influential 16C tea ceremony master)-style dish of steamed abalone and white taro with a sesame seed aroma. Dinner can last a good three hours, so allow yourself plenty of time.

■ Opening hours, last orders
Lunch = 12:00-13:00 (L.O.)
Dinner = 18:00-21:00 (L.O.)

■ Annual and weekly closing
Closed late December-early
January

■ Price
Lunch = set   ¥ 5,500-20,000
Dinner = set   ¥ 11,000-20,000
Service charge = 10%

TEL. 03-6410-7355
Azuma Building 2F,
2-19-5 Jingumae, Shibuya-ku,
Tokyo

Iconic

✿

✕✕✕✕

🛇 ♿ ↯ 🖵 40 🍽 ☼

This restaurant is a collaboration between celebrated British designer and restaurateur Sir Terence Conran and the Hiramatsu Group. Specialising in Italian cuisine, the chef also uses French techniques. Novel dishes can be enjoyed here, such as the orange-froth-covered foie gras terrine; charcoal grilled cured Japanese beef is also good. Wines are mostly French. Weddings are often held at weekends, so check beforehand.

■ Opening hours, last orders
Lunch = 11:30-14:00 (L.O.)
Dinner = 18:00-20:30 (L.O.)

■ Annual and weekly closing
Closed 1 January and Monday
except Public Holidays

■ Price
Lunch = set   ¥ 4,800-8,400
            à la carte ¥ 11,000-16,000
Dinner = set   ¥ 8,400-16,800
            à la carte ¥ 11,000-16,000
Service charge = 10%

TEL. 03-3562-7500
Ginza Velvia-kan 9F,
2-4-6 Ginza, Chuo-ku, Tokyo
www.danddlondon.jp/iconic

Ise NEW
いせ

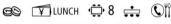

The owner-chef goes to Tsukiji to select the seafood himself; vegetables are from all over the country and the live young *saimaki ebi* come directly from Amakusa. In spring, his father sends edible wild plants from the mountains of Tohoku. The ingredients are fried in a homemade blend of cotton seed oil; the salt is also homemade. Prices are reasonable for what is included and once the rice runs out, the restaurant closes.

■ Opening hours, last orders
Lunch = 11:30-14:00 L.O.13:30
Dinner = 17:30-22:00 L.O.20:30

■ Annual and weekly closing
Closed mid-August, late December-early January and Sunday

■ Price
Lunch = set   ¥ 800-2,500
Dinner = set   ¥ 2,500-8,400
              à la carte ¥ 5,000-8,000

TEL. 03-3768-0750
3-29-8 Minamioi, Shinagawa-ku, Tokyo

Ishibashi
いし橋

 30

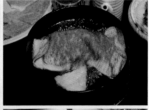

Established in 1879, this restaurant serves finely-marbled sirloin cuts of black-haired cattle beef from throughout Japan. The secret to the *sukiyaki* sauce, known only to the proprietress, has been passed down through generations. The staff take care of the pot and the serving, allowing you to enjoy the food and entertain your guests. The tile-roofed restaurant inexplicably blends in with the surrounding modern buildings.

■ Opening hours, last orders
Dinner = 17:00-21:30 L.O.20:30

■ Annual and weekly closing
Closed Golden week, mid-August,
late December-early January,
Saturday, Sunday and Public
Holidays

■ Price
Dinner = set   ¥ 9,765-11,865

TEL. 03-3251-3580
3-6-8 Sotokanda, Chiyoda-ku,
Tokyo

Ishibashi
石ばし

    20

The *unagi* comes from a designated farm in Shizuoka, with the feed, cultivation period, etc. all specified by Ishibashi's owner. Preparation begins only once the customer has arrived so expect something of a wait. The broiled eel, free of excess oil, is served on rice in a Wajima lacquered box with a light, slightly tangy sauce to flavour the rice. The pickles, prepared using rice bran in a time-honoured way are also good.

■ Opening hours, last orders
Lunch = 11:30-13:30 (L.O.)
Saturday 11:30-14:00 (L.O.)
Dinner = 18:00-19:30 (L.O.)
Saturday 17:30-20:00 (L.O.)

■ Annual and weekly closing
Closed mid-August, late
December-early January, Sunday,
Monday and Public Holidays

■ Prices
Lunch = set   ¥ 7,500-10,000
             à la carte ¥ 2,500-10,000
Dinner = set   ¥ 10,000-12,000
             à la carte ¥ 2,500-10,000
Service charge = 10%

TEL.03-3813-8038
2-4-29 Suido, Bunkyo-ku, Tokyo

Ishikawa
石かわ

✿ ✿ ✿   ✕✕

Hideki Ishikawa's cuisine is described as 'Ishikawa-style', bound only by his imagination. Innovative touches are incorporated to highlight the unique characteristics of each ingredient. Stewed beef tendon and wax gourd in stock is refined and creamy; the spiny lobster and abalone add an element of luxury. Sake is mainly from chef's birthplace of Niigata and the Hokuriku region. Look for a black fence behind Zenkokuji Temple.

■ Opening hours, last orders
Dinner = 17:30-24:00 L.O.22:00

■ Annual and weekly closing
Closed mid-August, late December-
early January, Sunday and Public
Holidays

■ Price
Dinner = set   ¥ 15,750-19,950
Service charge = 10%

TEL. 03–5225–0173
5-37 Kagurazaka, Shinjuku-ku,
Tokyo

Itosho
いと正

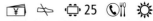

Hiroji Ito opened in 1960 to introduce Takayama meat-free cuisine rooted in Zen Buddhism. He uses vegetables from all over the country, including Takayama, and stock made from kelp, *shiitake* mushrooms, dried gourd shavings and other ingredients. The colourful appetiser, *matcha* jelly mixed with yams, laver boiled down in soy sauce and raw wheat gluten are eaten with a rich sauce with tofu, sesame and walnuts.

■ Opening hours, last orders
Lunch = 12:00-15:00 L.O.13:00
Dinner = 17:30-21:30 L.O.19:30

■ Price
Lunch = set   ¥ 6,000-10,000
Dinner = set   ¥ 8,000-10,000
Service charge = 10%

TEL. 03-3454-6538
3-4-7 Azabujuban, Minato-ku,
Tokyo

Izumi NEW
い津み

 12

The *omakase* comes in two types: *fugu kaiseki* and *fugu ryori*. If you are looking for *chirinabe* and *zosui*, we recommend the latter; the former is made up of several dishes that include *fugu*, like *nikogori* and *nanbanni*. *Sashimi* is cut thick and placed on a white porcelain dish. The speciality is the *zosui*; the rice is cooked in stock to fully absorb the flavour of the *fugu*. There are separate entrances for the 1st and 2nd floors.

■ Opening hours, last orders
Dinner = 17:00-22:00

■ Annual and weekly closing
Closed August, late December-early January, Saturday and Public Holidays from April-September and Sunday

■ Price
Dinner = set   ¥ 21,000-29,400
          à la carte ¥ 20,000-30,000
Service charge = 15%

TEL. 03-3582-0101
6-11-11 Akasaka, Minato-ku, Tokyo
www.izumi-akasaka.jp

Joël Robuchon

🕸 🕸 🕸   ✗✗✗✗✗

✂ ▭ 30 ☎♨ ☀ ❀

Located on the 2nd floor of an 18C French-style château at Yebisu Garden Place and under the auspices of the eponymous chef, Joël Robuchon. The room is furnished in black with Swarovski crystal adorning the golden walls and a dazzling Baccarat chandelier. The house specialities, ossetra caviar and crustacean gelée served with cauliflower cream, and ravioli stuffed with langoustine and truffles, are highly recommended.

■ Opening hours, last orders
Lunch = 11:30-14:00 (L.O.)
Dinner = 18:00-21:30 (L.O.)

■ Price
Lunch = set   ¥ 6,000-12,300
        à la carte ¥ 15,000-30,000
Dinner = set   ¥ 22,500-36,000
        à la carte ¥ 15,000-30,000
Service charge = 12% (private
                room 15%)

TEL. 03-5424-1347
Yebisu Garden Place,
1-13-1 Mita, Meguro-ku, Tokyo
www.robuchon.jp/ebisu

Kadowaki
かどわき

❀ ❀   ✂

🖼 6   🚇   🕐🍴   🕐   🍇   🍶

Toshiya Kadowaki's creativity is the attraction here. Along with local ingredients, he looks to Western produce like truffles and foie gras to help him make 'dishes to impress'. In April, *hanasansho* hotpot with fish or beef is available; in autumn, *matsutake* mushroom and beef *shabu-shabu* is recommended. *Soba* with foie gras sauce is also good and truffle rice is a speciality. There are private rooms but we recommend the counter.

■ Opening hours, last orders
Dinner = 18:00-1:00 L.O.23:00
Saturday L.O.22:00

■ Annual and weekly closing
Closed Golden week, mid-August,
late December-early January,
Sunday and Public Holidays

■ Price
Dinner = set   ¥ 21,000-26,250
Service charge = 10%

TEL. 03−5772−2553
2-7-2 Azabujuban, Minato-ku,
Tokyo
www.azabu-kadowaki.com

Kagura NEW
花楽

In 2010, Kanazawa brewery Fukumitsuya's restaurant Kagura was reborn. The head chef trained at a *ryotei* in Tokushima, and the menu offers plenty of vegetable dishes. One of the standard dishes is the *kagurazuke*—vegetables pickled in sake lees. Traditional techniques are used in simple, familiar dishes like *okara* and *shiraae*. When available, we recommend the salt grilled sweetfish; the monthly hotpot is also popular.

■ Opening hours, last orders
Dinner = 16:00-23:00

■ Annual and weekly closing
Closed mid-August, late December-early January and Sunday

■ Price
Dinner = set   ¥ 8,400-12,600
        à la carte ¥ 6,000-15,000
Private room fee = ¥ 10,500
Service charge = 10%

TEL. 03-3585-3030
5-5-9 Akasaka, Minato-ku, Tokyo

Kamiya Nogizaka
神谷 乃木坂

❀   🍴🍴

🍽 12 ◕🍴

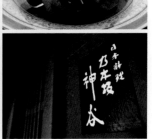

Masataka Kamiya expands the possibilities of Japanese cuisine by
also using French, Italian and Chinese ingredients. Meishanton
pork loin is used for the *shabu-shabu*, while the belly is cooked
with black vinegar and topped with a scallion sauce. French duck
is slowly cooked in its own fat and flavoured with a red wine sauce
that includes soy sauce. The handmade *soba* served before dessert
is another memorable feature.

■ Opening hours, last orders
Lunch = 11:30-15:00 L.O.14:30
Dinner = 17:30-22:00 L.O.21:30

■ Annual and weekly closing
Closed Golden week, mid-August,
late December-early January,
Sunday and Public Holidays

■ Price
Lunch = set   ¥ 5,250-10,500
Dinner = set   ¥ 10,500-21,000
Private room fee = ¥ 1,050/person
Service charge = 10%

TEL. 03-3497-0489
8-11-19 Akasaka, Minato-ku,
Tokyo
www.kamiya-m.com/nogizaka

Kanda
かんだ

❀ ❀ ❀

Hiroyuki Kanda makes the most of the natural flavour of quality ingredients to create dishes bursting with originality. The springtime broad bean cakes have a rich sweetness and pleasant texture. Tomatoes are used in the sweet *waridashi* for the beef *sukiyaki*, eaten with whipped eggs. Close attention is even paid to garnishes and the chef understands his customers' preferences and adjusts tastes and quantity to satisfy them.

■ Opening hours, last orders
Dinner = 18:00-22:00 (L.O.)

■ Annual and weekly closing
Closed mid-August, late December-early January, Sunday and Public Holidays

■ Price
Dinner = set   ¥ 15,750-24,150
Service charge = 10%

TEL. 03-5786-0150
3-6-34 Motoazabu, Minato-ku, Tokyo

Kanesada   NEW
兼定

This small 10-seater restaurant is always lively. The *mehikari ichiyaboshi* and *aji tsumire* are popular constants on the menu. Depending on the season, items like smooth, rich monkfish liver and deftly prepared salt-roasted *nodoguro* are available; the mild rice goes well with the fresh items. In addition to the hand-rolled sushi, the owner-chef's skills are particularly evident in the *saba bozushi* and the *aji oshizushi*.

■ Opening hours, last orders
Dinner = 18:00-23:00

■ Annual and weekly closing
Closed mid-August, late December-
early January, Sunday and Public
Holidays

■ Prices
Dinner = set   ¥ 21,000-26,250

TEL.03-3403-3648
4-4-6 Roppongi, Minato-ku,
Tokyo

Karin NEW
花梨

🔗 ♿ ⇥ ☞ 🅿 💺 60 ☎🍴 ☀

Here one can enjoy Cantonese and other cuisines from all over China. Popular items include Cantonese roast pork and pork dumplings. The peeled prawn in chilli sauce is skilfully cooked and the sauce is balanced between sweetness, sourness and spiciness. There are plenty of set menus; most popular are the weekday lunches that change weekly and the 'Health and Beauty Hong Kong Dim Sum' lunch served on weekends and holidays.

■ Opening hours, last orders
Lunch = 11:30-14:30 (L.O.)
Sat.,Sun. and Public Holidays
11:30-16:00 (L.O.)
Dinner = 17:00-21:30 (L.O.)

■ Price
Lunch = set   ¥ 2,300-7,300
           à la carte ¥ 3,000-10,000
Dinner = set   ¥ 8,500-25,000
           à la carte ¥ 6,000-30,000
Private room fee = ¥ 6,300-21,000
Service charge = 10%

TEL. 03-3505-1111
ANA Intercontinental Hotel 3F,
1-12-33 Akasaka, Minato-ku, Tokyo
www.anaintercontinental-tokyo.jp

Katsuzen   NEW
かつぜん

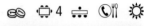

This restaurant is run by a family of four. In charge of the fluffy batter is the daughter, who sifts the bread crumbs by hand with a special sifter. The tonkatsu, enveloped in a delicate batter, is not oily and is accompanied by white rice that whets the appetite. The miso soup, made with sardine stock, is prepared while the tonkatsu is fried. The entrance to the tatami room is small, like a tea ceremony hut, so watch your head.

■ Opening hours, last orders
Lunch = 11:30-14:30 L.O.14:00
Sat.,Sun. and Public Holidays
11:30-15:00 L.O.14:30
Dinner = 17:00-22:30 L.O.21:30
Sat., Sun. and Public Holidays
17:00-21:30 L.O.20:00

■ Annual and weekly closing
Closed late December-early January
and Monday

■ Price
Lunch = à la carte   ¥ 2,500-8,000
Dinner = set   ¥ 7,500-12,000
           à la carte ¥ 3,500-10,000
Service charge = 10% (dinner)

TEL. 03-3289-8988
Kojun Building 4F,
6-8-7 Ginza, Chuo-ku, Tokyo

Kien
帰燕

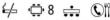

The head chef says he wants customers to return, just as swallows return to their nests ('Kien' means 'homecoming swallows'). The restaurant is divided into two: counter seats on one side and three tables with partitions on the other. The *omakase* is the main event, but there are also special menus featuring *wagyu* steak cooked on a lava rock or *suppon* nabe. The unwavering quality and value contribute to the restaurant's appeal.

■ Opening hours, last orders
Lunch = 12:00-15:00 L.O.13:30
Dinner = 18:00-23:00 L.O.21:00

■ Annual and weekly closing
Closed mid-August, late December-early January, Sunday except Public Holidays and Public Holiday Mondays

■ Price
Lunch = set ¥ 5,250
Dinner = set ¥ 10,500-13,650
Service charge = 10%

TEL. 03–3505–0728
2-18-8 Akasaka, Minato-ku, Tokyo

Kikuchi
き久ち

The owner-chef of this cosy *kappo* restaurant trained in a range of restaurants to learn various cuisines. To sample different ingredients, order *tsukuri* - the two varieties are served side-by-side. For roast dishes, try the charcoal-grilled seasonal fish. Rice cooked in kelp stock is served in small iron pots. Since he runs the restaurant on his own and purchases only enough ingredients for the day, book as early as possible.

■ Opening hours, last orders
Dinner = 18:00-21:30 (L.O.)

■ Annual and weekly closing
Closed early January and Sunday

■ Price
Dinner = set   ¥ 10,500-15,750

TEL. 03-6313-5599
Minatoya Sohonten Building 2F,
2-17-17 Nishiazabu, Minato-ku,
Tokyo

Kikunoi
菊乃井

Third-generation owner-chef Yoshihiro Murata reflects the seasons through exquisite dishes, prepared according to the restaurant's long-held traditions. April's grilled dish is smoked and grilled cherry salmon from Himi; it's first dipped in *miso* paste, sake, *mirin* and soy sauce. On the 1st floor are two counters; upstairs, a tearoom and *tatami* rooms are based on the *sukiya* style of architecture employed for tea houses.

■ Opening hours, last orders
Lunch = Tue.-Sat. 12:00-13:00 (L.O.)
Dinner = 17:00-21:00 (L.O.)

■ Annual and weekly closing
Closed mid-August, late December-early January and Sunday

■ Price
Lunch = set   ¥ 10,500
Dinner = set   ¥ 15,750-21,000
Service charge = 10% (tatami
                    room 15%)

TEL. 03–3568–6055
6-13-8 Akasaka, Minato-ku, Tokyo
www.kikunoi.jp/akasaka.htm

Kisaku NEW
喜作

Opened in 2010, the restaurant is named after the owner-chef's grandfather who invented a technique for artificially cultivating *shiitake* mushrooms. Prices are relatively low as he wants young people to enjoy Japanese cuisine. The elaborate *hassun*, thinly sliced white-fleshed *sashimi* with liver, and summer vegetable *nibitashi* are recommended. *Omakase* set menus are served, but after 8:30pm à la carte dishes can also be ordered.

■ Opening hours, last orders
Lunch = 11:30-13:30 (L.O.)
Dinner = 17:00-22:00 (L.O.)

■ Annual and weekly closing
Closed mid-August, late December-early January, Sunday and Public Holidays

■ Price
Lunch = set   ¥ 4,000
Dinner = set   ¥ 10,500-15,750
              à la carte ¥ 8,000-12,000

TEL. 03-5419-7332
Coms Azabu Jyuban 5F,
3-3-9 Azabujuban, Minato-ku,
Tokyo

Kodama
こだま

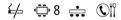

Owner-chef Tsutomu Kodama is self-taught and guided by his instincts. Emphasis is on the ingredients' true taste and food is transformed into inventive dishes. One of the most popular is *awabi-soba* and *tai-meshi*. The fish bone soup is made from seasonal fish after it has been stewed, and contains plenty of gelatine, bone marrow and other nutrients. In autumn, the *matsutake* mushroom ice cream is particularly innovative.

■ Opening hours, last orders
Dinner = 18:00-22:00 L.O.20:00

■ Annual and weekly closing
Closed Golden week, mid-August,
30,31 December, Sunday and
Public Holidays

■ Price
Dinner = set   ¥ 15,750-21,000
Private room fee = 10%
Service charge = 10%

TEL. 03-3408-8865
Nishiazabu 1106 2F,
1-10-6 Nishiazabu, Minato-ku,
Tokyo

Kogetsu
湖月

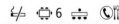

Whilst not spacious, it goes back a long way and has nine counter seats plus a further room. House specialities include *kasujiru* -the sake lees soup- with eight kinds of vegetables, steamed Shogoin turnip with conger eel, and thinly sliced crossbred duck loin cooked in a bonito and kelp stock. To finish, we recommend the fish roe with rice or sea bream with rice. The friendly chef previously taught Japanese cuisine overseas.

■ Opening hours, last orders
Dinner = 18:00-21:30

■ Annual and weekly closing
Closed mid-August, late December-early January, Sunday and Public Holidays

■ Price
Dinner = set   ¥ 13,650-15,750

TEL. 03-3407-3033
5-50-10 Jingumae, Shibuya-ku, Tokyo
www.aoyama-kogetsu.com

Koju
小十

✿ ✿ ✿   ✕

✌/ ⬚ 10 ⚌ ⦿Ⅱ 📅 ⊛ ⌂

The name comes from close friend and ceramicist Koju Nishioka.
Toru Okuda says he aims to use choice ingredients to excite his
customers. In addition to seafood ordered from Omaezaki, red
sea bream, *hamo*, tilefish, prawns and others are sent daily from
Naruto in Tokushima. The *unagi* is thick and both the *shirayaki*
and *kabayaki* are tasty. For dessert, strawberry sherbet with
champagne rosé shows the chef's creativity.

■ Opening hours, last orders
Dinner = 17:30-1:00 L.O.23:30
Saturday 17:30-24:00 L.O.21:30

■ Annual and weekly closing
Closed mid-August, late December-
early January, Sunday and Public
Holidays

■ Price
Dinner = set   ¥ 13,650-26,250
Service charge = 10%

TEL. 03–6215–9544
8-5-25 Ginza, Chuo-ku, Tokyo
www.kojyu.jp

Komuro

小室

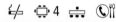

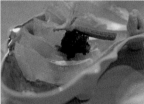

Mitsuhiro Komuro's philosophy is to use choice ingredients to emphasise seasonal flavours. The summer *hamo zukushi* menu is a treat and includes *tsukuri*, *oshizushi* and other *hamo* dishes. Chat with the chef while enjoying food served in ceramics by Seika Suda and Tosai Sawamura. Go up Kagurazaka-dori Avenue, take the side road just before Zenkoku-ji Temple and follow it until the white sign. The restaurant may relocate in 2011.

■ Opening hours, last orders
Lunch = Tue.-Sat. 12:00-13:00
(L.O.)
Dinner = 18:30-20:00 (L.O.)

■ Annual and weekly closing
Closed mid-August, 21 December-16
January, Sunday and Public
Holidays

■ Price
Lunch = set   ¥ 8,400-12,600
Dinner = set   ¥ 16,800-63,000
Service charge = 10%

TEL. 03-3235-3332
13 Wakamiyacho, Shinjuku-ku,
Tokyo

Kondo
近藤

Fumio Kondo opened this *tempura* restaurant in 1991, from a desire to treat customers to generous helpings of delicious vegetables. Because he wants to provide the tastes of the season, he travels to the production areas himself to buy ingredients directly. One 'must' is sweet potato: after frying, the cylindrical slices are left to cook in the remaining heat. Also worth trying is zucchini stuffed with *yuba*, his original recipe.

■ Opening hours, last orders
Lunch = 12:00-15:00 L.O.13:30
Dinner = 17:00-22:30 L.O.20:30

■ Annual and weekly closing
Closed Golden week, mid-August,
late December-early January,
Sunday and Public Holiday
Mondays

■ Price
Lunch = set   ¥ 6,300-8,400
Dinner = set   ¥ 10,500-17,850

TEL. 03–5568–0923
Sakaguchi Building 9F,
5-5-13 Ginza, Chuo-ku, Tokyo

Kuikiri Eguchi
喰切り 江ぐち

This 8 counter-seat restaurant is run by a conscientious owner-chef and his friendly wife. Originally a members-only establishment, Toru Eguchi opened to the public in 2009 after relocating to Ginza. There are three different *omakase* set menus; they do not come with very many items, so if you want to enjoy *suppon*, we recommend the most expensive one – prices are a little high, but the *suppon* dishes are carefully prepared.

■ Opening hours, last orders
Dinner = 18:00-22:00 (L.O.)

■ Annual and weekly closing
Closed mid-August, late December-early January, Sunday and Public Holidays

■ Price
Dinner = set   ¥ 15,750-26,250
          à la carte ¥ 6,300-15,000

TEL. 03-5537-5141
6-3-8 Ginza, Chuo-ku, Tokyo

JAPANESE MAP NO. 15/D-3

Kurogi NEW
くろぎ

Jun Kurogi relocated to a traditional Japanese house in 2007. Besides standard items like aromatic *goma-dofu* and tender tongue stew, the menu is determined by the day's ingredients. Prices are relatively low as he wants to introduce people to Japanese cuisine. The number of lunches served is limited; the *tai chazuke* comes with small appetisers and dessert. The name was changed from 'Yushima 121' to 'Kurogi' in autumn 2010.

■ Opening hours, last orders
Lunch = Tue.-Fri. 11:30-12:30
and 12:30-13:30
Dinner = 17:00-22:00 (L.O.)

■ Annual and weekly closing
Closed mid-August, late December-early January, Sunday and Public Holidays

■ Price
Lunch = set ¥ 1,050
Dinner = set ¥ 9,240-12,600
Service charge = 10% (dinner)

TEL. 03-5846-3510
3-35-1 Yushima, Bunkyo-ku, Tokyo

Kuwano
くわ野

Tatsuya Kuwano opened in 2005, having spent many years as chef of a sushi restaurant in Akasaka. Appetisers before the sushi could include oysters steamed in sake, tasty *kobashira* kebab seasoned with red pepper flakes or the grilled spicy marinated pollock roe. Examples of the sushi are gizzard shad and the prawn, which is boiled on the spot. Although a little pricey, the effort Kuwano puts into his work is worth it.

■ Opening hours, last orders
Dinner = 17:00-24:00 L.O.23:00

■ Annual and weekly closing
Closed Golden week, mid-August,
late December-early January,
Sunday and Public Holidays

■ Price
Dinner = set   ¥ 20,000-25,000

TEL. 03–3573–6577
Hiratsuka Building 3F,
8-7-6 Ginza, Chuo-ku, Tokyo

Kyoraku-tei
蕎楽亭

The faint sound of a *shamisen* drifting in from a music studio suits the atmosphere here. It is well-regarded for its stone-ground, hand-kneaded *soba* noodles made with *soba* flour from the Aizu, the owner's home town. For a summer treat try the tomato *soba*. There are drinking snacks like *zarudofu*, uncooked *yuba* and *anago tempura*, so be sure to order some sake. *Udon* is also a favourite. It fills up fast at lunch, so arrive early.

■ Opening hours, last orders
Lunch = Tue.-Sat. 11:30-15:00
L.O.14:30
Dinner = 17:00-21:00 L.O.20:30

■ Annual and weekly closing
Closed early January, mid-August,
Sunday and Public Holidays

■ Price
Lunch = à la carte ¥ 1,500-5,000
Dinner = à la carte ¥ 1,500-5,000

TEL. 03-3269-3233
3-6 Kagurazaka, Shinjuku-ku,
Tokyo

La Bombance

Although underpinned by Japanese culinary traditions, the cooking uses a variety of non-Japanese ingredients – one is unlikely to find these dishes elsewhere. With freshness as his credo, the owner-chef buys only the day's ingredients. He serves a monthly changing menu and foie gras appears as a constant. A degustation menu, with sake pairings, is also available. The amiable owner-chef gives his customers his full attention.

■ Opening hours, last orders
Dinner = 18:00-22:00 (L.O.)

■ Annual and weekly closing
Closed mid-August, late December-early January, Sunday and Public Holidays

■ Price
Dinner = set   ¥ 10,800
Service charge = 10%

TEL. 03–5778–6511
New City Residence Twin Tower I B1F, 2-26-21 Nishiazabu, Minato-ku, Tokyo
www.bombance.com

L'Anneau d'Or

A husband and wife team run this small restaurant; he buys ingredients from all over the country to create rich, but not heavy, cuisine. Specialities include carefully selected soft-steamed egg in a small cocotte with a sauce of truffles and foie gras; Lacan pigeon with a light salmis sauce and roasted Challans duck served with a Rouennaise sauce. The two-plate business lunch is served on Mondays, Tuesdays and Thursdays.

■ Opening hours, last orders
Lunch = 12:30-15:00 L.O.13:30
Dinner = 18:30-22:30 L.O.20:30

■ Annual and weekly closing
Closed mid-August, late December-
early January and Wednesday

■ Price
Lunch = set   ¥ 5,000-21,000
Dinner = set   ¥ 10,000-21,000
Service charge = 10% (lunch 5%)

TEL. 03-5919-0141
Yotsuya Sun Heights B1F,
4-6-1 Yotsuya, Shinjuku-ku, Tokyo
www.lanneaudor-tokyo.com

La Table de Joël Robuchon

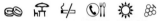

French *convivialité* is the underlying theme of the restaurant and a favourite word of Joël Robuchon. The cuisine is contemporary French, with original recipes combining Spain (gazpacho soup), Italy (millefeuille of eggplant, tomato and mozzarella cheese) and France (quail with a caramelised layer stuffed with foie gras). A special feature is an hors d'oeuvre of consommé jelly-covered sea urchin, served with fennel cream.

■ Opening hours, last orders
Lunch = 11:30-14:00 (L.O.)
Dinner = 18:00-21:30 (L.O.)

■ Price
Lunch = set   ¥ 2,950-5,250
          à la carte ¥ 7,000-14,000
Dinner = set   ¥ 4,800-13,800
          à la carte ¥ 7,000-14,000
Service charge = 10%

TEL. 03–5424–1338
Yebisu Garden Place,
1-13-1 Mita, Meguro-ku, Tokyo
www.robuchon.jp/ebisu

L'Atelier de Joël Robuchon

The stylish red and black interior is dominated by a long counter with seating for 44, in the style of a sushi restaurant or Spanish bar. The open kitchen is lively; the chefs and waiting team a friendly lot. Carefully selected ingredients include seafood from Japan, foie gras, asparagus and poultry from France and, from Spain, Jamón Ibérico de Bellota. The Dégustation menu allows guests to try a variety of à la carte dishes.

■ Opening hours, last orders
Lunch = 11:30-14:30 (L.O.)
Sun. and Public Holidays
11:30-15:00 (L.O.)
Dinner = 18:00-22:00 (L.O.)

■ Price
Lunch = set   ¥ 2,950-12,600
         à la carte ¥ 5,000-16,000
Dinner = set   ¥ 4,800-14,800
         à la carte ¥ 5,000-16,000
Service charge = 10%

TEL. 03–5772–7500
Roppongi Hills Hillside 2F,
6-10-1 Roppongi, Minato-ku,
Tokyo
www.robuchon.jp/roppongi

La Tour

Owner-chef Tadaaki Shimizu refined his skills at La Tour d'Argent in Paris and Tokyo. The Royale de Foie Gras is a house speciality: foie gras is cooked for four hours at 110℃, flavoured with Sauternes and refined by the sweetness of honey. Also recommended are duck dishes, which go well with the green pepper, fig or citrus sauces. There is also a wide choice of French cheeses. The restaurant uses classic French techniques.

■ Opening hours, last orders
Lunch = 11:30-15:00 L.O.13:30
Dinner = 18:00-23:00 L.O.20:30

■ Annual and weekly closing
Closed mid-August, 31 December,
1 January and Monday

■ Price
Lunch = set   ¥ 4,500-8,000
Dinner = set   ¥ 12,500-18,500
                à la carte ¥ 14,000-19,000

Service charge = 10%

TEL. 03–3569–2211
Kojun Building 5F,
6-8-7 Ginza, Chuo-ku, Tokyo
www.ginzalatour.com

La Tour d'Argent

♿ ✌ ☞ 🅿 📷 30 📞🍴 ☀ 🐾

The venerable Parisian establishment, serving diners since 1582, opened this Tokyo outpost in 1984. The restaurant spells graceful luxury at every turn. Among the specialities is roast duckling, imported from France. Two sauces are recommended: 'Tour d'Argent' is a rich sauce made from consommé and duck blood and liver, adjusted with cognac and Madeira - and "Marco Polo,' a duck stock seasoned with four types of pepper.

■ Opening hours, last orders
Dinner = 17:30-21:00 (L.O.)

■ Annual and weekly closing
Closed Monday

■ Price
Dinner = set   ¥ 21,000-35,000
              à la carte ¥ 15,000-25,000
Private room fee = less than 12 persons
                              ¥ 21,000
Service charge = 10%

TEL. 03-3239-3111
New Otani Hotel The Main 2F,
4-1 Kioicho, Chiyoda-ku, Tokyo
www.newotani.co.jp/tokyo

Lauburu NEW

Push the pig's foot shaped door knob to enter, and the sounds of Radio France, combined with the interior, will make you feel as though you stepped into Basque Country. The chef works with pork to this day, placing importance on the teachings of Madame Juliette. The menu includes pork dishes made from various parts, and the portions are large. Ham is all carefully home-cured; pork loin is cooked slowly over a charcoal flame.

■ Opening hours, last orders
Dinner = 18:00-22:00 (L.O.)

■ Annual and weekly closing
Closed mid-August, late December-
early January and Sunday

■ Price
Dinner = à la carte ¥ 3,500-7,000
Service charge = 10%

TEL. 03-3498-1314
6-8-18 Minamiaoyama,
Minato-ku, Tokyo

Le Bourguignon

Based on traditional French regional cuisine, the dishes of owner-chef Yoshinaru Kikuchi are refined according to his own style. His speciality is the *boudin noir* terrine with apple salad and purée: the dish is delicately flavoured. As offal is the chef's strong suit, the menu consists of many varied meat dishes, including a number of winter game dishes. Good wines, primarily from Burgundy, are offered at reasonable prices.

■ Opening hours, last orders
Lunch = 11:30-15:30 L.O.13:00
Dinner = 18:00-23:30 L.O.21:00

■ Annual and weekly closing
Closed 2 weeks in July, late December-early January, Wednesday and 2nd Tuesday of each month

■ Price
Lunch = set   ¥ 2,625-4,725
        à la carte ¥ 7,000-11,000
Dinner = set   ¥ 5,775-10,500
        à la carte ¥ 7,000-11,000
Service charge = 10%

TEL. 03-5772-6244
3-3-1 Nishiazabu, Minato-ku, Tokyo

Le Jeu de l'Assiette NEW

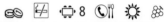

The second-generation chef's experiences in France inform his creative dishes, which do not use too much oil. The assortment of ingredients is original and the delicate seasoning is exquisite. Specialities are Tasmanian ocean trout, roasted duck breast and chocolate sphere rose. As the name of the restaurant – "play on the plate" – implies, the appealing, whimsical presentation of the food makes for a delightful experience.

■ Opening hours, last orders
Lunch = 11:30-13:30 (L.O.)
Dinner = 18:00-21:00 (L.O.)

■ Annual and weekly closing
Closed mid-August, late December-early January and Monday

■ Price
Lunch = set   ¥ 3,500-10,000
Dinner = set   ¥ 7,500-13,500
Service charge = 10%

TEL. 03–6415–5100
Sun Village Daikanyama 2F,
2-17-5 Ebisunishi, Shibuya-ku,
Tokyo
www.lejeudelassiette.com

Le Mange-Tout

✿✿   ✕✕

                                          ⇗ ☏⏱

Chef Noboru Tani is an avid follower of Auguste Escoffier and offers traditional French cuisine but with a modern twist. In winter expect game dishes using Japanese deer and boar from West Izu in Shizuoka; game consommé is based on a classic venison dish with sauce poivrade. *Omble chevalier*, a European mountain trout, is served lightly smoked. The *pêche Melba* combines juicy peach, vanilla ice cream and raspberry sauce.

■ Opening hours, last orders
Dinner = 18:30-21:00 (L.O.)

■ Annual and weekly closing
Closed late December-early
January and Sunday

■ Price
Dinner = set   ¥ 12,600
Service charge = 10%

TEL. 03–3268–5911
22 Nandomachi, Shinjuku-ku,
Tokyo
www.le-mange-tout.com

L'Embellir

Relocated in 2010, when the adjoining *pâtisserie* was also established. The small dining room has a modern interior and only set menus are offered; just one course is served at lunch unless reservations are made. More use is made now of domestic ingredients, but the delicate seasoning remains unchanged. Specialities like the market garden vegetable terrine, *akaza ebi* wrapped in crispy potatoes or almond blancmange feature.

■ Opening hours, last orders
Lunch = 11:30-14:00 (L.O.)
Dinner = 18:00-21:00 (L.O.)

■ Annual and weekly closing
mid-August, late December-early
January, Sunday and Monday

■ Price
Lunch = set   ¥ 5,250-10,500
Dinner = set   ¥ 12,600-15,750
Private room fee = ¥ 10,500 (dinner)
Service charge = 10%

TEL. 03-6427-3209
R2-A B1F, 5-2-11 Minamiaoyama,
Minato-ku, Tokyo
www.lembellir.com

Le Pergolèse

🐧 XXXX

♿ ⚕ P 🚇8 ☏🍴 ☀ 🐝

A branch of Parisian restaurant Le Pergolèse, supervised by owner-chef Stéphane Gaborieau. Emphasis is placed on the natural taste of the ingredients and, from time to time, they are combined to create unique dishes; originality is also evident in the elaborate arrangements on the plate. There is also a 'Wine Marriage' menu, which offers wines from around the world which are carefully selected to complement the dishes.

■ Opening hours, last orders
Dinner = 17:30-22:00 L.O.21:30

■ Annual and weekly closing
Closed Monday

■ Price
Dinner = set   ¥ 12,600-18,900
           à la carte ¥ 12,000-20,000
Private room fee = ¥ 8,820
Service charge = 10%

TEL. 03-3344-5111
Hilton Hotel 2F,
6-6-2 Nishishinjuku, Shinjuku-ku,
Tokyo
www.hilton.co.jp/tokyo

Les Créations de Narisawa

Yoshihiro Narisawa offers creative and modern dishes which are underpinned by the basics of French cuisine, hence the restaurant's name. Take note, too, of the novel combinations of ingredients. Organic vegetables come directly from farmers, while fish is sourced nationwide and delivered on the same day as caught. Located in the courtyard of a modern building, this chic restaurant is ideally suited for special occasions.

■ Opening hours, last orders
Lunch = 12:00-13:00 (L.O.)
Dinner = 18:30-21:00 (L.O.)

■ Annual and weekly closing
Closed Sunday

■ Price
Lunch = set   ¥ 7,350-21,000
Dinner = set   ¥ 21,000
Service charge = 10%

TEL. 03-5785-0799
2-6-15 Minamiaoyama, Minato-ku, Tokyo
www.narisawa-yoshihiro.com

FRENCH MAP NO. 27/B-2

Les Enfants Gâtés

The first thing to catch your eye is the refrigerator filled with colourful terrine containers. Flavours vary from traditional to inventive, such as the aged country-style pâté or the pressed terrine of organic vegetables; duck foie gras terrine is a speciality. Seafood, including lobster, is also made into sublime terrines. Expect too a range of sophisticated dishes, based on traditional recipes using contemporary techniques.

■ Opening hours, last orders
Lunch = 12:00-14:00 (L.O.)
Dinner = 18:00-21:30 (L.O.)

■ Annual and weekly closing
Closed late December-early January
and Monday except Public Holidays

■ Price
Lunch = set   ¥ 3,150-5,775
Dinner = set   ¥ 7,140-11,550
              à la carte ¥ 6,000-11,000
Service charge = 10%

TEL. 03-3476-2929
2-3 Sarugakucho, Shibuya-ku,
Tokyo
www.terrine-gates.com

Le 6eme Sens d'Oenon

The dishes conceived by chef Dominique Corby are creative; French and Japanese ingredients are used and plates come attractively presented. The basement private room is well worth a visit and is ideal for special occasions, small parties and business entertaining. Specialities include wild duck, sabayon of *homard* lobster and soufflé. Set menus change monthly and the à la carte every season. Lunch menus are well priced.

■ Opening hours, last orders
Lunch = 12:00-14:00 (L.O.)
Dinner = 18:00-21:00 (L.O.)

■ Annual and weekly closing
Closed mid-August, late December-early January, Sunday and Public Holidays

■ Price
Lunch = set		¥ 4,500-10,000
	à la carte	¥ 12,500-21,000
Dinner = set		¥ 12,000-18,000
	à la carte	¥ 12,500-21,000

TEL. 03-3575-2767
6-2-10 Ginza, Chuo-ku, Tokyo
www.6eme.com

Les Saisons

The 'classic-modern' style fuses traditional design elements with a contemporary elegance. While the menu is grounded in tradition, dishes incorporate a modern spirit. For example, roast flounder with truffles and a white asparagus purée; and Bresse chicken breast stuffed with morels and served with Comté cheese gnocchi. The spacious dining has warmly lit oak walls and, in addition to 4 private rooms, also has a cigar salon.

■ Opening hours, last orders
Lunch = 11:30-14:30 (L.O.)
Dinner = 17:30-22:00 (L.O.)

■ Price
Lunch = set   ¥ 6,800-10,500
            à la carte ¥ 13,000-28,000
Dinner = set   ¥ 16,800-29,000
            à la carte ¥ 13,000-28,000
Private room fee = ¥ 10,500-21,000
Service charge = 10%

TEL. 03–3539–8087
Imperial Hotel-Main Building M2F,
1-1-1 Uchisaiwaicho, Chiyoda-ku,
Tokyo
www.imperialhotel.co.jp

Lugdunum Bouchon Lyonnais

Owner-chef Christophe Paucod was born in Lyon and in tribute to his hometown has faithfully replicated a typical *bouchon* restaurant. As well as Lyonnaise salad and *boudin nouvelle*, there are other dishes that add touches of creativity and lightness to tradition. Burgundy and Rhône wines account for the majority of the wine list. French music plays in the background and Mr Paucod provides friendly service in fluent Japanese.

■ Opening hours, last orders
Lunch = 11:30-14:30 (L.O.)
Dinner = 18:00-22:00 (L.O.)

■ Annual and weekly closing
Closed 2 weeks in August, late December-early January, Monday and 3rd Tuesday of each month

■ Price
Lunch = set Tue.-fri. ¥ 1,850-3,850
          set Sat., Sun.¥ 2,850-3,850
Dinner = set   ¥ 3,850-4,850
          à la carte ¥ 4,000-6,000

TEL. 03-6426-1201
4-3-7 Kagurazaka, Shinjuku-ku, Tokyo
www.lyondelyon.com

CHINESE

Maison de Yulong

XX

      🍴 18 ☏🍴 ✿

Maison de Yulong serves nouvelle Chinese cuisine that uses many local ingredients. The focus is on fixed price menus, but at lunch there are other items such as noodles and fried rice. The carefully adjusted seasoning is the highlight of dishes like freshwater shrimp simmered in fermented been curd, delicately textured jellyfish and rock salt sautéed seasonal vegetables and reef squid. The head chef specialises in stir-fry.

■ Opening hours, last orders
Lunch = 11:30-15:00 L.O.13:30
Sat.,Sun. and Public Holidays
11:30-15:00 L.O.14:00
Dinner = 17:30-23:00 L.O.21:30

■ Annual and weekly closing
Closed late December-early January
and Sunday

■ Price
Lunch = set   ¥ 2,940-6,300
      à la carte ¥ 2,000-12,000
Dinner = set   ¥ 6,300-15,750
      à la carte ¥ 6,000-25,000
Service charge = 10%

TEL. 03-3589-3955
4-13-18 Akasaka, Minato-ku,
Tokyo
www.yulong.jp

Maison Paul Bocuse

A partnership between celebrated chef Paul Bocuse, and Hiroyuki Hiramatsu. Try specialities from the chef's Lyon restaurant: oven-baked black truffle consommé covered with pie dough, served in 1975 to then French President Valéry Giscard d'Estaing; the sea bass pie with Choron sauce uses a whole sea bass, and is good to share; *poularde de Bresse en vessie*, which requires pre-ordering. Popular for weekend wedding receptions.

■ Opening hours, last orders
Lunch = 12:00-13:30 (L.O.)
Dinner = 18:00-20:30 (L.O.)

■ Annual and weekly closing
Closed early January and Monday
except Public Holidays

■ Price
Lunch = set   ¥ 2,860-6,300
          à la carte ¥ 11,000-23,000
Dinner = set   ¥ 12,000-25,000
          à la carte ¥ 11,000-23,000
Service charge = 10%

TEL. 03-5458-6324
Daikanyama Forum B1F,
17-16 Sarugakucho, Shibuya-ku,
Tokyo
www.hiramatsu.co.jp/restaurants/
maison-paulbocuse

Makimura
まき村

Warm hospitality is a feature of this simple restaurant, with counter and table seating. Akio Makimura uses a light stock and two different kinds of dried bonito - with or without *chiai*. The former is used to make a richer stock for the fried eggplant dish; the latter for the clear soup of pike conger and egg tofu. *Tai-chazuke*, refined over years, has a rich flavour. Recommended is the *fugu kaiseki* from December to February.

■ Opening hours, last orders
Lunch = Tue.-Sat. 12:00-14:00
L.O.13:00
Dinner = 17:30-22:00 L.O.21:00

■ Annual and weekly closing
Closed Golden week, mid-August, late December-early January, Sunday and Public Holiday Mondays

■ Price
Lunch = set   ¥ 6,300-8,400
Dinner = set   ¥ 10,500-16,800
Service charge = 10%

TEL. 03-3768-6388
3-11-5 Minamioi, Shinagawa-ku, Tokyo

Masa's Kitchen 47

Dishes are largely traditional and from all over China—but primarily Sichuan—and are prepared in a modern style so as not to be too heavy. The predominant feature is the delicate seasoning which highlights the freshness of the ingredients; for example, in the cold eggplant and raw sea urchin and the 'Zabuton' beef *sashimi* dish with its rare cuts. At lunch, set menus with pork dumplings and noodles are also offered.

■ Opening hours, last orders
Lunch = 11:30-14:00 (L.O.)
Dinner = 18:00-23:30 L.O.22:30

■ Annual and weekly closing
Closed Golden week, mid-August, late December-early January and Monday

■ Price
Lunch = set   ¥ 3,500-5,500
        à la carte ¥ 1,400-20,000
Dinner = set   ¥ 7,850-15,750
        à la carte ¥ 4,500-20,000
Service charge = 10% (dinner)

TEL. 03–3473–0729
Comforia Ebisu Building B1F,
1-21-13 Ebisu, Shibuya-ku, Tokyo

Masumi
ます味

Using the techniques he learned at a *kaiseki* restaurant, Tsukasa
Masui serves a wide variety of *anago* dishes. The thinly sliced
tsukuri resembles *fugu* and is served with *ponzu*, and in summer
anago shabu-shabu, reminiscent of *hamo*, comes with plum pulp
sauce. Staples include the fluffy *shirayaki* and the seared *anago*
hotpot with thinly sliced burdock served in an iron pot. The
anago should keep you coming back for more.

■ Opening hours, last orders
Lunch = 12:00-14:00 L.O.13:00
Dinner = 17:00-22:30 L.O.21:00

■ Annual and weekly closing
Closed mid-August, late December-
early January, Sunday and Public
Holidays

■ Price
Lunch = set   ¥ 3,700-5,300
Dinner = set   ¥ 6,500-12,000
Service charge = 10%

TEL. 03-3356-5938
Hokuto Yotsuya Building B1F,
11-2 Arakicho, Shinjuku-ku,
Tokyo

Mikawa Keyakizaka-dori
みかわ けやき坂通り

In addition to the nine seats at a red lacquered counter, there is a private room. The proprietress and skilled staff handle all the work. There are only a few vegetable items, but the focus lies on seafood as is the tradition with *Edomae tempura*. The *saimaki ebi* and squid are cooked just right and served medium-done, and the *anago* is crispy, fragrant and evenly golden brown; everything has a light sesame fragrance to it.

■ Opening hours, last orders
Lunch = 11:30-14:00
Dinner = 17:30-21:30
Sun. and Public Holidays
17:30-21:00

■ Annual and weekly closing
Closed mid-August, late December-
early January and Wednesday

■ Prices
Lunch = set   ¥ 5,880-10,500
Dinner = set   ¥ 10,500

TEL. 03-3423-8100
Roppongi Hills Residence B, 3F,
6-12-2 Roppongi, Minato-ku,
Tokyo

Mikawa Zezankyo
みかわ 是山居

10

Tetsuya Saotome opened this restaurant in 2009 as the realisation of his dreams. His tastes are evident, from the golden duct modelled on his favourite borsalino to the lacquered floor and stained glass. The flow of the meal goes from light to strongly flavoured items, moving from *makiebi* to smelt-whiting, squid, *megochi* and *anago*; their degree of cooking also varies. The soup is a rare experiment for a tempura restaurant.

■ Opening hours, last orders
Lunch = 11:30-14:00 L.O.13:30
Dinner = 17:00-22:30 L.O.20:30

■ Annual and weekly closing
Closed mid-August, late December-early January and Wednesday

■ Prices
Lunch = set ¥ 10,500
Dinner = set ¥ 15,750-16,800

TEL. 03-3643-8383
1-3-1 Fukuzumi, Koto-ku, Tokyo

Minoichi
未能一

Owner-chef Yasuji Tatsumi and his wife run this small but charming *kappo* restaurant, paying attention to the smallest of details. Each dish leaves you with a real appreciation of the skill of a traditional Japanese chef. The *konnyaku* and scallion mixed with salted and fermented bonito gut is perfectly seasoned and provides a nice chewy texture, while the sea urchin pickled in *miso* is richly flavoured and satisfying.

■ Opening hours, last orders
Dinner = 17:30-22:30 L.O.21:00

■ Annual and weekly closing
Closed Golden week, mid-August, late December-early January and Sunday

■ Price
Dinner = set   ¥ 12,600-21,000
Service charge = 10%

TEL. 03-3289-3011
Suzuryu Building 5F,
8-7-19 Ginza, Chuo-ku, Tokyo

Mitsuta
三ツ田

Diners sit on *tatami* at this *tempura* restaurant, opened in 1958. Through a specially made glass cover you can watch the chef at work. Meals begin with several *makiebi*, thinly battered and fried, with a raw centre to bring out their sweetness. The taste of the pickled vegetables, *miso* soup and *tentsuyu* dipping sauce comes from a secret recipe from the proprietress' aunt. Don't forget to remove your shoes at the entrance.

■ Opening hours, last orders
Lunch = 12:00-14:30 (L.O.)
Dinner = 17:30-20:30 (L.O.)

■ Annual and weekly closing
Closed mid-August, late December-early January, Sunday and Public Holidays

■ Price
Lunch = set ¥ 14,700
Dinner = set ¥ 16,800
Service charge = 10%

TEL. 03-3541-5577
1-12-15 Tsukiji, Chuo-ku, Tokyo

Momonoki
桃の木

Although the menu mostly consists of Cantonese and Shanghainese dishes, those from Beijing and Sichuan are not overlooked. Takeshi Kobayashi prefers 'less familiar home-style dishes' and avoids pricey dried ingredients like shark's fin and abalone. Lightly fried *A-sai* and *fu ru* is their specialty. *Mapo tofu*, a typical Sichuan offering, is made using hot pepper rather than *dou ban jiang*. One unique Beijing dish is duck tongue.

■ Opening hours, last orders
Lunch = 11:30-14:30 L.O.14:00
Dinner = 17:30-22:30 L.O.21:30

■ Annual and weekly closing
Closed mid-August, late December-early January, Wednesday and 2nd Tuesday of each month

■ Price
Lunch = set   ¥ 2,500-15,000
        à la carte   ¥ 3,000-6,500
Dinner = set   ¥ 8,500-20,000
        à la carte   ¥ 3,000-6,500

TEL. 03-5443-1309
2-17-29 Mita, Minato-ku, Tokyo
www.mitamachi-momonoki.com

Monnalisa Ebisu

The menu changes quarterly, with new dishes being added each year. In spring, examples could include *blanc-manger d' asperges blanches et crevettes facon*; in summer you might find *rocace de tomate farcie au crabe et laitue*. Only a minimal amount of butter is ever used and all dishes beautifully match the plates designed by the chef himself. A smaller portion à la carte menu is available only at lunch on weekdays.

■ Opening hours, last orders
Lunch = 11:30-15:30 L.O.14:00
Dinner = 17:30-23:30 L.O.21:30

■ Annual and weekly closing
Closed late December-early January

■ Price
Lunch = set   ¥ 5,064-10,550
Dinner = set   ¥ 7,174-15,825
                    à la carte ¥ 8,000-15,000
Service charge = 10%

TEL. 03-5458-1887
1-14-4 Ebisunishi, Shibuya-ku,
Tokyo
www.monnalisa.co.jp

Monnalisa Marunouchi

Toru Kawano favours set menus and offers a large variety of seasonal dishes, taking care not to overlap cooking methods and seasoning combinations. He also looks to indigenous ingredients - wild plants in spring and ginkgo and *matsutake* mushrooms in autumn - to create a distinctly Japanese sense of season. The speciality is roast lamb with a herb and salt pie dough. Wide windows offering a city panorama is another treat.

■ Opening hours, last orders
Lunch = 11:30-15:30 L.O.14:00
Dinner = 17:30-23:30 L.O.21:30

■ Annual and weekly closing
Closed 1 January

■ Price
Lunch = set   ¥ 3,956-10,550
Dinner = set   ¥ 7,174-16,880
               à la carte ¥ 8,000-15,000
Service charge = 10%

TEL. 03-3240-5775
Marunouchi Building 36F,
2-4-1 Marunouchi, Chiyoda-ku,
Tokyo
www.monnalisa.co.jp

Motoyoshi NEW
元吉

Offering three *omakase* set menus, owner-chef Kazuhito Motoyoshi says he is keen to see people eat lots of vegetables, which is why the menu ends up with so many vegetable dishes. Be sure to try the standard 'kakumorokoshi' summer dish and the firm asparagus. The savoury *mizunasu* is kept juicy, and the *kamonasu* is cooked slowly to draw out the flavour. Open late; after 9pm you can order your favourite dishes or just *tencha*.

■ Opening hours, last orders
Dinner = 17:30-23:00 (L.O.)

■ Annual and weekly closing
Closed mid-August, late December-early January and Sunday

■ Prices
Dinner = set   ¥ 7,350-10,500
Service charge =10 %

TEL.03-3401-0722
Central Aoyama No.6 B1F
3-2-4 Minamiaoyama, Minato-ku, Tokyo
www.motoyoshi-1120.com

JAPANESE MAP NO. 22/A-3

Muroi
室井

8

Masao Muroi opened his restaurant in 1980 and the 'Muroi-style' results from his culinary flexibility. Original dishes include curry made with a bonito and kelp broth and others using wild plants. Another appealing feature is wild mushrooms collected by the chef and his staff in autumn; about 40kg of over 70 varieties are picked in a single day. The wild mushroom set menu offers a pasta dish, risotto and a clear soup.

■ Opening hours, last orders
Dinner = 17:30-22:00 (L.O.)

■ Annual and weekly closing
Closed Golden week, mid-August, late December-early January, Sunday and Public Holidays

■ Price
Dinner = set ¥ 15,750-31,500
Service charge = 10%

TEL. 03–3571–1421
Suzuryu Building 2F,
8-7-19 Ginza, Chuo-ku, Tokyo

Muto NEW
むとう

  LUNCH

Soft lighting and background jazz set the mood. The *soba* flour arrives daily from a long-time supplier in Nagano. It is basically *juwari*, but a small amount of flour is added depending on the weather. The noodles are thick and glossy, while rich sauce made with 2-year old dried bonito accents the aroma and sweetness of the *soba*. At dinner, there is only a set menu featuring *sashimi* and broiled fish, ending with *soba*.

■ Opening hours, last orders
Lunch = 11:30-14:30 L.O.14:00
Sat. 12:00-16:00 L.O.15:30
Dinner = Mon.-Fri. 17:30-21:00
L.O.20:30

■ Annual and weekly closing
Closed early January, mid-August,
Sunday , 2nd and 4th Saturday of
each month and Public Holidays

■ Price
Lunch = set   ¥ 4,000
           à la carte   ¥ 2,000-5,000
Dinner = set   ¥ 5,250-7,350
Service charge = 5% (dinner)

TEL. 03-3231-7188
1-13-1 Nihonbashimuromachi,
Chuo-ku, Tokyo

Nabeya NEW
なべ家

Hiroshi Fukuda, the second-generation owner-chef of this restaurant founded in 1935, is an expert in Edo cuisine. Kelp is not used in the stock; instead, it is made with sake and *katsuobushi*. The *katsuo sashimi* with mustard and the sweet fried eggs are good examples of *Edomae* cuisine. Look for *negima* hotpot in April, brook trout in May, *ayu* from June to August, *matsutake* in September, and *fugu* and *Horai nabe* in winter.

■ Opening hours, last orders
Dinner = 17:00-21:00

■ Annual and weekly closing
Closed mid-August, late December-early January, Sunday and Public Holidays

■ Prices
Dinner = set   ¥ 15,750-23,100
Service charge = 10%

TEL. 03–3941–2868
1-51-14 Minamiotsuka,
Toshima-ku, Tokyo
http://www.gourmet.ne.jp/nabeya/

Nadaman Honten Sazanka-so
なだ万本店 山茶花荘

✿ ✿   ❌❌❌❌

🏮 ✈ ☞ 🅿 💺 16 ☎🍴 ☀

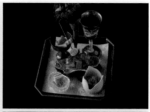

All four rooms, named from *The Tale of Genji*, have a view of the manicured garden from the veranda. Waiting staff in kimono offer polished service, making this a suitable venue for a reception. The traditional cuisine focuses on seasonal tastes; one example in winter is yellowtail covered with turnip; simmered beef cheek and Sakurajima radish dish is also tasty. Prices may not be that low but lunch menus are less expensive.

■ Opening hours, last orders
Lunch = 11:30-15:00
Dinner = 17:00-22:00

■ Annual and weekly closing
Closed late December-early January

■ Price
Lunch = set   ¥ 21,000-42,000
Dinner = set   ¥ 42,000
Private room fee = ¥ 8,000/person
                 (Mon.-Fri. for dinner)
Service charge = 20%

TEL. 03-3264-7921
New Otani Hotel Japanese Garden,
4-1 Kioicho, Chiyoda-ku, Tokyo
www.nadaman.co.jp/sazankaso

Nagazumi   NEW
ながずみ

The name comes from the owner-chef's hometown in Fukuoka City. He stands behind the 10-seater, U-shaped counter, wearing a white *samue* with his hair pulled back. There are three *omakase* set menus, featuring creative combinations of aromas and textures. The *oden*, which is the speciality, features a stock made not only from kelp and *katsuo-bushi* but also flying fish and small horse mackerel. It is always lively at night.

■ Opening hours, last orders
Dinner = 18:00-22:30 (L.O.)

■ Price
Dinner = set   ¥ 7,000-10,000

TEL. 03–5410–1919
1-5-3 Motoakasaka, Minato-ku, Tokyo

Nakajima
中嶋

  LUNCH 20

The owner-chef Sadaharu Nakajima can trace his culinary roots back to his grandfather. He aims to create original cuisine guided by Kansai traditions, while remaining loyal to his family's craft. Nakajima pays close attention to both his cooking and his customers; he also develops many young cooks. At lunch, customers can choose from several set menus that feature sardines, as well as the traditional multi-course menu.

■ Opening hours, last orders
Lunch = 11:30-14:00 L.O.13:45
Dinner = 17:30-22:00 L.O.20:30

■ Annual and weekly closing
Closed mid-August, late December-early January, Sunday and Public Holidays

■ Price
Lunch = set   ¥ 800-5,250
Dinner = set   ¥ 8,400-13,650
Service charge = 10%

TEL. 03–3356–4534
Hihara Building B1F,
3-32-5 Shinjuku, Shinjuku-ku, Tokyo
www.shinjyuku-nakajima.com

Nico NEW
二戀

First timers may be a little confused by the members-only like appearance. The platinum finished walls and interior were designed by Yasumichi Morita. The chef honed his skills at a Naniwa *kappo* restaurant and places emphasis on natural flavours. Only set menus are available, but creative dishes using Western ingredients are combined with more traditional ones. The kimono-clad staff all leave a favourable impression.

■ Opening hours, last orders
Dinner = 18:00-22:00 (L.O.)

■ Annual and weekly closing
Closed mid-August, late December-early January and Sunday

■ Price
Dinner = set   ¥ 11,550-15,750
Service charge = 10%

TEL. 03-3498-3330
4-2-9 Nishiazabu, Minato-ku, Tokyo
www.nico-nishiazabu.jp

Nodaiwa
野田岩

5th-generation owner-chef Kanejiro Kanemoto keeps alive a family tradition as this is one of the few places serving natural *unagi*. Numbers are decreasing, but between mid-April to early December, he receives *unagi* caught at Kasumigaura, the Tone River and the Ariake. The *shirayaki*, the steamed *unagi* with its excess fat removed, is normally eaten with wasabi and rock salt, but try it here with caviar, an original combination.

■ Opening hours, last orders
Lunch = 11:00-13:30 (L.O.)
Dinner = 17:00-20:00 (L.O.)

■ Annual and weekly closing
Closed mid-August, late December-early January and Sunday

■ Price
Lunch = set   ¥ 4,500-15,700
          à la carte ¥ 2,100-10,000
Dinner = set   ¥ 4,500-15,700
          à la carte ¥ 2,100-10,000
Service charge = 10%

TEL. 03–3583–7852
1-5-4 Higashiazabu, Minato-ku, Tokyo

Obana NEW
尾花

Lines form before it opens and the hall with rows of small dining tables is reminiscent of the Showa era. The *unagi* is prepared once an order is placed and takes at least 40 minutes, so try drinking snacks like *koi-no-arai*, *umaki* and *uzaku* while waiting. The almost melting *shirayaki* is eaten with soy sauce and *wasabi*; the *unaju* is packed tight in the multi-tiered box with just the right amount of sauce soaking into the rice.

■ Opening hours, last orders
Lunch = 11:30-13:30
Sat., Sun. and Public Holidays
11:30-19:30
Dinner = 16:00-19:30

■ Annual and weekly closing
Closed mid-August, late December-
early January and Monday

Private room:
Closed July-September, Sunday
and Public Holidays

■ Prices
Lunch = set(private room only)
¥ 13,000
à la carte ¥ 3,500-12,000
Dinner = set (private room only)
¥ 13,000
à la carte ¥ 3,500-12,000

TEL.03–3801–4670
5-33-1 Minamisenju,
Arakawa-ku, Tokyo

Ogasawara Hakushaku-tei
小笠原伯爵邸

The current owner renovated this Spanish-style building, which was once the residence of Count Nagayoshi Ogasawara. Its air of elegance allows your mind to wander back in time to the life of the nobles. The Spanish chef offers colourful dishes based on Spanish cuisine with a modern twist, using Japanese ingredients. Only one set menu consisting of many small dishes is served. Suitable for both business or private occasions.

■ Opening hours, last orders
Lunch = 11:30-15:00 L.O.13:30
Dinner = 18:00-23:00 L.O.20:30

■ Annual and weekly closing
Closed 31 December-5 January

■ Price
Lunch = set   ¥ 7,350
Dinner = set   ¥ 10,500-15,750
Private room fee = ¥ 10,500
Service charge = 10%

TEL. 03-3359-5830
10-10 Kawadacho, Shinjuku-ku, Tokyo
www.ogasawaratei.com

Ohara's

Kei Ohara honed his skills in a number of famous restaurants in France, where he lived for a decade. He offers traditional French cuisine, placing particular attention on the pairing of sauces: Choron sauce is used for fish dishes and béarnaise is paired with grilled Hiba beef. The *boudin noir* served with herb salad is particularly recommended. Warm service provided by the chef's German wife makes for a friendly atmosphere.

■ Opening hours, last orders
Lunch = 11:30-15:00 L.O.14:00
Dinner = 18:00-23:00 L.O.21:00

■ Annual and weekly closing
Closed late December-mid-January,
Monday and 3rd Tuesday of each
month

■ Price
Lunch = set   ¥ 3,150-7,350
         à la carte ¥ 7,000-13,000
Dinner = set   ¥ 7,350-10,500
         à la carte ¥ 7,000-13,000
Service charge = 10%

TEL. 03–5436–3255
Yacmo Building B1F,
5-4-18 Osaki, Shinagawa-ku,
Tokyo

Okina
翁

The proprietress is an 8th-generation descendant of the founder of a long-established Sarashina *soba* restaurant. The buckwheat noodles are made and boiled on the spot for maximum freshness. While set menus ending with *soba* are generally served, other dishes can also be enjoyed: seaweed; fish and shellfish. Unique *soba* dishes are also available: tea flavoured *soba* with *yuzu* and winter *soba* kneaded with black or white truffles.

■ Opening hours, last orders
Dinner = 18:00-22:30 (L.O.)

■ Annual and weekly closing
Closed early January, Sunday and
Public Holidays

■ Price
Dinner = set   ¥ 15,750-26,250
Service charge = 10%

TEL. 03-3477-2648
Five Annex B1F,
1-3-10 Ebisunishi, Shibuya-ku,
Tokyo

Ozaki
おざき

✄ 🍱6 🚋 ☎🍴 🕐 ⚜ 🍶

As the son of a sushi chef, owner-chef Ichiro Ozaki sticks to what he knows best. He offers only an *omakase* set menu, which naturally includes sushi. After appetisers, two pieces of tasty tuna sushi are served as a 'greeting'. Grilled crab in its shell follows as a regular year-long dish. Seasonal dishes include cold sea-urchin *chawanmushi*, and fried soft-shelled turtle seasoned with the chef's original Asian spice blend.

■ Opening hours, last orders
Dinner = 18:00-24:00 L.O.22:00

■ Annual and weekly closing
Closed late December-early
January and Sunday

■ Price
Dinner = set   ¥ 17,325-21,000
Service charge = 10%

TEL. 03–3454–1682
3-4-5 Azabujuban, Minato-ku,
Tokyo

Pachon

André Pachon, who has lived in Japan for about 40 years, has contributed to the cultures of both France and Japan, thanks to his classic French cuisine. You may be surprised by the firewood stove burning all year long until learning that it is used to cook the lamb, duck, suckling pig and other fine ingredients. The speciality is *cassoulet* and, as the chef is from Carcassonne, he puts an extra touch into this hometown dish.

■ Opening hours, last orders
Lunch = 11:30-15:30 L.O.14:00
Dinner = 18:00-22:00 (L.O.)
Sun. and Public Holidays 18:00-
21:00 (L.O.)

■ Annual and weekly closing
Closed late December-early
January

■ Price
Lunch = set   ¥ 3,200-8,400
          à la carte   ¥ 4,500-6,500
Dinner = set   ¥ 6,300-16,800
          à la carte ¥ 9,000-24,000
Service charge = 10%

TEL. 03-3476-5025
Hillside Terrace B1F,
29-18 Sarugakucho, Shibuya-ku,
Tokyo
www.pachon.co.jp

Piatto Suzuki

Located by Azabujuban Station, which is a constant hive of activity. Owner-chef Yahei Suzuki serves traditional, regional Italian cuisine and the strictness with which he runs his kitchen is palpable. *Agu* pork, a delicacy, is ordered from Okinawa; chicken comes from Miyazaki and beef fillet from Hitachi in Ibaraki; most of the vegetables come directly from Kyoto. There's also a wide choice of Italian and French desserts.

■ Opening hours, last orders
Dinner = 18:00-2:00 L.O.24:00

■ Annual and weekly closing
Closed Golden week, late December-
early January, Sunday and Public
Holiday Mondays

■ Price
Dinner = set   ¥ 10,500
          à la carte ¥ 6,500-12,000

TEL. 03-5414-2116
Hasebeya Building 4F,
1-7-7 Azabujuban, Minato-ku,
Tokyo

FRENCH CONTEMPORARY

MAP NO. 21/C-2

Pierre Gagnaire   NEW

Opened in 2010 by famous chef Pierre Gagnaire, this restaurant serves creative dishes prepared with Japanese and French ingredients in set menus. Each dish is served on multiple plates for an enjoyable mix of tastes and arrangements. For lunch there is also a low-priced 'Express Gourmet' set consisting of the weekly appetiser and a main dish. The cityscape can be enjoyed from the bench seats, which are ideal for couples.

■ Opening hours, last orders
Lunch = 11:30-14:00 (L.O.)
Dinner = 18:00-21:00 (L.O.)

■ Annual and weekly closing
Closed Monday

■ Price
Lunch = set Tue.-Fri.¥ 3,800-10,000
           Sat., Sun.¥ 6,000-10,000
Dinner = set   ¥ 12,000-20,000
Service charge = 10%

TEL. 03–3505–1111
ANA Intercontinental Hotel 36F,
1-12-33 Akasaka, Minato-ku,
Tokyo
www.anaintercontinental-tokyo.jp

199

Quintessence

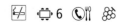

After training in Japan, Chef Shuzo Kishida's perfected his skills in France, notably at Parisian restaurant, Astrance. So inspired was he that he bases the menu *carte blanche* -under which different dishes are created for each table - on available ingredients as well as his own inclination. Particular care is paid to the roasting and broiling of meat and fish. Reservation calls are only accepted 09:30-11:00 and 15:30-17:00.

■ Opening hours, last orders
Lunch = 12:00-15:00 L.O.13:00
Dinner = 18:30-23:00 L.O.20:30

■ Annual and weekly closing
Closed late December-early January
and Sunday

■ Price
Lunch = set   ¥ 7,875
Dinner = set   ¥ 16,800
Service charge = 10%

TEL. 03–5791–3715
5-4-7 Shirokanedai, Minato-ku,
Tokyo
www.quintessence.jp

Raku-tei
楽亭

A subdued atmosphere and a plain wooden counter with seating for 12 greet you at this *tempura* restaurant. There is a choice of two set menus and the mild oil is specially blended to enhance the flavour of sesame and gives the *tempura* a light, pleasant taste. Owner-chef Shuji Ishikura fries *makiebi* only after receiving an order. The oil temperature for each ingredient is adjusted; while it is being changed try some *sashimi*.

■ Opening hours, last orders
Lunch = 12:00 (L.O.)
Dinner = 17:00-20:30 (L.O.)

■ Annual and weekly closing
Closed Golden week, mid-August, late December-early January and Monday

■ Price
Lunch = set   ¥ 10,500-12,600
Dinner = set   ¥ 10,500-12,600

TEL. 03-3585-3743
6-8-1 Akasaka, Minato-ku, Tokyo

Ranjatai NEW
蘭奢待

The atmosphere may be unremarkable but the *yakitori* will surprise you. We recommend the counter seats so you can see the chef's passion up close. Only Akita Hinai chicken is used; while difficult to prepare, its strong flavours come out through careful roasting and the skin produces a delicious aroma as it is cooked over *bincho*. First timers should try the set menu which includes liver pâté, six spit roasts and rice.

■ Opening hours, last orders
Dinner = Mon.-Fri. 17:00-2:00 L.O.1:00
Sat. 17:00-22:00 L.O.21:00

■ Annual and weekly closing
Closed mid-August, late December-early January, Sunday and Public Holidays

■ Price
Dinner = set   ¥ 2,310-3,360
          à la carte ¥ 4,000-6,000
Seat charge=¥ 500/person

TEL. 03–3263–0596
2-12-3 Kandajinbocho,
Chiyoda-ku, Tokyo
www.ranjatai.com

Reikasai
厲家菜

🍴 24 📞🍴 ☀

The female chef has access to imperial recipes, thanks to her grandfather who was a high-ranking courtier in the Qing Dynasty and supervised the preparation of meals for Empress Dowager Cixi. The chef's choice menu, which includes dishes such as smoked pork flavoured with jasmine and peanuts and coloured with beetroot, is bound to satisfy. Each colourful, memorable dish offers a sense of the rich history of the Li family.

■ Opening hours, last orders
Lunch = 11:30-15:30 L.O.13:30
Dinner = 18:00-23:30 L.O.20:30

■ Price
Lunch = set   ¥ 6,300-47,250
Dinner = set   ¥ 10,500-47,250
Service charge = 10%

TEL. 03-5413-9561
Roppongi Hills Residence B, 3F,
6-12-2 Roppongi, Minato-ku,
Tokyo

Ren   NEW
蓮

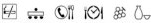

The sacred lotus (*ren*) symbolises purity and is used in the restaurant's name to express the approach of cooking with a pure heart. Dishes that deliver honest flavours are prepared behind the counter, like the bamboo shoots, charbroiled skin and all, and *hamo*, placed in the stock with onions. The young chef's interaction with the customers is just right. Only an *omakase* is offered, but after 9pm there are small set menus.

■ Opening hours, last orders
Dinner = 17:30-24:00 L.O.22:30

■ Annual and weekly closing
Closed mid-August, late December-early January, Sunday and Public Holidays

■ Price
Dinner = set   ¥ 12,600
Service charge = 5%

TEL. 03-6265-0177
Omiya Building 4F,
4-3-2 Kagurazaka,
Shinjuku-ku, Tokyo

Restaurant-I NEW

The glass-enclosed dining room, surrounded by trees, has a spacious feel. The chef also owns a restaurant in Nice, but here dishes are prepared primarily with ingredients from the outskirts of Tokyo. The speciality is Edo vegetable and foie gras terrine, which goes well with *miso* sauce. Whole pigs are purchased, and each part is prepared using the most suitable technique. Dessert is the Harajuku crepe, which changes monthly.

■ Opening hours, last orders
Lunch = 11:30-15:00 L.O.13:30
Dinner = 18:00-22:00 L.O.21:00

■ Annual and weekly closing
Closed mid-August and late
December-early January

■ Price
Lunch = set   ¥ 3,500-8,000
Dinner = set   ¥ 6,500-15,000
Service charge = 10% (lunch 5%)

TEL. 03-5772-2091
1-4-20 Jingumae, Shibuya-ku,
Tokyo
www.restaurant-i.jp

Ristorante Aso

Ristorante Aso opened in 1997, with chef Tatsuji Aso's original and creative cooking going far beyond the boundaries of Italian and French cuisine. Dishes overflow with innovation, both in their arrangement and the colour combinations. Selected beef is grilled on charcoal and served with peppered mascarpone; sautéed foie gras is topped with zabaione and black truffle sauce. The customers leave immeasurably satisfied.

■ Opening hours, last orders
Lunch = 12:00-15:30 L.O.13:30
Dinner = 18:00-23:00 L.O.20:30

■ Annual and weekly closing
Closed early January, Saturday,
Sunday and Public Holidays

■ Price
Lunch = set   ¥ 5,250-10,500
          à la carte ¥ 13,000-19,000
Dinner = set   ¥ 10,500-21,000
          à la carte ¥ 13,000-19,000
Service charge = 13%

TEL. 03-3770-3690
29-3 Sarugakucho, Shibuya-ku,
Tokyo
www.hiramatsu.co.jp/restaurants/aso

Ristorante Honda

Tetsuya Honda's menu is characterised by sophisticated dishes, full of originality in the way the food is arranged and the colour combinations. His distinct approach is also reflected in his cooking methods which, although based on Italian cuisine, incorporate some French elements. The tableware is also unique. *Tagliolini* with sea urchin is a year-long speciality. Dishes on the set menus can be ordered individually.

■ Opening hours, last orders
Lunch = 12:00-15:00 L.O.14:00
Dinner = 18:00-22:00 (L.O.)

■ Annual and weekly closing
Closed late December-early January
and Monday except Public Holidays

■ Price
Lunch = set   ¥ 2,940-6,825
Dinner = set   ¥ 7,875-12,600
Service charge = 10%

TEL. 03-5414-3723
2-12-35 Kitaaoyama, Minato-ku,
Tokyo
www.ristorantehonda.jp

Ristorante La Primula

The chef spent three years studying Italian cuisine in northern Italy. His last position in Friuli was at a restaurant called Primula (primrose), from which this establishment takes its name. *Cjalçons*, pasta stuffed with potato purée, cinnamon, mint and raisins and topped with parmesan, is one of the Friulian speciality dishes. Only set menus are served and they showcase the flavours of regional Italian cuisine.

■ Opening hours, last orders
Lunch = Wed.-Sat. 12:00-14:30
L.O.13:00
Dinner = 18:00-23:00 L.O.21:00

■ Annual and weekly closing
Closed late December-early January,
Sunday and 3rd Monday of each
month

■ Price
Lunch = set   ¥ 3,500-5,500
Dinner = set   ¥ 8,400-15,750
Service charge = 10%

TEL. 03–5439–9470
Patio Azabu Juban 3F,
2-8-10 Azabujuban, Minato-ku,
Tokyo

Rokkaku
六角

Rokkaku is a Japanese-style pub, where one can eat in a simply-adorned, laid-back atmosphere. Since opening, this establishment has shunned advertising while quietly catering to its regulars. An assortment of starters, soups and appetisers are brought to your table, followed by the menu. First-timers should ask the chef for recommendations. Prices may be higher than a typical pub but here you can enjoy real artisanal cuisine.

■ Opening hours, last orders
Dinner = 18:00-23:30 (L.O.)

■ Annual and weekly closing
Closed Golden week, mid-August
and late December-early January

■ Price
Dinner = à la carte ¥ 10,000-20,000
Service charge = 5%

TEL. 03–3401–8516
Yuken Azabu Building 4F,
1-5-5 Azabujuban, Minato-ku,
Tokyo

Rokukaku-tei
六覺燈

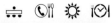

This *kushikatsu* restaurant, originally from Nipponbashi in Osaka, opened in Ginza in 2004. It has a single set menu which varies in price depending on the number of skewers ordered —the standard being twenty. The minced white-fleshed fish is wrapped in *oba*, fried and topped with *tonburi*, and there is also lotus root stuffed with curry-flavoured minced beef. The sliced and stacked *konnyaku* has an interesting texture.

■ Opening hours, last orders
14:00-22:30 (L.O.)

■ Annual and weekly closing
Closed mid-August, late December-
early January and Tuesday

■ Price
Dinner = set   ¥ 10,500
Service charge = 10%

TEL. 03–5537–6008
Kojun Building 4F,
6-8-7 Ginza, Chuo-ku, Tokyo

Ryuan
劉安

The specialities are the *kanpo* herbal soups reproduced according to books passed down over thousands of years. The set menus all include 1 of 9 varieties of soup, each with their own health benefits and eaten before other liquids to ensure it is absorbed. Also try the colourful fried vegetable dish, made up of over 20 different vegetables. The owner-chef hopes to establish a research institute for clinical *kanpo* in the future.

■ Opening hours, last orders
Lunch = 12:00-15:00 L.O.14:00
Dinner = 17:30-23:00 L.O.21:00

■ Annual and weekly closing
Closed mid-August, late December-
early January and Monday

■ Price
Lunch = set   ¥ 6,500-28,800
          à la carte ¥ 3,000-30,000
Dinner = set   ¥ 10,000-28,800
          à la carte¥ 3,000-30,000
Service charge = 10% (dinner)

TEL. 03–3448–1978
5-13-35 Shirokanedai, Minato-ku,
Tokyo
www.shirokane-ryuan.com

Ryugin
龍吟

The owner-chef Seiji Yamamoto says that new things can be created by bringing together various classics. Focusing on Japanese cuisine, he exercises his natural curiosity in the pursuit of new possibilities and original dishes. He shaves the dried bonito after receiving the order so that the stock is at its tastiest when served. A daily-changing omakase set menu is available and its contents vary according to the season.

■ Opening hours, last orders
Dinner = 18:00-1:00 L.O.22:30

■ Annual and weekly closing
Closed mid-August, late December-
early January, Sunday and Public
Holidays

■ Price
Dinner = set   ¥ 23,100
                à la carte ¥ 10,000-20,000
Service charge = 10% (private
                    room 15%)

TEL. 03–3423–8006
7-17-24 Roppongi, Minato-ku,
Tokyo
www.nihonryori-ryugin.com

Ryutenmon
龍天門

Take one step in and you'll find yourself in an exotic atmosphere
created by the furnishings, paintings and decoration. It's divided
into several rooms; we recommend 'Suiren' as it faces the garden.
The focus is on Cantonese cuisine, with a wide selection of à la
carte dishes and several set menus. The grilled duck, crispy on the
outside and deliciously tender on the inside, is understandably
popular and well worth ordering.

■ Opening hours, last orders
Lunch = 11:30-15:00 (L.O.)
Sat., Sun. and Public Holidays
11:30-16:30 (L.O.)
Dinner = 17:30-21:30 (L.O.)

■ Price
Lunch = set   ¥ 3,470-40,000
           à la carte ¥ 9,500-16,000
Dinner = set   ¥ 9,500-40,000
           à la carte ¥ 9,500-16,000
Private room fee = ¥ 6,930-23,100

TEL. 03-5423-7787
Westin Hotel 2F,
1-4-1 Mita, Meguro-ku, Tokyo
www.westin-tokyo.co.jp/
restaurant/ryutenmon

Sakuragaoka
桜ヶ丘

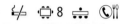

While *Kyo-ryori* is the base, owner-chef Tomohiko Kubo also offers a variety of creative dishes; his repertoire goes beyond the boundaries of Japanese cuisine and combines elements of old-style *yoshoku* and Chinese cuisine. Imaginative options include *matsutake* mushroom croquettes; omelette stuffed with rice; bamboo shoots and *yuba*; and Japanese-style beef stew. The *omakase* set menus changes monthly according to tradition.

■ Opening hours, last orders
Dinner = 17:00-23:00 L.O.20:30

■ Annual and weekly closing
Closed mid-August, late December-early January, Sunday and Public Holidays

■ Price
Dinner = set   ¥ 12,600-21,000
Service charge = 15% (private
                 room 20%)

TEL. 03–5770–5250
6-8-21 Roppongi, Minato-ku, Tokyo
www.sakuraoka.com

Sakuragawa
櫻川

                       ✗✗

         ♿ ✄ 🚇 20 ☎🍴 ☀

Owner-chef Yoshiaki Kurahashi named the restaurant after his hometown to remember his heritage. Keeping traditional sensibilities alive, seasonal flowers and leaves are used for *hassun*; *warabimochi* dessert, sprinkled with salt-pickled cherry blossom petals, is served with *matcha*. The set menu changes monthly and so does the tableware, with motifs depicting seasonal blossoms such as cherry, camellia, plum, iris and hydrangea.

■ Opening hours, last orders
Lunch = 12:00-15:30 L.O.14:00
Dinner = 18:00-22:00 L.O.20:00

■ Annual and weekly closing
Closed mid-August

■ Price
Lunch = set   ¥ 6,050
Dinner = set   ¥ 13,200
Private room fee=¥3,150-5,250 (lunch)
              ¥5,250-10,500 (dinner)

TEL. 03-3279-0039
Mitsui Tower 2F,
2-1-1 Nihonbashimuromachi,
Chuo-ku, Tokyo

Sanda NEW
さんだ

This *kappo* restaurant serves Japanese beef, with an emphasis on offal. The thinly sliced Achilles tendon is reminiscent of *fugu* skin, and there is variety in the cooking techniques and seasoning. The rumen is seasoned with curry powder and salt; soft-boiled cheek has a Western taste and there's a hint of *wamono* in the beef tongue *tsumire* soup with cartilage. Well priced and suitable for casual business dinners.

■ Opening hours, last orders
Dinner = 17:30-23:30 L.O.21:30
Saturday 17:30-23:00 L.O.21:00

■ Annual and weekly closing
Closed mid-August, late December-
early January, Sunday and Public
Holidays

■ Price
Dinner = set   ¥ 6,300

TEL. 03-3423-2020
4-5-9 Roppongi, Minato-ku,
Tokyo

Sangoan
三合菴

Hiroyuki Kato opened his restaurant in 2000. Recently renovated, it is now half its original size but the warm lighting creates a soothing atmosphere. The *toichi soba* is made with 10 parts buckwheat and 1 part wheat flour; it includes moderate amounts of the black inner skin of the buckwheat, making it fragrant and visually pleasing. The slightly strong sauce served with the *seiro* brings out the sweetness of the *soba*.

■ Opening hours, last orders
Lunch = 11:30-14:00 L.O.13:30
Dinner = 17:30-21:30 L.O.21:00

■ Annual and weekly closing
Closed early January, early September, Wednesday, 1st and 3rd Thursday of each month

■ Price
Lunch = à la carte   ¥ 2,000-5,000
Dinner = set   ¥ 5,500-7,500
         à la carte   ¥ 2,000-5,000
Seat charge=¥ 850/person (dinner)

TEL. 03-3444-3570
5-10-10 Shirokane, Minato-ku, Tokyo

Sankame

三亀

  LUNCH 6

 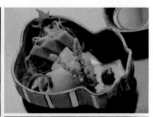 

Sankame has been serving Kansai-style cuisine since 1946. As well as set menus, à la carte dishes are available at dinner; only *teisyoku* are served at lunch. Try the simmered *zenmai*, its bitterness removed by being plunged in water or steamed tilefish wrapped in glutinous rice and cherry tree leaves. The restaurant is always lively with a diverse clientele. Owner-chef Isao Nanjo's personality and humour add to the appeal.

■ Opening hours, last orders
Lunch = 12:00-14:00 L.O.13:00
Dinner = 17:00-22:00 L.O.21:30

■ Annual and weekly closing
Closed mid-August, late December-early January, Saturday in July-August, Sunday and Public Holidays

■ Price
Lunch = set   ¥ 1,950-2,950
Dinner = set   ¥ 13,650
            à la carte ¥ 8,000-12,000

TEL. 03-3571-0573
6-4-13 Ginza, Chuo-ku, Tokyo

Sant Pau

♣♣   𝖳𝖳𝖳𝖳

♿ 🚩 P 📻 8 ☎🍴 ☀ ⅋

This is the Tokyo branch of Sant Pau, near Barcelona. Diners can experience traditional Spanish cuisine that makes much of Catalonia's natural bounty, albeit with extra twists courtesy of Carme Ruscalleda, the owner-chef of the parent restaurant. Ingredients such as Iberico pork, salted cod, olive oil, Majorca salt and dried pimientos are imported from Catalonia, while others are sourced locally. Presentation is also original.

■ Opening hours, last orders
Lunch = 11:30-15:30 L.O.13:30
Sat.and Sun.12:00-15:30 L.O.13:30
Dinner = 18:00-23:30 L.O.21:00

■ Annual and weekly closing
Closed 1 January and Monday

■ Price
Lunch = set   ¥ 5,500-22,000
         à la carte   ¥ 16,000-17,000

Dinner = set   ¥ 18,000-22,000
          à la carte ¥ 16,000-17,000
Private room fee = ¥10,000 (lunch),
                              ¥18,000 (dinner)
Service charge = 10%

TEL. 03-3517-5700
Coredo Nihonbashi Annex,
1-6-1 Nihonbashi, Chuo-ku,
Tokyo
www.santpau.jp

Sanyukyo NEW
三友居

Opened by Kyoto's *chakaiseki* catering establishment Sanyukyo, out of a desire to have people enjoy their cooking in a casual atmosphere and to make lives even richer. Most ingredients arrive daily from Kyoto. The main item of the set menus changes with the seasons and is prepared in several different ways to keep your taste buds guessing. The thick sesame seed dressing accompanying the Kyoto vegetables has a rich taste.

■ Opening hours, last orders
Lunch = 11:30-15:00 L.O.14:00
Dinner = 17:30-21:30 L.O.20:00

■ Annual and weekly closing
Closed late December-late January
and Monday

■ Price
Lunch = set   ¥ 4,700
Dinner = set   ¥ 8,900

TEL. 03-5449-7155
1-27-19 Takanawa, Minato-ku,
Tokyo

Sasada

笹田

❀❀

Run by Hidenobu Sasada and his wife, this small restaurant has an intimacy that guarantees individual care and attention. Try the *oden* in winter - this dish balances flavours such as Shamo gamecock skin and fried fish cakes with seasonal vegetables such as Shogoin turnip, yam and *kyo-ninjin* carrot containing generous amount of Kansai-style soup stock. The *omakase* menu ends with a serving of fragrant rice cooked in a clay pot.

■ Opening hours, last orders
Dinner = 18:00-21:00 (L.O.)

■ Annual and weekly closing
Closed mid-August, late December-
early January, Sunday and Public
Holidays

■ Price
Dinner = set   ¥ 12,600-31,500

TEL. 03-3507-5501
1-18-8 Nishishinbashi, Minato-ku,
Tokyo

Sawada
さわ田

Koji Sawada is a sushi chef with an unusual background because, before setting up his restaurant, he worked in the transport industry. One of the features here is the chef's commitment to maturing each ingredient, allowing their full flavour to come out. Rice is cooked slightly hard and is well seasoned with white vinegar so that its flavour is as distinctive as that of the ingredients that top it. Sawada is reservation-only.

■ Opening hours, last orders
Lunch = 12:00-14:00
Dinner = 18:00-21:00 and
22:00-1:00 L.O.22:00
Sat. and Sun. 17:00-20:00 L.O.17:00

■ Annual and weekly closing
Closed mid-August, late December-
early January and Monday

■ Price
Lunch = set   ¥ 21,000
Dinner = set   ¥ 32,000

TEL. 03-3571-4711
MC Building 3F,
5-9-19 Ginza, Chuo-ku, Tokyo

Seiju

清壽

In such a dignified atmosphere you may feel obliged to sit up straight, but Yoshiaki Shimizu's friendly manner creates a sense of ease. There is only one *omakase* set menu, but drinking snacks can be added as desired. The specialities are prawn and kidney beans from the owner's parents' farm. During the new sake season, rare sake lees *tempura* is available. Along with sake are reasonably priced wines selected by the sommelier.

■ Opening hours, last orders
Dinner = 17:00-21:00 (L.O.)

■ Annual and weekly closing
Closed Golden week, mid-August, late December-early January and Monday

■ Price
Dinner = set ¥ 12,600
Service charge = 5%

TEL. 03-3546-2622
Urban Mates Building B1F,
3-16-9 Tsukiji, Chuo-ku, Tokyo

Seika Kobayashi NEW
青華 こばやし

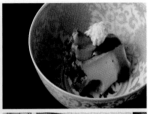

The owner-chef of this homely restaurant says he opened it after collecting a full set of serving dishes. The set menus are largely comprised of seafood, except when bamboo shoots, wax gourds, turnips and *ebi-imo* are in season; sugar and *mirin* are used sparingly and the volume is plentiful. At the end comes rice from his parents' farm prepared in an earthenware pot. Only one party is served at lunch and two at dinner.

■ Opening hours, last orders
12:00-21:30 (L.O.)

■ Annual and weekly closing
Closed late December-early January

■ Price
Lunch = set ¥ 10,000-13,800
Dinner = set ¥ 13,800-18,000

TEL. 03–6459–2210
7-10-30 Roppongi, Minato-ku,
Tokyo
www.seikakobayashi.com

Seisoka
青草窠

Hidden on the 1st floor of a building near Tengenji Temple. All dishes emphasise the four seasons and the serving dishes, from the mid Edo era and made by a 5th-generation potter, are used for the *mukozuke*. The *hassun* is served on lotus leaves laid out, according to the restaurant, on a Tenpyo roof tile from the Nara era (710-794) and exemplifying traditional beauty. The easy-going hospitality makes you feel right at home.

■ Opening hours, last orders
Lunch = 12:00-15:00
Dinner = 17:30-23:00

■ Annual and weekly closing
Closed mid-August and late December-early January

■ Price
Lunch = set   ¥ 6,300-20,000
Dinner = set   ¥ 20,000
Service charge = 10%

TEL. 03-3473-3103
4-2-34 Minamiazabu, Minato-ku, Tokyo

225

Sekiho-tei
赤寶亭

Traditional techniques and high quality ingredients are used here. Stock is made only with the core parts of back meat and belly of a special kind of bonito produced in Makurazaki; water comes from Shiga to highlight the taste of the Rishiri kelp. Cards that read '*risshun daikichi* (with luck on the first day of spring)' are placed on plates in February; and *chimaki-zushi* are served on the May 5 Boys' Festival.

■ Opening hours, last orders
Lunch = Wed.-Sat.12:00-14:30
L.O.13:30
Dinner = 18:00-23:00 L.O.21:30

■ Annual and weekly closing
Closed Golden week, mid-August, late December-early January and Sunday

■ Price
Lunch = set   ¥ 5,250-18,900
Dinner = set   ¥ 11,500-18,900
Private room fee = ¥ 3,150-5,250
Service charge = 10%

TEL. 03-5474-6889
3-1-14 Jingumae, Shibuya-ku, Tokyo

Sense

The Japanese chef prepares modern Cantonese cuisine based on traditional recipes, with the focus on set menus. Authentic Chinese ingredients and seasonings are used, such as Napoleon fish – a Hong Kong favourite – local grouper, and Chinese vegetables grown in Japan, cooked according to each diner's preference. A casual lunch is always appealing, but ambient lighting and panoramic city views make dinner even more attractive.

■ Opening hours, last orders
Lunch = 11:30-14:30 (L.O.) Sat.,
Sun. and Public Holidays 11:30-
16:00 (L.O.)
Dinner = 17:30-22:00 (L.O.)

■ Price
Lunch = set   ¥ 3,800-10,000
          à la carte ¥ 7,000-29,000
Dinner = set   ¥ 14,000-26,000
          à la carte ¥ 7,000-35,000

Private room fee = ¥10,000
Service charge = 13%

TEL. 03-3270-8188
Mandarin Oriental Hotel 37F,
2-1-1 Nihonbashimuromachi,
Chuo-ku, Tokyo
www.mandarinoriental.co.jp/tokyo

7chome Kyoboshi
七丁目 京星

❀ ❀ ❀   ✕

Shigeya Sakakibara's *tempura* is made of small ingredients to be popped into the mouth whole; small, sweet *saimaki ebi*, purple asparagus, abalone, quail eggs and figs. *Ten-cha* is recommended to finish the meal. The chef's constant trial of new ingredients accounts for his wide repertoire, giving diners the chance to savour some rare treats, albeit at a high price. Reservations for the weekend must be made two days in advance.

■ Opening hours, last orders
Lunch = 12:00-15:00 (L.O.)
Dinner = 17:00-21:00 (L.O.)

■ Annual and weekly closing
Closed mid-August and late December-
early January

■ Price
Lunch = set   ¥ 31,500
Dinner = set   ¥ 31,500

TEL. 03-3572-3568
Ozio Ginza Building 6F,
5-5-9 Ginza, Chuo-ku, Tokyo

Shigetsu NEW
指月

After operating in Yugawara for years as an inn, Shigetsu relocated to Tokyo in 2009. It has a 5-seater counter and a private room and serves an *omakase kaiseki* set menu. The head chef has been in charge since the Yugawara days. Most popular are the bamboo shoots in spring, spiny lobster in mid August and the *tai meshi* in autumn. Prices are a little high, but worth it for the fine flavours arranged on exquisite tableware.

■ Opening hours, last orders
Dinner = 17:30-23:00 L.O.22:00

■ Price
Dinner = set ¥ 25,000-30,000

TEL. 03-6438-0918
3-9-1 Minamiaoyama, Minato-ku, Tokyo

Shigeyoshi
重よし

Head downstairs to the first floor of Co-op Olympia on Omotesando-dori near Harajuku Station. Diners can sit at the counter, at tables or in a private room. Kenzo Sato is a keen researcher and he developed a soup of *suppon* without ginger after a year of trials. You can expect to enjoy high quality sea urchin from Naruto from May to September. In May, a jelly of a rare type of citrus called *hyuganatsu* is also very good.

■ Opening hours, last orders
Lunch = 12:00-13:30 (L.O.)
Dinner = 17:30-22:00 L.O.21:00

■ Annual and weekly closing
Closed Golden week, mid-August,
late December-early January,
Sunday and Public Holiday Mondays

■ Price
Lunch = set   ¥ 5,250-15,750
Dinner = set   ¥ 18,900-31,500
Private room fee = 10%

TEL. 03–3400–4044
Co-op Olympia 1F,
6-35-3 Jingumae, Shibuya-ku,
Tokyo

Shimizu NEW
しみづ

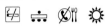

Shimizu is on a street lined with small restaurants and serves traditional but larger than usual hand-rolled sushi. The *Edomae* spirit is evident in the red vinegar flavoured rice, marinated tuna, gizzard shad marinated with salt and vinegar, and other items. The prices are reasonable. Only regulars can make advance reservations, but same-day reservations are possible. If you don't speak Japanese, go with someone who does.

■ Opening hours, last orders
Lunch = 11:30-13:00 (L.O.)
Dinner = 17:00-21:30 (L.O.)

■ Annual and weekly closing
Closed 31 December, 1 January and Monday

■ Prices
Lunch = set ¥ 5,500-8,500
Dinner = set ¥ 12,000-14,000

TEL. 03–3591–5763
2-15-10 Shinbashi, Minato-ku, Tokyo

Shin
真

Shintaro Suzuki looks to traditional *Edomae* techniques and the ingredients are salted, vinegared or seared—sometimes with straw. Rice is a blend of two from Niigata and Ibaraki; *nigari* is added and it is cooked quite hard so that the texture of each grain is distinguishable. The sushi is comparatively large but can be adjusted. Sea bream is used as a topping with radish and kelp; gizzard shad is combined with shredded kelp.

■ Opening hours, last orders
Lunch = 12:00-14:00
Dinner = 18:00-23:00

■ Annual and weekly closing
Closed Monday

■ Price
Lunch = set   ¥ 5,750-9,450
Dinner = set   ¥ 16,800

TEL. 03–5485–0031
H·T Nishiazabu Building XI 3F,
4-3-10 Nishiazabu, Minato-ku,
Tokyo

Shinsuke NEW
シンスケ

Once an established liquor store, it became a Japanese-style pub in 1924 and is now run by the fourth-generation of the family. The onion *nuta* with mustard-vinegar-*miso* dressing offers a nostalgic taste; the *Kitsune Raclette* with cheese inside deep-fried tofu is popular. Try draft sake ordered by the barrel between autumn and spring. Seats on the 1st floor, which has a Showa feel to it, cannot be reserved so arrive early.

■ Opening hours, last orders
Dinner = 17:00-22:00

■ Annual and weekly closing
Closed mid-August, late December-early January, Sunday and Public Holidays

■ Prices
Dinner = à la carte ¥ 4,500-8,000
Seat charge=¥ 315/person

TEL.03–3832–0469
3-31-5 Yushima, Bunkyo-ku,
Tokyo

Shofukuro NEW
招福楼

Boasting a prime location on the top floor of Marunouchi Building, this restaurant has counter seats, *tatami* rooms and table seating, all with views of the Imperial Palace and northern Tokyo. There are more modern rooms but the elegant *tatami* rooms offer traditional Japanese beauty. The way the *suiji* (the soup) is prepared depends on the season to bring out the sweetness of the *kombu* and the natural flavour of the *katsuo*.

■ Opening hours, last orders
Lunch = 11:30-15:00
Dinner = 17:00-23:00
Sun. and Public Holidays 17:00-22:00

■ Annual and weekly closing
Closed 1 January

■ Price
Lunch = set ¥ 6,300-31,500
Dinner = set ¥ 12,600-31,500
Private room fee = ¥ 1,050/person
Service charge = 10%

TEL. 03-3240-0003
Marunouchi Building 36F,
2-4-1 Marunouchi, Chiyoda-ku, Tokyo
www.shofukuro.jp

Shunnoaji Ichi NEW
旬の味 いち

Enjoy seasonal seafood fresh from the port and vegetables from the owner-chef's parents' home. In spring, regulars come for the nearly 10 different wild plants cooked in various ways: in summer tomato *surinagashi*, in autumn pacific saury with rice, and in winter *sawani nabe* with boar meat and plenty of edible roots. We recommend the *omakase* and adding meat dishes and rice according to how hungry you are. Prices are reasonable.

■ Opening hours, last orders
Dinner = 18:00-24:00

■ Annual and weekly closing
Closed late December-early January,
Sunday and Public Holidays

■ Price
Dinner = set   ¥ 3,500-10,500
Service charge = 10%

TEL. 03-3402-9424
7-10-30 Roppongi, Minato-ku,
Tokyo

Signature

The chef mixes ingredients from both France and Japan to create delicate, refined contemporary French cuisine. Using sweet and sour flavours from fruits and accents of herbs and spices, he makes each dish stand out. Specialities include toasted scallops, foie gras and persimmon two ways and cacao-crusted pigeon breast. The reasonably priced lunch menus are particularly attractive. Ask for window table to enjoy the cityscape.

■ Opening hours, last orders
Lunch = 11:30-14:30 (L.O.)
Dinner = 17:30-22:00 (L.O.)

■ Price
Lunch = set   ¥ 5,000-12,000
       à la carte   ¥ 12,000-19,000
Dinner = set   ¥ 14,000-20,000
       à la carte   ¥ 12,000-19,000
Private room fee = ¥10,000
Service charge = 13%

TEL. 03–3270–8188
Mandarin Oriental Hotel 37F,
2-1-1 Nihonbashimuromachi,
Chuo-ku, Tokyo
www.mandarinoriental.co.jp/tokyo

Sukiyabashi Jiro Honten
すきやばし 次郎 本店

The 'left-handed master craftsman', Jiro Ono, creates the finest sushi with swift, fluid movements. At his authentic sushi restaurant, he serves only *omakase nigiri* sushi; one should go with a 'When in Rome, do as the Romans do' mentality. The 20 or so pieces may not come cheap but just consider the exquisite tastes. Everything is carefully timed so be punctual; and if you don't speak Japanese, go with someone who does.

■ Opening hours, last orders
Lunch = 11:30-14:00
Dinner = Mon.-Fri. 17:30-20:30

■ Annual and weekly closing
Closed mid-August, late December-early January, Sunday and Public Holidays

■ Price
Lunch = set   ¥ 31,500
Dinner = set   ¥ 31,500

TEL. 03-3535-3600
Tsukamoto Sozan Building B1F,
4-2-15 Ginza, Chuo-ku, Tokyo

Sukiyabashi Jiro Roppongi
すきやばし 次郎 六本木

A branch of 'Sukiyabashi Jiro', this is run by Takashi Ono, second son of the world-famous sushi master, Jiro Ono. His creed is 'No compromise' and the occasional reprimand to the young cooks is an expression of this attitude. Try the 15-item *omakase* for lunch and the 20-item *omakase* for dinner. The rice is carefully cooked so that each grain stands out. Prices may be high but the restaurant attracts plenty of sushi lovers.

■ Opening hours, last orders
Lunch = 11:30-14:00
Dinner = 17:00-21:00

■ Annual and weekly closing
Closed late December-early January
and Wednesday

■ Price
Lunch = set   ¥ 17,850
Dinner = set   ¥ 25,200

TEL. 03-5413-6626
Roppongi Hills Residence B, 3F,
6-12-2 Roppongi, Minato-ku,
Tokyo

Sushi Aoki Ginza
鮨 青木 銀座

   10

Owner-chef, Toshikatsu Aoki, uses *Edomae* techniques handed down from his father but also seeks out new ideas. Specialities inherited from his father are still favourites: simmered octopus; smelt-whiting between sheets of kelp; and pickled young tiger prawns. Perch or red rockfish are good either as snacks, or lightly seared, served as sushi. On Sunday lunch, the number of well priced 'okimari' and 'chirashi-zushi' is limited.

■ Opening hours, last orders
Lunch = 12:00-14:00
Dinner = 17:00-22:00

■ Annual and weekly closing
Closed late December-early January

■ Price
Lunch = set ¥ 3,150-20,000
Dinner = set ¥ 21,000

TEL. 03–3289–1044
Ginza Takahashi Building 2F,
6-7-4 Ginza, Chuo-ku, Tokyo
www.sushiaoki.com

Sushi Aoki Nishiazabu
鮨 青木 西麻布

The owner-chef often refers to 'Team Aoki'— he believes sushi cannot be made alone and that it is important to nurture young sushi chefs. The Kyushu disk abalone, the *Edomae* horse mackerel and the Hokkaido *uni* are recommended. There is also rarely found oyster sushi; the *nitsume* that coats the steamed oysters is based on an *Edomae* technique, similar to oyster sauce. While expensive, the exquisite interior is a delight.

■ Opening hours, last orders
Lunch = 11:30-14:00
Dinner = 18:00-23:00

■ Annual and weekly closing
Closed late December-early January

■ Price
Lunch = set   ¥ 3,150-20,000
Dinner = set   ¥ 21,000

TEL. 03-5771-3344
3-23-7 Nishiazabu, Minato-ku,
Tokyo
www.sushiaoki.com

Sushi Fukumoto
鮨 福元

A menu listing the items of the day and where they were produced sits on the counter. An appetiser of Chinese yam and sea urchin dressed with soy sauce is one speciality; conger eel and ark shells *shiroyaki* is also flavoursome. Rice is boiled quite hard and blended with a mild *akazu*. It's fun to have sake with the sushi while listening to his owner-chef's stories about fish. A dental clinic's green board acts as a marker.

■ Opening hours, last orders
Dinner = 18:00-23:00 (L.O.)
Sun. and Public Holidays 17:00-
21:00 (L.O.)

■ Annual and weekly closing
Closed mid-August, late December-
early January and Wednesday

■ Price
Dinner = set   ¥ 14,667
Service charge = 5%

TEL. 03-5481-9537
Hanabu Building B1F,
5-17-6 Daizawa, Setagaya-ku,
Tokyo
www17.ocn.ne.jp/~fuku3411

Sushi Hashiguchi NEW
鮨 はしぐち

The owner-chef cherishes *Edomae* style in his preparation of sushi. How the fish is handled when caught is key; working with trusted fish merchants and fishermen, he places his orders late at night. Watching him prepare the sushi with his large hands is a sight to see. Rice is cooked to just the right firmness so it breaks up in your mouth; the amount of wasabi is adjusted with each item. His wife provides charming service.

■ Opening hours, last orders
Dinner = 18:00-22:00

■ Annual and weekly closing
Closed mid-August, late December-early January, Sunday and Public Holidays

■ Prices
Dinner = set   ¥ 15,750-21,000

TEL.03-5275-5877
Kioicho Tower Building 2F
5-7 Kojimachi, Chiyoda-ku, Tokyo

Sushiichi NEW
鮨一

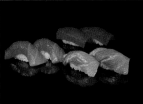

The entrance is on the first floor, but not noticeable from the street; alert the staff over the intercom and they will come to greet you. The modern interior, with Japanese paper and bamboo, is comfortable. Red vinegar and rice vinegar are used with the rice to cut down on the sweetness; chub mackerel and *nodoguro* are grilled and white-fleshed fish are garnished with salt and *sudachi*. There are several *omakase* set menus.

■ Opening hours, last orders
Lunch = 12:00-14:30 L.O.14:00
Dinner = 17:30-23:00 L.O.21:30
Sat. and Public Holidays
17:30-22:00 L.O.20:30

■ Annual and weekly closing
Closed Golden week, mid-August,
late December-early January,
Sunday and Public Holiday
Mondays

■ Price
Lunch = set   ¥ 3,150-30,000
Dinner = set   ¥ 10,500-30,000

TEL. 03-3567-0014
3-4-4 Ginza, Chuo-ku, Tokyo
www.3567-0014.com

Sushi Imamura NEW
鮨 いむら

The counter runs alongside the kitchen, so you can watch the food being prepared. The rice blend is cooked firm in a cast iron rice cooker and seasoned with *akazu*, rice vinegar and salt. The salt-vinegar mix for the gizzard shad is perfect, the bitterness complementing the sweetness of the rice. *Anago* is boiled soft and then charbroiled and pressed gently onto the rice. The owner-chef's wife provides meticulous service.

■ Opening hours, last orders
Lunch = Sat. and Sun. 12:00-14:00
Dinner = 18:00-23:30
Sat., Sun. and Public Holidays
18:00-22:00

■ Annual and weekly closing
Closed mid-August, late December-
early January and Monday

■ Price
Lunch = set   ¥ 3,150-5,250
Dinner = set   ¥ 12,600

TEL. 03–5789–3637
5-8-13 Shirokane, Minato-ku,
Tokyo

Sushi Isshin Asakusa

鮨 一新 浅草

Abalone from Chiba is a house appetiser. *Maguro-no-zuke* sees tuna marinated in a blend of dried tuna stock and soy sauce to ensure a richer taste. Winter dishes include *karasumi* and seared *shirako*. Rice is steamed on charcoal and seasoned with *akazu*. Popular sushi toppings include gizzard, conger eel, boiled clams and spear squid with egg in spring and salmon roe. Asakusa-4 Post Office or the Police Station act as landmarks.

■ Opening hours, last orders
Dinner = 18:00-22:00 (L.O.)

■ Annual and weekly closing
Closed mid-August, late December-early January, Sunday and Public Holidays

■ Price
Dinner = set   ¥ 15,750

TEL. 03–5603–1108
4-11-3 Asakusa, Taito-ku, Tokyo
www.sushi-issin.com

Sushi Isshin Ginza 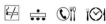 NEW
鮨 一新 銀座

This Ginza branch of an Asakusa sushi restaurant is run single-handedly by the owner-chef's right-hand man. It shares the same philosophy as the parent restaurant, but offers a bigger selection of drinking snacks, and the sushi is a little smaller. The standard dish is the *nidako*, cooked in *bancha* together with red beans; boiled *anago* is cooked on a charcoal stove for a smoky flavour. Items include *nihamaguri* and *zuke-maguro*.

■ Opening hours, last orders
Dinner = 18:00-23:00 (L.O.)

■ Annual and weekly closing
Closed mid-August, late December-early January, Sunday and Public Holidays

■ Price
Dinner = set   ¥ 18,900-21,000

TEL. 03–3575–0150
MC Building B1F,
5-9-19 Ginza, Chuo-ku, Tokyo
www.sushi-issin.com/pc/free01.html

Sushi Iwa
鮨 いわ

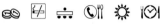

Located near Taimei Elementary School, in a narrow alleyway. To ensure the best flavour of the tuna, Iwa leaves the cut slices to sit for a while before transforming them into sushi and uses several sections of the tuna, including *harakami*, a delicacy. Three pieces of sushi -topped respectively with *akami*, *chu-toro* and *o-toro* - are served in well-timed succession. This is an intimate restaurant that is good for small groups.

■ Opening hours, last orders
Lunch = 12:00-14:00
Dinner = 17:00-23:00
Sun.12:00-20:00

■ Annual and weekly closing
Closed Golden week, mid-August
and late December-early January

■ Price
Lunch = set   ¥ 4,725-8,400
Dinner = set   ¥ 15,750-26,250

TEL. 03-3571-7900
6-3-17 Ginza, Chuo-ku, Tokyo

Sushi Kanesaka
鮨 かねさか

While the owner-chef Shinji Kanesaka attaches much importance to *Edomae* sushi techniques, new ideas are also adopted in pursuit of the ultimate taste: this is the style of 'Sushi Kanesaka.' The basic rules are still observed: priority is given to the freshness of ingredients and close attention paid to the way they are matured. The oft-felt barrier of respect between customers and sushi chefs gives way to a cosy atmosphere.

■ Opening hours, last orders
Lunch = 11:30-14:00 L.O.13:00
Dinner = 17:00-22:00 L.O.21:00

■ Annual and weekly closing
Closed Golden week, mid-August,
late December-early January and
Public Holiday Mondays

■ Price
Lunch = set   ¥ 5,250-15,750
Dinner = set   ¥ 15,750-21,000

TEL. 03-5568-4411
Misuzu Building B1F,
8-10-3 Ginza, Chuo-ku, Tokyo

Sushi Kazui NEW
鮨 嘉瑞

❀❀  ✕✕

Despite being raised in Osaka, the owner-chef is particular about
Edomae. His passion for tuna can be seen in how he serves 5
pieces in a row that have been aged. Without breaking from the
mainstream of *Edomae* sushi, he makes use of Kansai techniques
and adds twists, like rolling pickled vegetables with *samatsu* in
summer. At the end comes rolled sushi with *unagi* and *kanpyo*. If
you want the *oshizushi*, let him know when booking.

■ Opening hours, last orders
Lunch = 12:00-13:00 (L.O.)
Dinner = 17:00-21:00 (L.O.)

■ Annual and weekly closing
Closed mid-August, late December-
early January and Wednesday

■ Price
Lunch = set ¥ 5,250-16,800
Dinner = set ¥ 16,800

TEL. 03-5707-8008
4-27-1 Nakamachi, Setagaya-ku,
Tokyo

Sushiko Honten
寿司幸本店

🚇 10

Mamoru Sugiyama, the 4th generation owner-chef, uses only sun-dried rice whose texture, when cooked, is never too hard. Seasoning consists of the merest hint of salt and red vinegar and the serving temperature is key: the cooked rice is stored in a wooden container and placed in a warmed basket to keep it at body temperature. Sweet *atsuyaki tamago* is prepared using a technique from the Edo Period. Open all day with no breaks.

■ Opening hours, last orders
11:30-23:00 L.O.21:45

■ Annual and weekly closing
Closed mid-August and late December-early January

■ Price
Lunch = set   ¥ 9,450-26,250
Dinner = set   ¥ 9,450-26,250

TEL. 03-3571-1968
6-3-8 Ginza, Chuo-ku, Tokyo

Sushi Mizutani
鮨 水谷

✿ ✿ ✿

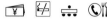

The appeal lies in the quality of ingredients and Hachiro Mizutani's sushi-making techniques. It is slightly more slender than usual and beautifully crafted. Innovative ideas are used to enhance the taste of the toppings, which include fragrant steamed abalone, high-quality tuna, and smoked bonito. Two time slots are available for dinner - it's easier to get a lunch booking. Sushi Mizutani moved to its address here in 2010.

■ Opening hours, last orders
Lunch = 11:30-13:30
Dinner = 17:00-21:30

■ Annual and weekly closing
Closed Golden week, mid-August,
late December-early January,
Sunday and Public Holidays

■ Price
Lunch = set   ¥ 18,000-30,000
Dinner = set   ¥ 18,000-30,000

TEL. 03-3573-5258
Juno Ginza Seiwa Building 9F,
8-7-7 Ginza, Chuo-ku, Tokyo

Sushi Musashi

鮨 武蔵

Owner-chef Hiroyuki Musashi places emphasis on the rice which is seasoned well with white vinegar and seaweed salt. His *nikiri* and *nitsume* are subtle so as to emphasise the natural flavours. A popular dish to complete the meal is the medium-sized sushi rolls. This is a traditional and immaculate sushi restaurant, with a cypress counter, wickerwork ceiling and granite floor, hiding in the basement of a modern building.

■ Opening hours, last orders
Dinner = 18:00-21:00 (L.O.)

■ Annual and weekly closing
Closed mid-August, late December-early January, Sunday and Public Holidays

■ Price
Dinner = set ¥ 15,750

TEL. 03–5464–3634
Tokyo Morris Building III B1F
5-18-10 Minamiaoyama,
Minato-ku, Tokyo

Sushi Nakamura
鮨 なかむら

As well as fish from Tsukiji market, white fish and shellfish come from Noto. Masanori Nakamura is particular about tuna: in summer it's from Sado and in winter from Oma. Sun-dried rice from Fukushima is steamed at a high heat, seasoned with aged black vinegar from Kagoshima and a mild salt from Okinawa for a good match with the tuna. A summer soup of boiled abalone slices is recommended. It is open late and always busy.

■ Opening hours, last orders
Dinner = 18:00-1:00 L.O.23:30

■ Annual and weekly closing
Closed Golden week, mid-August,
late December-early January,
Sunday and Public Holidays

■ Price
Dinner = set   ¥ 16,800

TEL. 03-3746-0856
7-17-16 Roppongi, Minato-ku,
Tokyo

Sushi Ohno
すし おおの

The chef offers originality and a variety of tastes before sushi, serving not only *sashimi*, but also *kobujime* alongside dishes that may be steamed, grilled or salted. Soft, tasty abalone is steeped in sake and kelp for half a day before being steamed; the *chawanmushi* with Japanese plum made with a clear golden stock is also memorable; its cold version is recommended in summer. In early autumn, homemade *karasumi* features.

■ Opening hours, last orders
Dinner = 17:30-22:00 (L.O.)

■ Annual and weekly closing
Closed Golden week, mid-August, late December-early January, Sunday and Public Holidays

■ Price
Dinner = set　¥ 17,850-24,150

TEL. 03–3572–0866
7-2-17 Ginza, Chuo-ku, Tokyo

Sushi Saito
鮨 さいとう

❀ ❀ ❀

As you enter the parking lot of the Nihon Jitensha Kaikan building, this restaurant, with its counter for six, is on your right – there is no sign. Takashi Saito takes great care to achieve the right balance between rice, topping, *wasabi* and *nikiri*. The texture of each grain of rice is constant; seasoning is slightly saltier than usual, the red vinegar milder. This is ideal for tuna, of which the chef is particularly proud.

■ Opening hours, last orders
Lunch = 12:00-14:00 (L.O.)
Dinner = 17:00-22:00 (L.O.)

■ Annual and weekly closing
Closed mid-August, late December-early January, Sunday and Public Holiday Mondays

■ Price
Lunch = set   ¥ 5,250-15,750
Dinner = set   ¥ 15,750-26,250

TEL. 03-3589-4412
Nihon Jitensha Kaikan 1F,
1-9-15 Akasaka, Minato-ku,
Tokyo

Sushiya Mao
すし屋 真魚

Opened by Shinji Kanesaka, owner-chef of Sushi Kanesaka, in 2009 but, somewhat differently, the décor here was handled by *kabuki* actor Ebizo Ichikawa XI; the wooden door at the entrance features the pattern of his guild, Naritaya. Like Sushi Kanesaka, the sushi is prepared in the *Edomae* style and care is taken with the glittering gizzard shad and chub mackerel sushi. Note that there is a table charge per party in the evening.

■ Opening hours, last orders
Lunch = 11:30-14:00 (L.O.)
Dinner = 17:00-22:00 (L.O.)

■ Annual and weekly closing
Closed Public Holiday Mondays

■ Price
Lunch = set   ¥ 5,250-12,600
         à la carte ¥ 8,000-25,000
Dinner = set   ¥ 12,600-21,000
          à la carte ¥ 8,000-25,000
Seat charge = ¥ 1,050/group (dinner)

TEL. 03-3562-7890
Seiyo Ginza Hotel 1F,
1-11-2 Ginza, Chuo-ku, Tokyo

Suzuki
すずき

Chinese and French techniques combine with Suzuki's flair to bring out natural flavours, while the menu is determined by what's good at the market each day. Bamboo shoots brought in directly from Tanba offer a taste of spring; tilefish is soaked in salted water, dried then roasted. As he offers a home-cooking class in his kitchen every day at noon, only one lunch reservation is accepted and *tatami* seating is the only option.

■ Opening hours, last orders
Lunch = 12:00-14:00 L.O.12:30
Dinner = 18:00-22:00 L.O.21:00

■ Annual and weekly closing
Closed Golden week, mid-August,
late December-early January and
Monday

■ Price
Lunch = set   ¥ 6,300
Dinner = set   ¥ 10,500-15,750

TEL. 03-3710-3696
2-16-3 Takaban, Meguro-ku,
Tokyo
www.kappou.jp

Tajima NEW
たじま

Enjoy refreshing Ibaraki summer *soba* and savoury Hokkaido autumn *soba* when they are in season. De-hulled buckwheat is ground both coarse and fine, and the flours are mixed to make the *soba* which is cut thin. The spicy sauce gives off a savoury *katsuo* aroma. There are also drinking snacks like *itawasa* and *dashimaki*, making for a hearty selection of items. The fixed priced menu is recommended for those who like vegetables.

■ Opening hours, last orders
Lunch = Tue.-Sat. and Public
Holiday Mondays 11:30-14:30 (L.O.)
Dinner = 17:30-21:30 (L.O.)
Public Holidays 17:30-20:30 (L.O.)

■ Annual and weekly closing
Closed early January and Sunday

■ Price
Lunch = set   ¥ 3,000-5,100
      à la carte ¥ 2,000-5,000
Dinner = set   ¥ 3,000-5,100
      à la carte ¥ 2,000-5,000

TEL. 03-3445-6617
3-8-6 Nishiazabu, Minato-ku,
Tokyo
www.sobatajima.jp

Takahashi
たかはし

Yuji Takahashi opened here in 2005, having previously had a French restaurant. He works alone so order the chicken liver terrine and wine while waiting. Influences from western cuisines are adapted: chicken oysters come with violet mustard, and the *eringi* mushrooms are seasoned with *pancetta* and olive oil. To conclude, try the spicy *keema* curry. There are two starting times for dinner; at lunch only *oyakodon* is available.

■ Opening hours, last orders
Dinner = 17:00-20:00 and
            20:15-22:30

■ Annual and weekly closing
Closed mid-August, late December-
early January, Sunday, 1st and 3rd
Mondays of each month

■ Price
Dinner = à la carte ¥ 2,800-8,000

TEL. 03–5436–9677
Pragma. G-Tower 2F,
1-7-1 Nishigotanda, Shinagawa-ku,
Tokyo

Takeyabu
竹やぶ

The interior overflows with decorative touches that reflect the owner-chef's personality. Needless to say, the *soba* also reflects his unique senses. The un-threshed buckwheat is ground with a millstone and new ideas and methods are constantly being applied, such as the cold *sobagaki* and the egg soufflé with balsamic vinegar topped with buckwheat seeds. Unfortunately, the owner-chef plans to close the restaurant in July 2011.

■ Opening hours, last orders
Lunch = 11:30-15:30
Dinner = 18:00-21:30
Sunday and Public Holidays
11:30-20:30

■ Annual and weekly closing
Closed 1-3 January

■ Price
Lunch = set   ¥ 5,250
        à la carte ¥ 3,000-8,000
Dinner = set   ¥ 9,240
         à la carte ¥ 3,000-8,000
Private room fee = 10%

TEL. 03-5786-7500
Roppongi Hills Residence B, 3F,
6-12-2 Roppongi, Minato-ku,
Tokyo

Taku
拓

Co-owned by a sushi chef and sommelière, Taku offers interesting pairings of sushi and wine. Takuya Sato trained in Japanese cuisine which gives extra depth to his sushi craftsmanship; the high-quality fish, for example, is seasoned with kelp or salt before being served, to bring out its natural flavour. The *omakase* begins with a wide variety of elaborate appetisers including *sashimi*, before moving on to nigiri. Open late.

■ Opening hours, last orders
Dinner = 18:00-1:00 (L.O.)

■ Annual and weekly closing
Closed mid-August, late December-early January, Sunday and Public Holidays

■ Price
Dinner = set   ¥ 16,800-21,000

TEL. 03–5774–4372
2-11-5 Nishiazabu, Minato-ku, Tokyo

MAP NO. 20/B-3

Tamao
玉青

As there is no sign, look for the building entrance on the left of the *izakaya* on the 1st floor and call 301 on the intercom. You will then feel as though you have been invited to a private retreat. Tamao is known for its *rogama* cuisine: in spring, roasted bamboo shoots; in summer, lightly baked abalone and, in winter, hotpot of salt-grilled *suppon*. Organic rice is cooked in the oven and served straight to the plate.

■ Opening hours, last orders
Dinner = 18:00-23:00 (L.O.)

■ Annual and weekly closing
Closed Golden week, mid-August, late December-early January and Sunday

■ Price
Dinner = set   ¥ 10,500-18,900
à la carte ¥ 10,000-20,000
Service charge = 10%

TEL. 03–3455–1407
Sanrakukan 301,
3-3-7 Azabujuban, Minato-ku, Tokyo
www.i-anbai.com/pc/rest6.html

Tapas Molecular Bar

Innovative interpretations of dishes from assorted countries are served at this counter bar, and dinner is made up of least 20 small, creative dishes. The chefs create and deconstruct dishes in an entertaining way, using cylinders, pipettes and syringes for delicacies like 'blood orange caviar' and '*miso* soup'. To experience this 'food magic' at the corner of the Oriental Lounge, guests are strongly advised to arrive on time.

■ Opening hours, last orders
Dinner = 18:00-20:15 and 20:30-22:45

■ Price
Dinner = set   ¥ 14,000
Service charge = 13%

TEL. 03–3270–8188
Mandarin Oriental Hotel 38F,
2-1-1 Nihonbashimuromachi,
Chuo-ku, Tokyo
www.mandarinoriental.co.jp/tokyo

Tateru Yoshino Ginza

The Ginza branch of Yoshino's restaurant group is its third. As with the other locations, the focus is on what the chef calls '*terroir* cooking', although here the modern presentation of the food and its lighter seasoning set it apart. Specialities include 'Stella Maris-style pâté en croûte' and 'red tuna and eggplant millefeuille with Ossetra caviar'. The set lunch menu is quite a bargain and includes the specialities.

■ Opening hours, last orders
Lunch = 11:30-14:00 (L.O.)
Dinner = Mon.-Sat. 18:00-21:00 (L.O.)

■ Annual and weekly closing
Closed late December-early January

■ Price
Lunch = set   ¥ 4,800-21,000
Dinner = set   ¥ 10,000-21,000
Private room fee = ¥ 3,150 (lunch),
                            ¥ 5,250 (dinner)
Service charge = 10%

TEL. 03-3563-1511
Pias Ginza 12F,
4-8-10 Ginza, Chuo-ku, Tokyo
www.tateruyoshino.com

Tateru Yoshino Shiba

✿✿

⊖ ⅍ 🅿 🚌 12 📞🍴 ⵙ

Tateru Yoshino is also the owner-chef of Stella Maris in Paris. *Duo de foie gras* is a duck foie gras terrine infused with dried fruits, while *saumon fumé mi-cuit à la Stella Maris* is Yoshino's fish speciality. *Tourte de gibier*, wild game meat pie, is a traditional winter dish that uses several types of game and foie gras. Compared to his other locations, dishes here are more classic. An extensive wine list is also available.

■ Opening hours, last orders
Lunch = 11:30-14:00 (L.O.)
Dinner = Mon.-Sat. 18:00-21:00
(L.O.)

■ Price
Lunch = set   ¥ 3,675-15,750
          à la carte ¥ 10,000-17,000
Dinner = set   ¥ 4,725-15,750
          à la carte ¥ 10,000-17,000
Service charge = 10%

TEL. 03-5405-7800
Shiba Park Hotel Annex 1F,
1-5-10 Shibakoen, Minato-ku,
Tokyo
www.tateruyoshino.com

Tateru Yoshino Shiodome

The compact dining room is on the 25th floor of the Shiodome Media Tower. Menus are mainly fixed price but there is also a chef's choice menu available. Accent is placed on the combination of classic ingredients and dishes are kept quite light to please today's palate. We recommend the roast lamb with rock salt. Bar à vins Tateru Yoshino, the adjacent wine bar, offers a collection of wines from France and other countries.

■ Opening hours, last orders
Lunch = 11:30-14:00 (L.O.)
Dinner = 18:00-21:00 (L.O.)

■ Price
Lunch = set   ¥ 3,675-8,400
Dinner = set   ¥ 7,875-15,750
Private room fee = ¥ 5,250-29,400
Service charge = 10%

TEL. 03-6252-1155
Park Hotel Shiodome Media Tower 25F,
1-7-1 Higashishinbashi,
Minato-ku, Tokyo
www.tateruyoshino.com

Tatsumura
たつむら

There is just one set menu, consisting of about 10 dishes. Masahiko Miyagawa employs various techniques so as not to bore diners' palates: he uses a different soup stock base (bonito flakes, scallops or clams) depending on the dish to add variety and the *takikomi-gohan* changes each season. The interior is simple but is often used for business occasions. One of their *tatami* rooms has a lovely view of the spring cherry blossom.

■ Opening hours, last orders
Dinner = 17:30-23:00 L.O.21:00

■ Annual and weekly closing
Closed mid-August, late December-early January, Sunday and Public Holidays

■ Price
Dinner = set   ¥ 12,600
Service charge = 10%

TEL. 03-3585-7285
Trade Akasaka Building 2F,
5-4-14 Akasaka, Minato-ku,
Tokyo

Tenmo
てん茂

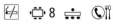

This family-operated *tempura* restaurant opened in 1885. Today, third-generation owner-chef Nobuo Okuda looks after the customers and his son does the cooking. Traditional flavours are preserved through the use of sesame oil, as has always been the practice. Seasonal tastes include ice fish and butterbur sprouts in spring, young *ayu* and the *Edomae anago*. The specialities are abalone in summer and fried chestnuts in the autumn.

■ Opening hours, last orders
Lunch = 12:00-14:00 L.O.13:30
Dinner = 17:00-20:00 L.O.19:00

■ Annual and weekly closing
Closed mid-August, late December-
early January, Saturdays in August,
Sunday and Public Holidays

■ Price
Lunch = set   ¥ 6,300-12,600
Dinner = set   ¥ 9,450-12,600

TEL. 03-3241-7035
4-1-3 Nihonbashihoncho, Chuo-ku,
Tokyo
www.tenmo.jp

Tetsuan
哲庵

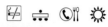

The quiet owner-chef's personality is reflected in the restaurant's tranquil atmosphere. There are three set menus, each offering a different number of dishes, including *nabe ryori* and *takikomi-gohan*. In summer, *nabe* is served cold with ice made from stock; in winter, *mizore-nabe* is flavoured with *yuzu* and tilefish. The stock varies depending on the dish, while salt is used for seasoning in summer and soy sauce in winter.

■ Opening hours, last orders
Dinner = 18:00-21:30 (L.O.)

■ Annual and weekly closing
Closed early January and Monday

■ Price
Dinner = set　　¥ 10,500-16,800

TEL. 03-3423-1850
1-5-26 Azabujuban, Minato-ku, Tokyo

Tomura
と村

Chiba-native Kimio Tomura not only selects ingredients each day from Tsukiji, he also buys items not available in Tokyo directly from the producing area. The steamed lobster is a speciality served all year round; after cooking, he carefully peels off the shell in front of you. The meal concludes either with *jakomeshi* or a noodle dish. The warm and friendly owner-chef will happily answer questions about ingredients or dishes.

■ Opening hours, last orders
Dinner = 18:00-21:30 (L.O.)

■ Annual and weekly closing
Closed Golden week, mid-August,
late December-early January,
Sunday and Public Holiday Mondays

■ Price
Dinner = set   ¥ 24,150-52,500
Service charge = 10%

TEL. 03-3591-3303
1-11-14 Toranomon, Minato-ku,
Tokyo

Toriki
とり喜

Yasuhito Sakai serves up varieties of free-range poultry, including Daisen local chicken and Tokyo *shamo* gamecock; carefully skewered, lightly salted and then grilled. Although set menu selections—comprising eight *yakitori* and four vegetable skewers—are popular, you will get faster service ordering individual kebabs. Whole chicken hearts must be ordered in advance. Reservations can only be made between 10:00-16:00.

■ Opening hours, last orders
Dinner = Mon.-Fri. 17:30-22:00 (L.O.)
Sat. 17:00-22:00 (L.O.)

■ Annual and weekly closing
Closed Golden week, mid-August,
late December-early January,
Sunday and Public Holidays

■ Price
Dinner = set   ¥ 3,360-4,940
           à la carte ¥ 3,000-7,000

TEL. 03-3622-6202
1-8-13 Kinshi, Sumida-ku, Tokyo

Torishiki NEW
鳥しき

The main feature of the menu here is *omakase*, ensuring a nicely balanced assortment of various cuts and parts; simply indicate when you've had enough. The vegetables are succulent, and the date chicken has a light texture with sweet skin. The outside is cooked with a fuller flame to seal in the juices, and the inside is cooked slowly with the residual heat, so you may have to wait although the regulars never seem to mind.

■ Opening hours, last orders
Dinner = 18:00-23:00

■ Annual and weekly closing
Closed mid-August, late December-
early January, Monday and Public
Holidays

■ Price
Dinner = set   ¥ 4,000-5,500
Seat charge=¥ 500/person

TEL. 03-3440-7656
2-14-12 Kamiosaki,
Shinagawa-ku, Tokyo

Totoya Uoshin
とゝや魚新

As the name suggests - totoya means 'fish dealer'- dishes revolve around seasonal fish. A word or two with the chef will have him serve you your favourite. The Pacific sea bream comes in various ways, including *sashimi*, *kombujime*, *ushiojiru*, *arataki*, and also the steamed *kotsumushi*. There is a large selection of sake, chosen by the head chef who visits small breweries all over the country - ask the chefs for recommendations.

■ Opening hours, last orders
Lunch = 11:30-14:00 (L.O.)
Dinner = 17:30-21:30 (L.O.)

■ Annual and weekly closing
Closed mid-August, late December-early January, Sunday and Public Holidays

■ Price
Lunch = set   ¥ 5,250-7,350
Dinner = set   ¥ 10,500-15,750
Private room fee = ¥ 3,150 (lunch),
                              ¥ 5,250 (dinner)
Service charge = 10% (dinner)

TEL. 03-3585-4701
5-1-34 Akasaka, Minato-ku, Tokyo

Toyoda
とよだ

Seasonal ingredients are selected for their texture and flavour: in spring, thick bamboo shoots grilled over charcoal; in summer, sweetfish, dried and marinated with *shuto* before being grilled and served with *honesenbei*. In autumn it is kelp hotpot with pike conger and *matsutake* mushrooms; grilled *matsubagani* crab is popular in the cold months. The owner-chef welcomes customers at the entrance and the waitress is pleasant.

■ Opening hours, last orders
Lunch = 11:30-14:30 L.O. 13:30
Dinner = 17:30-22:00 L.O. 20:30

■ Annual and weekly closing
Closed mid-August, late December-early January, Sunday and Public Holidays

■ Price
Lunch = set   ¥ 5,250-10,500
Dinner = set   ¥ 10,500-21,000
Service charge = 10%

TEL. 03-5568-5822
La Vialle Ginza Building 2F,
7-5-4 Ginza, Chuo-ku, Tokyo

Tsujitome
辻留

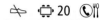

The chef serves *kaiseki* dishes with respect for the *chanoyu* spirit. *Tofu-dengaku* dressed with *miso* is a March dish; in September, *maruage-dofu* is used in a soup to recreate the season inside the bowl. As in *chakaiseki*, *usucha* finishes the meal. Attention to detail is apparent in everything, from the alcove with its hanging scrolls and *ikebana* to the attractive tableware and the service of the waiters in neat, simple *kimono*.

■ Opening hours, last orders
Lunch = 12:00-14:00
Dinner = 17:00-21:00

■ Annual and weekly closing
Closed Golden week, mid-August, late December-early January and Sunday

■ Price
Lunch = set   ¥ 15,750-36,750
Dinner = set   ¥ 26,250-45,150
Service charge = 10%

TEL. 03-3403-3984
1-5-8 Motoakasaka, Minato-ku, Tokyo
www.tsujitome.co.jp

Tsukasa
司

Opened in 1960, this warm and friendly *kappo* restaurant serves high-grade, natural white tiger puffer fish. There is a set menu, which can be a little expensive, but you can talk with the chef and order what you like. The *sashimi* is thickly sliced and the milt soup is a popular item and features strong-tasting dried bonito stock, white *miso* and smooth, seasoned milt. The hotpot is made with green onions, tofu and *shungiku*.

■ Opening hours, last orders
Dinner = 17:00-22:30

■ Annual and weekly closing
Closed 16 April-10 September

■ Price
Dinner = set ¥ 30,000-38,000
à la carte ¥ 25,000-40,000
Private room fee = 10%

TEL. 03-3405-9397
1-9-1 Minamiaoyama, Minato-ku, Tokyo

Uchitsu
うち津

 4

Uchitsu is a new style of *tempura* restaurant, opened by Takahisa Uchitsu in 2008. Just a set menu is usually served, which includes staples like *anago* and smelt-whiting as well as seasonal items such as summer oyster, pike conger and crab meat. Assorted items, including raw vegetables, are served in between the various tempura pieces. You will see a private room on your left and a cypress counter at the end of a stone path.

■ Opening hours, last orders
Dinner = 18:00-23:00 L.O.22:00

■ Annual and weekly closing
Closed mid-August, late December-early January, Sunday except Public Holidays and Public Holiday Mondays

■ Price
Dinner = set   ¥ 15,000-18,000

TEL. 03-6408-9591
5-25-4 Hiroo, Shibuya-ku, Tokyo
www.tempura-uchitsu.com

Uchiyama
うち山

The spirit of *chakaiseki* holds special importance for the owner-chef and the purchasing of *tai* and abalone is done with his own keen eye. His modesty and the staff's friendly service is expressed in the 'the spirit of tea.' Specialities are sesame tofu, with its fragrant skin and soft inner texture, and *ochazuke*-style rice and broth with raw sea bream. The dessert *kuzukiri* is made from Yoshino *kudzu* and Okinawan *kuromitsu*.

■ Opening hours, last orders
Lunch = 11:30-14:00 (L.O.)
Dinner = 17:00-23:00
Sun. and Public Holidays
17:00-22:00

■ Annual and weekly closing
Closed Golden week, mid-August
and late December-early January

■ Price
Lunch = set   ¥ 5,000-15,000
Dinner = set   ¥ 13,650-26,250
Service charge = 10% (dinner)

TEL. 03–3541–6720
Light Building B1F,
2-12-3 Ginza, Chuo-ku, Tokyo
www.nk-net.jp/uchiyama

Uemura Honten
植むら 本店

✕✕✕

🪑 12 📞🍴

The head chef uses Kyoto vegetables like Kamo eggplants, carrots and Shogoin turnips, as well as seafood from various parts of the country. The *hassun* features elaborate seasonal arrangements; sweet tomato soup made with chicken stock and *junsai* is a refreshing dish in summer. Each floor offers a different seating option: table seating, private rooms or a large main room; the counter on the 1st floor only opens in the evening.

■ Opening hours, last orders
Lunch = 11:30-15:00 L.O.14:00
Dinner = 17:00-22:00 L.O.20:00

■ Annual and weekly closing
Closed Golden week, mid-August,
late December-early January,
Sunday and Public Holidays

■ Price
Lunch = set   ¥ 7,000-25,000
Dinner = set   ¥ 7,000-25,000

TEL. 03–3541–1351
1-13-10 Tsukiji, Chuo-ku, Tokyo
www.tukijiuemura.com/shop/101.
html

Ukai-tei Ginza

The French Belle Époque-style décor fits well with the building, which served as the main house of a wealthy farmer, before being relocated from Tokamachi. Kobe beef is used, as well as black-haired cattle bred on a designated farm in Tottori. The speciality dish of abalone steamed in rock salt is also good. Other options make the best of the seasons: spring vegetables, autumn *matsutake* mushrooms and truffles in winter.

■ Opening hours, last orders
Lunch = 12:00-14:00 (L.O.)
Sat., Sun. and Public Holidays
12:00-15:00 (L.O.)
Dinner = 17:00-23:00 L.O.21:00

■ Annual and weekly closing
Closed 31 December-4 January

■ Price
Lunch = set   ¥ 6,830-9,450
           à la carte ¥ 14,000-43,000
Dinner = set   ¥ 16,800-24,150
           à la carte ¥ 14,000-43,000
Service charge = 10%

TEL. 03-3544-5252
Jiji-Tsushin Building,
5-15-8 Ginza, Chuo-ku, Tokyo
www.ukai.co.jp/ginza

Ukai-tei Omotesando

❀   ✗✗✗✗

✈ ≪ 🖵 8 �] ☏❢ ☀ 🍇

Opened in Omotesando-dori in 2007, but its interior dates back about 150 years. Its construction centres around a merchant's house from Kanazawa; it was moved and reassembled here. For the cooking, black-haired cattle, known as 'ukai-gyu', come from a designated farm in Tottori and abalone steamed in rock salt is a speciality. After dinner, you will be invited to take dessert in the salon. Terrace seating is available.

■ Opening hours, last orders
Lunch = 12:00-14:30 (L.O.)
Dinner = 17:30-23:00 L.O.21:00
Sat., Sun. and Public Holidays
11:30-23:00 L.O.21:00

■ Annual and weekly closing
Closed 1 January

■ Price
Lunch = set   ¥ 6,830-9,450
          à la carte   ¥ 14,000-43,000
Dinner = set   ¥ 12,600-24,150
          à la carte   14,000-43,000
Service charge = 10%

TEL. 03-5467-5252
Omotesando Gyre 5F,
5-10-1 Jingumae, Shibuya-ku,
Tokyo
www.omotesando-ukaitei.jp

Umi
海味

High quality fresh ingredients are what draws one to Umi. Rare fish come from Kyushu and Hokkaido and, with sushi and appetisers, up to 30 different types can be sampled. Rice is prepared slightly harder and saltier than usual and the mellow-flavoured vinegar is a blend of two red vinegars: one aged for three years with a bouquet of sake lees and another, thinner variety. This lively restaurant runs like clockwork.

■ Opening hours, last orders
Dinner = 18:00-23:00 (L.O.)

■ Annual and weekly closing
Closed mid-August, late December-
early January, Sunday and Public
Holidays

■ Price
Dinner = set   ¥ 20,000

TEL. 03–3401–3368
3-2-8 Minamiaoyama, Minato-ku,
Tokyo

Uotoku
うを徳

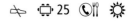

Uotoku has a history dating back to the beginning of the Meiji Era, when a fish dealer in Hatchobori moved his business to Kagurazaka and changed the name to Uotoku. The *ebi-shinjo* deserves a mention: the shrimps are carefully minced with a knife to maintain their firm texture before being deep-fried. *Tai-no matsukawa-zukuri* uses a method passed down from the founder, parboiling the fish with its skin. Service is excellent.

■ Opening hours, last orders
Lunch = 11:30-14:30
Dinner = 17:00-22:30

■ Annual and weekly closing
Closed mid-August and late December-early January

■ Price
Lunch = set　　¥ 10,500-15,750
Dinner = set　　¥ 21,000-26,250
Service charge = 10%

TEL. 03-3269-0360
3-1 Kagurazaka, Shinjuku-ku, Tokyo
www.uotoku.com

JAPANESE FUGU   MAP NO. 20/B-3

Usukifugu Yamadaya
臼杵ふぐ山田屋

❀ ❀ ❀   ✗✗✗

This is a *fugu* restaurant on Ushizaka in Nishiazabu which opened as a branch of a *ryotei* in Usuki, Oita in 2006. In season, *tora fugu* is delivered daily from Oita. Thick slices of *fugu* are served with homemade *ponzu* dipping sauce made from soy sauce and juicy citrus *kabosu* fruit harvested in Oita. A speciality is a sushi of the local Usuki dish *o-han* -yellow rice coloured with gardenia fruit- topped with grilled *shirako*.

■ Opening hours, last orders
Dinner = 18:00-24:00 L.O.22:30

■ Annual and weekly closing
Closed Golden week, mid-August,
late December-early January,
Sunday and Public Holidays

■ Price
Dinner = set   ¥ 21,000-31,500
            à la carte ¥ 12,000-22,000
Service charge = 10%

TEL. 03-3499-5501
Fleg Nishi-Azabu Vierge B1F,
4-11-14 Nishiazabu, Minato-ku,
Tokyo
www.usuki.info/yamadaya

Waketokuyama
分とく山

❀❀   ✕✕

🔲 🛋8 📞🍴

Waketokuyama provides cuisine in touch with the times. The head chef offers a variety of creative dishes, sourcing up to as many as 100 different ingredients nationwide. The speciality is *awabi-no-isoyaki*: lightly baked in its shell, the steamed Sanriku abalone is covered with a sauce of puréed offal, *kudzu* and topped with seaweed. Besides the counter and table seating, the annexe has a private room overlooking a garden.

■ Opening hours, last orders
Dinner = 17:00-23:00 L.O.21:00

■ Annual and weekly closing
Closed late December-early January
and Sunday

■ Price
Dinner = set   ¥ 15,750
Service charge = 10%

TEL. 03–5789–3838
5-1-5 Minamiazabu, Minato-ku,
Tokyo

Wako
和幸

'Live in harmony and to be grateful to nature for its bounty', owner-chef's philosophy is the origin of his restaurant's name. Only wild seafood is used: sea bream from Akashi is served as *kobujime* seasoned with soy sauce; sweetfish comes from Gifu. Dishes are prepared adhering to the *kaiseki* tradition and there are four *tatami* rooms, including one for tea ceremonies. Hidden in a residential area, Wako is not easy to find.

■ Opening hours, last orders
Lunch = 11:30-13:30 (L.O.)
Dinner = 17:30-20:00 (L.O.)

■ Annual and weekly closing
Closed Golden week, mid-August,
late December-early January,
Sunday and Public Holidays

■ Price
Lunch = set   ¥ 15,750-52,500
Dinner = set   ¥ 21,000-52,500
Service charge = 10%

TEL. 03–3982–2251
2-16-3 Mejiro, Toshima-ku, Tokyo

Yamaji
山路

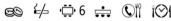

The speciality here is sea bream, fresh from the owner-chef's hometown, Ehime. All the fish is used: the body for *sashimi*, the head is salt-grilled or used for *tsukeyaki* or steamed with sake and kelp; lean parts are for soup. Another speciality is *tai-chazuke* with aged black sesame sauce. Only a set menu is served but adjustments can be made. At lunch there are also rice bowl dishes; try the grilled beef or salmon belly.

■ Opening hours, last orders
Lunch = 12:00-14:00 L.O.13:00
Dinner = 17:30-23:00 L.O.22:00

■ Annual and weekly closing
Closed mid-August, late December-early January, Sunday and Public Holidays

■ Price
Lunch = set ¥ 2,625-15,750
Dinner = set ¥ 18,900-31,500

TEL. 03-5565-3639
Ginza 7 Building B1F,
7-14-14 Ginza, Chuo-ku, Tokyo

Yamamoto
やまもと

❀ ❀   ✕✕✕

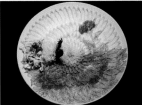

Run by the same family for three generations, Yamamoto is in a traditional house; its antique scrolls and decorative pieces chosen by the owner-chef. *Tora-fugu* features, with traditional dishes such as *kiku-zukuri* and *nikogori*, alongside original ones like milt crêpes and clear soup made with *fugu* skin. English menus, with drawings of *fugu* done by the chef, are available so it's a good place to entertain foreign nationals.

■ Opening hours, last orders
Dinner = 17:00-22:30

■ Annual and weekly closing
Closed April-September, Sunday and Public Holidays

■ Price
Dinner = set   ¥ 36,750
Service charge = 10%

TEL. 03-3541-7730
2-15-4 Tsukiji, Chuo-ku, Tokyo
www8.plala.or.jp/tsukijiyamamoto

Yamane
やま祢

⌗ 12 ☎¶

The founder trained at a *fugu* restaurant in Shimonoseki once frequented by Hirobumi Ito, Japan's first prime minister. The present owner-chef succeeded his father to become the 3rd generation chef. The *sashimi* comes highly recommended as the *nimaibiki* cutting technique used ensures thicker slices with added firmness. Deep-fried *fugu*, a speciality, has the fragrant flavour of soy-sauce. For the *miso* hotpot, white *miso* is used.

■ Opening hours, last orders
Dinner = 17:30-19:30 (L.O.)

■ Annual and weekly closing
Closed Golden week, mid-August, late December-early January and Sunday

■ Price
Dinner = set   ¥ 31,500-38,850
Service charge = 10% (tatami
                 room 15%)

TEL. 03–3541–1383
7-15-7 Ginza, Chuo-ku, Tokyo

Yamanochaya
山の茶屋

   30

An *unagi* restaurant in the grounds of Sanno Hie Shrine; the entrance is opposite the rear gate of Hibiya High School. *Kabayaki* is the speciality: *unagi* from areas such as Shizuoka and Kagoshima are broiled without seasoning, steamed slowly, then broiled over *bincho* charcoal with a sweet sauce. We recommend *horigotatsu*-style sunken seating in the annexe. Prices are high but lunch and Saturday evening menus are more reasonable.

■ Opening hours, last orders
Lunch = 11:30-13:00 (L.O.)
Dinner = 17:00-19:00 (L.O.)

■ Annual and weekly closing
Closed mid-August, late December-early January, Sunday and Public Holidays

■ Price
Lunch = set   ¥ 9,450-16,170
Dinner = set   ¥ 13,650-18,270
Service charge = 10%

TEL. 03-3581-0585
2-10-6 Nagatacho, Chiyoda-ku, Tokyo

Yamasaki
山さき

On the 2nd floor of a building in front of Zenkokuji Temple, but hard to spot. During October-May, the owner-chef offers *negima nabe*. Tasty *setoro* is dipped in soup and goes well with scallion and seaweed, watercress and parsley. Also recommended are scallops, clams and pen shells, offered in February and March. Summer staples include *ainame*; *moryo nabe* uses chicken or Shamo gamecock. Prices are modest considering the quality.

■ Opening hours, last orders
Dinner = 18:00-22:00 L.O.20:00

■ Annual and weekly closing
Closed mid-August, late December-early January, Sunday and Public Holidays

■ Price
Dinner = set ¥ 7,350-15,750
Service charge = 5%

TEL. 03-3267-2310
Fukuya Building 2F,
4-2 Kagurazaka, Shinjuku-ku,
Tokyo

Yokota
よこ田

Tsuneo Yokota goes to Tsukiji with his son, in search of ingredients for his *omakase* set menu. The light-tasting oil is a mix of sesame and corn oils, and the chef varies the amount of batter used. All pieces come with *tentsuyu*, salt, lemon juice and curry powder—the chef will advise you which to use for each ingredient. *Tempura* with curry powder is a new concept and, according to the chef, best with flathead fish and *anago*.

■ Opening hours, last orders
Dinner = 17:30-20:30 (L.O.)

■ Annual and weekly closing
Closed Golden week, mid-August, late December-early January and Wednesday

■ Price
Dinner = set   ¥ 10,500

TEL. 03–3408–4238
Patio Azabu-Juban II 3F,
3-11-3 Motoazabu, Minato-ku,
Tokyo

Yokoyama
よこやま

Tadashi Yokoyama trained at a *tempura* restaurant in Kyoto before gaining more experience at its Tokyo branch. Ingredients include tiger prawns, *megochi*, white asparagus, sweetfish in spring and pike conger in summer. No dipping sauce is served, just salt and lemon juice. Seasoned grated radish is for refreshing the palate. *Tencha*, a speciality, is a must to finish with. Please refrain from using strong perfume or cologne.

■ Opening hours, last orders
Dinner = 17:30-22:00 L.O.20:00

■ Annual and weekly closing
Closed mid-August, late December-early January, Wednesday, Sunday and Public Holidays

■ Price
Dinner = set ¥ 13,125

TEL. 03–3631–3927
2-7-10 Kotobashi, Sumida-ku, Tokyo

Yonemura
よねむら

Having started his career specialising in French cuisine, Masayasu Yonemura is "not concerned about the categories of cuisine, I have established my own style by responding to my customer's requests; always searching for new ideas" and serves 'Yonemura-style' dishes, rich in creativity. A small toasted rice ball placed on a spoon and topped with a layer of sautéed foie gras and another of roasted duck breast are two examples.

■ Opening hours, last orders
Lunch = 12:00-15:30 L.O.14:00
Dinner = 17:30-23:00 L.O.21:00

■ Annual and weekly closing
Closed mid-August, late December-
early January and Monday

■ Price
Lunch = set   ¥ 6,000-10,00
Dinner = set   ¥ 12,500-14,500

TEL. 03-5537-6699
Kojun Building 4F,
6-8-7 Ginza, Chuo-ku, Tokyo

Yoneyama
よねやま

Spring dishes include giant clams seasoned with a little soy sauce and sake; abalone, moistened in hot bonito soup stock then sliced and served with strained liver sauce, is a summer speciality. *Sashimi* of *tai* is the chef's pick. The typical winter dish is *matsuba* crab mixed with sweet white *miso*. A *fugu* set menu is also available until February. The owner-chef's speaks mostly through the diligent efforts of his cooking.

■ Opening hours, last orders
Dinner = 18:00-21:30 (L.O.)

■ Annual and weekly closing
Closed mid-August, late December-early January and Sunday

■ Price
Dinner = set   ¥ 10,500-15,750

TEL. 03-3341-3117
15 Arakicho, Shinjuku-ku, Tokyo

Yorozuya Okagesan NEW
萬屋 おかげさん

The warmth and dedication of the owner-chef has added to the popularity of this restaurant, whose theme is 'seasonal vegetables and local sake'. Order the assortment of *sashimi* first; everything is carefully prepared, including straw-smoked young tuna and *kinmedai* dusted with *karasumi*. The salted rice ball is a popular item to end with. The sake menu resembles a wine list. If you don't speak Japanese, go with someone who does.

■ Opening hours, last orders
Dinner = 18:00-23:00 L.O.22:15

■ Annual and weekly closing
Closed Golden week, mid-August,
late December-early January,
Sunday, Monday and Public Holidays

■ Price
Dinner = set   ¥ 4,200-5,250
         à la carte ¥ 4,500-5,500
Seat charge=¥ 420/person

TEL. 03-3355-8100
Matsumoto Building B1F,
2-10 Yotsuya, Shinjuku-ku, Tokyo
www.okagesan.net

Yoshicho
よし鳥

Yoshicho, well-known for its *negima*, specialises in Aomori *shamorokku* gamecock cuisine. All *yakitori* - served as a set 5 or 7-skewer meal, including one vegetable item - are seasoned with salt and grilled over Kishu *bincho* charcoal. Start with some snacks and sake before ordering the set menu. Depending on the size of your appetite, you can either order more skewers or complete the meal with chicken *zosui* or *ontama soborodon*.

■ Opening hours, last orders
Dinner = 17:00-23:30 L.O.22:30

■ Annual and weekly closing
Closed mid-August, late December-early January, Sunday and Public Holidays

■ Price
Dinner = à la carte ¥ 6,000-8,000

TEL. 03-5793-5050
Il Viare Gotanda Building 2F,
1-12-9 Higashigotanda,
Shinagawa-ku, Tokyo

Yoshifuku
与志福

The young owner-chef opened this restaurant in his hometown in 2008, having trained in Kyoto. Particular effort goes into the making of stocks and soups. The set menus include original ideas such as the seared and marinated *hamo* and spring onion salad with sesame flavoured dressing. There are two *omakase* set menus, each with *sashimi*. There are also *suppon*, *hamo* and crab menus. Kenji Takahashi and his mother run the restaurant.

■ Opening hours, last orders
Dinner = 18:00-22:00 L.O.20:00

■ Annual and weekly closing
Closed mid-August, late December-early January and Wednesday

■ Price
Dinner = set   ¥ 10,500-15,750

TEL. 03-6905-7767
New Island Higashikitazawa 2F,
3-1-10 Kitazawa, Setagaya-ku,
Tokyo
www013.upp.so-net.ne.jp/
yoshifuku

Yoshihashi
よしはし

 LUNCH   12

The high-quality marbled beef is chosen not because of the origin but by its quality. Thickly cut meat is coated with comparatively dense *sukiyaki* sauce and pan-roasted to the preferred tenderness. To create an egg dipping sauce, the egg white is beaten quickly with chopsticks into a meringue-like foam, while the yolk is left whole. Three *sukiyaki* set menus are available. Visitors are advised not to wear strong perfume.

■ Opening hours, last orders
Lunch = 11:30-15:00 L.O.13:30
Dinner = 17:30-22:30 L.O.20:30

■ Annual and weekly closing
Closed mid-August, late December-
early January, Sunday and Public
Holidays

■ Prices
Lunch = set   ¥ 2,100-3,700
Dinner = set   ¥ 12,000-17,000
                à la carte¥ 10,000-20,000
Private room fee = less than 4 persons
                        ¥ 5,000/hour
Service charge = 15% (dinner)

TEL.03-3401-3129
1-5-25 Motoakasaka, Minato-ku,
Tokyo

Yotaro
与太呂

This speciality sea bream and *tempura* restaurant is run by owner-chef Motohiro Kawaguchi and his son. The *tai* comes from ports throughout Japan, as regional variations complement different dishes: wild *tai* with a firm texture is used for *sashimi*, while *tai* with a more tender texture is used for *tai-meshi*. Thinly battered *tempura* is lightly fried, enclosing the flavour of fish and the natural fragrance of seasonal vegetables.

■ Opening hours, last orders
Dinner = 18:00-22:00 (L.O.)

■ Annual and weekly closing
Closed Golden week, mid-August, late December-early January and Sunday

■ Price
Dinner = set   ¥ 13,650

TEL. 03–3405–5866
4-11-4 Roppongi, Minato-ku, Tokyo
www.roppongi-yotaro.com

Yotsuha
四つ葉

The proprietress runs this *suppon* restaurant with the chef, who is also a qualified tea ceremony instructor. With only 8 counter seats, reservations are vital. *Suppon mushi* is a staple dish; salt-grilled sweetfish is cooked to release its aroma and retain the softness. *Takikomi-gohan* and pickles, served at the end, are prepared by the proprietress. Wild white-finned puffer fish is also available in January and February.

■ Opening hours, last orders
Dinner = 18:30-20:30 (L.O.)

■ Annual and weekly closing
Closed mid-August, late December-
early January, Sunday and Public
Holidays

■ Prices
Dinner = set   ¥ 14,700-15,750

TEL.03-3398-7093
2-20-7 Kamiogi, Suginami-ku,
Tokyo

Yukicho
有季銚

From October to March, the chef serves a traditional menu using ocean-caught tiger puffer fish. Summer is the time for stonefish; along with *sashimi*, the lightly boiled head is good with *ponzu* sauce. Oysters are fried after being char-grilled with kelp. An exquisite range of tableware includes *Kyoyaki*, *Wajimanuri* and Baccarat glass. Private rooms are the only option; some have counters. Yukicho may move, so check first.

■ Opening hours, last orders
Lunch = Thu.-Sat. 11:30-14:30
L.O.13:30
Dinner = 17:30-22:00 L.O.21:00

■ Annual and weekly closing
Closed Golden week, mid-August, late December-early January, Sunday and Public Holidays

■ Price
Lunch = set   ¥ 5,000-35,000
Dinner = set   ¥ 16,000-35,000
Service charge = 15% (lunch 10%)

TEL. 03-3544-2700
Success Ginza 7 Building B1F,
7-13-10 Ginza, Chuo-ku, Tokyo
www.four-seeds.co.jp/brand/
yukicho

Yukimura
幸村

✿ ✿ ✿

🍴🍴

As there is no sign, look for the blue board with the address on the wall. Having worked for 25 years in Kyoto, Yukimura Jun bases his cooking on the city's culinary traditions. Deserving of mention are *shabu-shabu* with *hanasansho* in spring, and the *ayu* in summer; charcoal-grilled *matsutake* mushrooms wrapped in hamo feature in autumn and, in winter, snow crab. The originality of the cuisine leaves a lasting impression.

■ Opening hours, last orders
Dinner = 17:30-20:00 (L.O.)

■ Annual and weekly closing
Closed Golden week, mid-August and late December-early January

■ Price
Dinner = set   ¥ 23,100-31,500
Service charge = 10%

TEL. 03-5772-1610
Yuken Azabu Building 3F,
1-5-5 Azabujuban, Minato-ku,
Tokyo

HOTELS

HOTELS BY ORDER OF COMFORT

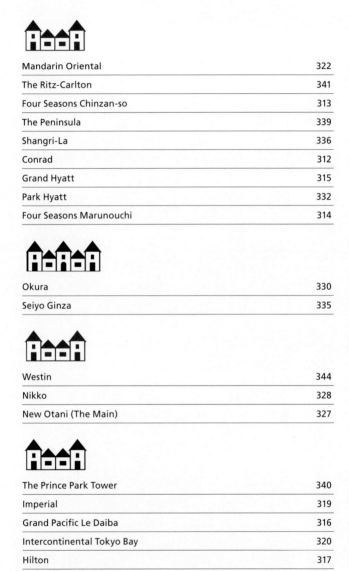

ANA Intercontinental

♿ ⟨ ☞ 🅿 ⟊ 🏊 🎿 🧖

Opened in 1986, at the same time as Akasaka Ark Hills. Rooms are on the 7-35th floors; the front lobby is on the 2nd. Standard rooms are between 28 - 32m^2 and have a comfortable, chic feel. Those staying on the Club Intercontinental Floor can use the newly created lounge – the biggest in Japan. The three sides of the triangular-shaped hotel provide views of the Imperial Palace Outer Garden, Tokyo Tower and Roppongi Hills.

■ Price
† = ¥ 38,850-51,450
†† = ¥ 43,050-51,450
Suite = ¥ 78,750-252,000
☲ = ¥ 2,100

Rooms = 800
Suites = 43
Restaurants = 7

TEL. 03–3505–1111
FAX. 03–3505–1155
1-12-33 Akasaka, Minato-ku, Tokyo
www.anaintercontinental-tokyo.jp

Century Southern Tower

   ♿ ≤ **P** ∷ ⛷ ⛸

This hotel occupies the 19-35th floors of the Odakyu Southern Tower; the lobby is on the 20th floor. Although next to a busy railway, rooms are soundproofed. Those on the eastern side boast views of Shinjuku Gyoen; rooms on the west look onto the Shinjuku skyscraper and Yoyogi Park. Despite cutting out services such as bell and room service, it caters for its guests through vending machines and a small convenience store.

■ Price
♦ = ¥ 18,480-57,750
♦♦ = ¥ 27,720-63,525
☲ = ¥ 2,194

Rooms = 375
Restaurants = 3

TEL. 03-5354-0111
FAX. 03-5354-0100
2-2-1 Yoyogi, Shibuya-ku, Tokyo
www.southerntower.co.jp

Cerulean Tower Tokyu

♿ ⪡ 🅿 ⚟ 🛉 🗺 ♿

All the rooms feature soothing décor with Japanese design elements and views across the capital. The 33-37th are executive floors; guests here have access to the executive salon. French cuisine can be enjoyed on the top floor; the jazz club has live music (except on Sundays and public holidays). Those interested in traditional Japanese performing arts can take in a *Noh* or *Kyogen* performance at the Cerulean Tower Noh Theatre.

■ Price
🕴 = ¥ 33,000-79,000
🕴🕴 = ¥ 43,500-81,500
Suite = ¥ 100,000-485,000
☕ = ¥ 3,003

Rooms = 402
Suites = 9
Restaurants = 8

TEL. 03–3476–3000
FAX. 03–3476–3001
26-1 Sakuragaokacho,
Shibuya-ku, Tokyo
www.ceruleantower-hotel.com

Claska

P

Rooms comes in three different types: 'Japanese Modern', with elegant furniture collected from all over Asia; 'Tatami', furnished with low beds and natural wood, and 'Weekly Residence', which feature a conceptual design and are geared to those on long stays. There are also distinctive 'DIY' rooms that were personally created by the designer. The hotel has a multi-purpose studio for exhibitions, photo shoots and events.

■ Price
♦ = ¥ 9,450-12,600
♦♦ = ¥ 19,950-89,250
☕ = ¥ 900
Service charge = 10%

Rooms = 18
Restaurants = 1

TEL. 03–3719–8121
FAX. 03–3719–8122
1-3-18 Chuocho, Meguro-ku,
Tokyo
www.claska.com

Conrad

    👨‍🦽 🔻 🖐️ 🅿️ 🚭 🏋️ 🏊 Spa 🚲

The front desk of this hotel is on the 28th floor of the Tokyo Shiodome Building, along with the main lobby, bar & lounge. Mizuki Spa and fitness centre with a 25m indoor pool has floor-to-ceiling windows and offers various relaxation facilities and treatments. Rooms are spacious and divide into two types: City Rooms, facing the Shiodome area, and Garden Rooms facing Hamarikyu Gardens. The hotel is convenient and fashionable.

■ Price
🕴 = ¥ 71,000-86,000
🕴🕴 = ¥ 76,000-91,000
Suite = ¥ 89,000-622,000
☕ = ¥ 2,800

Rooms = 222
Suites = 68
Restaurants = 4

TEL. 03–6388–8000
FAX. 03–6388–8001
1-9-1 Higashishinbashi, Minato-ku, Tokyo
www.conradtokyo.co.jp

MAP NO. 14/A-2

Four Seasons Chinzan-so

Chinzan-so was built by Aritomo Yamagata, a military leader and politician of the Meiji Era, in the scenic surroundings of Mejirodai; this smart and tranquil hotel opened in the garden in 1992. As well as streams flowing along gentle natural slopes and abundant greenery, the gardens are dotted with 3-storey pagodas and stone lanterns reminiscent of those at Hannyaji Temple. Guests can use the hot spring baths, pool or spa.

■ Price
👤 = ¥ 45,150-65,100
👥 = ¥ 45,150-65,100
Suite = ¥ 72,450-577,500
☕ = ¥ 2,970
Service charge = 10%

Rooms = 259
Suites = 24
Restaurants = 4

TEL. 03–3943–2222
FAX. 03–3943–2300
2-10-8 Sekiguchi, Bunkyo-ku, Tokyo
www.fourseasons-tokyo.com

Four Seasons Marunouchi

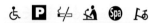

All its exterior walls are glass, providing cityscape views. The vibe is one of urban sophistication: rooms have a contemporary, elegant feel, in tones of beige and grey. Staff numbers are high in relation to the hotel's size and they provide attentive service. A greetings service is also available and can be arranged for guests arriving at Narita Airport or Tokyo Station. Facilities include a spa and fitness centre.

■ Price
♦ = ¥ 47,250-63,000
♦♦ = ¥ 47,250-63,000
Suite = ¥ 84,000-525,000
⚏ = ¥ 2,900
Service charge = 10%

Rooms = 48
Suites = 9
Restaurants = 1

TEL. 03–5222–7222
FAX. 03–5222–1255
Pacific Century Place Building,
1-11-1 Marunouchi, Chiyoda-ku,
Tokyo
www.fourseasons.com/jp/
marunouchi

Grand Hyatt

  👨‍🦽   ≤   ☞   🅿   ⚡   🧖   🏊   Spa   💆

This modern hotel marks a clear departure from competitors in terms of design, comfort and size. A contemporary ambience is created with materials unique to Japan, such as the Nagomi Spa & Fitness and its stone pool. A wide variety of cosmopolitan restaurants attract many guests beyond those staying in the hotel. It also offers extensive amenities, from sophisticated interior design to state-of-the-art telecommunications.

■ Price
♦ = ¥ 50,820-73,920
♦♦ = ¥ 56,595-79,695
Suite = ¥ 102,795-801,570
☕ = ¥ 2,860

Rooms = 361
Suites = 28
Restaurants = 7

TEL. 03–4333–1234
FAX. 03–4333–8123
6-10-3 Roppongi, Minato-ku, Tokyo
www.tokyo.grand.hyatt.jp

Grand Pacific Le Daiba

A 30-storey hotel connected directly to Daiba Station. Each room has a different panoramic view: the Rainbow Bridge, central Tokyo, Tokyo Bay or Haneda Airport. Standard rooms range from 30 to 50m^2 and are decorated in an 18C European style; those renovated in 2009 comes in chic brown tones and have large bathrooms with marble finishing. As the front desk is often crowded, a flexible check-out service is available.

■ Price
† = ¥ 33,000-61,000
†† = ¥ 39,000-67,000
Suite = ¥ 96,000-500,000
☲ = ¥ 1,850

Rooms = 860
Suites = 24
Restaurants = 10

TEL. 03–5500–6711
FAX. 03–5500–4507
2-6-1 Daiba, Minato-ku, Tokyo
www.grandpacific.jp

Hilton

                                                   ♿ ≼ 🅿 ⚟ 🚣 ⛰ ♨

This 38-storey hotel, with its distinctive S-shaped wave, is in Nishishinjuku. The 808 rooms take on a simple, modern style with Japanese touches. The 12 Gallery Suites each feature fine art by one of 12 young artists and are available for small meetings. The 32-38th floors are Executive Floors and offer a higher level of comfort for business and leisure guests. There is a fitness centre, and the gym is open around the clock.

■ Price
♀ = ¥ 23,900-49,900
♀♀ = ¥ 27,400-53,400
Suite = ¥ 31,900-191,400
☲ = ¥ 2,600

Rooms = 684
Suites = 124
Restaurants = 6

TEL. 03–3344–5111
FAX. 03–3342–6094
6-6-2 Nishishinjuku, Shinjuku-ku, Tokyo
www.hilton.co.jp/tokyo

Hyatt Regency

Bedrooms are divided into Regency Club rooms and standard rooms and are further classified according to their view; choose from a cityscape of high-rises or an outlook across Shinjuku Chuo Park. The Regency Club rooms, renovated in 2009, have a check in/out service in the executive lounge. There is also restaurant Cuisine[s] Michel Troisgros, recommended in this guide. A complimentary shuttle bus runs from Shinjuku Station.

■ Price
🛉 = ¥ 35,700-57,750
🛉🛉 = ¥ 38,850-60,900
Suite = ¥ 73,500-262,500
🛏 = ¥ 1,900
Service charge = 10%

Rooms = 726
Suites = 18
Restaurants = 6

TEL. 03–3348–1234
FAX. 03–3344–5575
2-7-2 Nishishinjuku, Shinjuku-ku, Tokyo
www.hyattregencytokyo.com

Imperial

This hotel has been hosting overseas dignitaries since 1890 and its history reflects the ebb and flow of Japan's modernisation. The Wright building, designed by American architect Frank Lloyd Wright and opened in 1923, was replaced by the Main Building in 1970. Dining and bar options include the Old Imperial Bar and Les Saisons. The suite on the 14th floor of the Main Building incorporates elements of Wright's design.

■ Price
♦ = ¥ 37,800-89,250
♦♦ = ¥ 43,050-94,500
Suite = ¥ 84,000-262,500
⌷ = ¥ 2,700
Service charge = 10%

Rooms = 875
Suites = 56
Restaurants = 13

TEL. 03–3504–1111
FAX. 03–3581–9146
1-1-1 Uchisaiwaicho, Chiyoda-ku, Tokyo
www.imperialhotel.co.jp

Intercontinental Tokyo Bay

♿ ⟨ ☞ **P** 🛏 🛀 🚴

All rooms offer commanding views: of the Rainbow Bridge and Ferris wheel in Odaiba or of the Sumida-gawa river threading among high-rise buildings. Guests staying on the Club Floors (20th to top) can check in and out at a dedicated desk. The restaurants are on the 3rd floor which connects to Takeshiba Station. Combining functionality with the feel of a resort, this hotel is popular with businesspeople and holidaymakers.

■ Price
♦ = ¥ 41,780-71,810
♦♦ = ¥ 41,980-72,010
Suite = ¥ 115,700-346,900
⌒ = ¥ 1,848

Rooms = 331
Suites = 8
Restaurants = 5

TEL. 03–5404–2222
FAX. 03–5404–2111
1-16-2 Kaigan, Minato-ku, Tokyo
www.interconti-tokyo.com

Keio Plaza

& ⮜ ☞ **P** ⤲ 🏌 ⚓ 🚴

Rooms are spread over two buildings: the 47-storey Main Tower, opened in 1971, and the South Tower, in 1980. Around half of the rooms have been upgraded as part of a renovation program. Contemporary décor and comprehensive facilities create strong comfort levels in the completed Plaza Premier rooms. For overseas guests keen to experience tradition, there are older Japanese rooms with a *hinoki* bathtub.

■ Price
♦ = ¥ 26,250-58,800
♦♦ = ¥ 34,650-58,800
Suite = ¥ 97,650-378,000
☕ = ¥ 2,310
Service charge = 10%

Rooms = 1409
Suites = 27
Restaurants = 13

TEL. 03–3344–0111
FAX. 03–3345–8269
2-2-1 Nishishinjuku, Shinjuku-ku, Tokyo
www.keioplaza.co.jp

Mandarin Oriental

Rooms use bamboo and other natural materials, while the fabrics carry a nature motif. The Japanese-inspired decoration adds to the air of elegance and tranquillity. The west side offers views of the gardens of the Imperial Palace; to the east you can see Odaiba in Tokyo Bay and the Sumida-gawa river. The Oriental Lounge is the place to try 'molecular cuisine.' We also recommend Cantonese food at Sense and French at Signature.

■ Price
= ¥ 73,500-85,050
= ¥ 73,500-85,050
Suite = ¥ 141,750-997,500
= ¥ 2,800
Service charge = 10%

Rooms = 157
Suites = 22
Restaurants = 5

TEL. 03–3270–8800
FAX. 03–3270–8828
2-1-1 Nihonbashimuromachi,
Chou-ku, Tokyo
www.mandarinoriental.co.jp/tokyo

Marunouchi

Located in front of Tokyo Station's Marunouchi North Exit, this hotel is convenient for both businesspeople and tourists. Rooms on the east side overlook the busy, red bricked station; those on the west face the Marunouchi business district – but both sides are quiet. Single rooms are not especially large, but their coved or arched ceilings add a feeling of space. This is a distinguished hotel with all modern conveniences.

■ Price
♦ = ¥ 23,300-52,175
♦♦ = ¥ 31,385-52,375
Suite = ¥ 115,900
☕ = ¥ 1,900

Rooms = 204
Suites = 1
Restaurants = 3

TEL. 03–3217–1111
FAX. 03–3217–1115
1-6-3 Marunouchi, Chiyoda-ku, Tokyo
www.marunouchi-hotel.co.jp

MAP NO. 29/B-2

Meguro Gajoen

Meguro Gajoen, well known as a wedding venue, opened in 1931. The house that lies within the property, known as Hyakudan Kaidan, is a registered cultural property and served as inspiration for the film 'Spirited Away'. Rooms provide a tranquil space, in contrast to the lavishly decorated public areas. The Western rooms include Ryukyu tatami in the corner; those on the west overlook the Meguro-gawa River and the cherry blossom.

■ Price
- (1 person) = ¥ 70,000-116,000
- (2 persons) = ¥ 70,000-116,000
- (breakfast) = ¥ 2,400

Rooms = 23
Restaurants = 4

TEL. 03-3491-4111
FAX. 03-5434-3931
1-8-1 Shimomeguro, Meguro-ku, Tokyo
www.megurogajoen.co.jp

Metropolitan Marunouchi

Connecting directly to Tokyo Station, Sapia Tower opened in 2007 and has a private elevator that takes you to the front lobby on the 27th floor. Guests can admire Tokyo Bay or look out in the Makuhari direction or the mountains of Chiba; at night there is modern metropolitan scenery like Tokyo Tower and Shinjuku to enjoy. The staff at the front desk can make arrangements for JR tickets including for the limited express.

■ Price
♦ = ¥ 18,680-25,610
♦♦ = ¥ 30,230-40,825
⌘ = ¥ 2,300

Rooms = 343
Restaurants = 1

TEL. 03–3211–2233
FAX. 03–3211–2244
1-7-12 Marunouchi, Chiyoda-ku, Tokyo
www.hm-marunouchi.jp

MAP NO. 22/B-3

Mitsui Garden Ginza

The lobby is situated on the 16th floor overlooking Tsukiji market. The hotel has a large number of compact rooms, in stylish brown and white basic tones. Guests choosing the View Bath Double or Twin rooms can luxuriate in the bathtub against the backdrop of Tokyo at night. For an even higher level of comfort, book a 25th or Executive Floor room. Mitsui Garden Ginza impresses with its functional yet contemporary design.

■ Price
🚹 = ¥ 18,900-44,100
🚹🚹 = ¥ 25,200-44,100
☕ = ¥ 2,100

Rooms = 361
Restaurants = 1

TEL. 03–3543–1131
FAX. 03–3543–5531
8-13-1 Ginza, Chou-ku, Tokyo
www.gardenhotels.co.jp

New Otani (The Main)

This hotel consists of the Main Building and the Garden Tower - this guide covers only the Main Building, which underwent a major renovation in 2007. Rooms feature a simple décor which includes elements of Japanese design. For greater comfort levels, try a well-equipped deluxe room with a contemporary design; a concierge service at the exclusive lounge is also available. There is an art museum, tennis courts and a golf range.

■ Price
♦ = ¥ 31,500-73,500
♦♦ = ¥ 39,900-73,500
Suite = ¥ 126,000-273,000
⌂ = ¥ 1,890
Service charge = 10%

Rooms = 614
Suites = 29
Restaurants = 29

TEL. 03-3265-1111
FAX. 03-3221-2619
4-1 Kioicho, Chiyoda-ku, Tokyo
www.newotani.co.jp/tokyo

Nikko

Nikko describes itself as 'the balcony of Tokyo' as every room has one. The lobby on the 2nd floor, with its atrium and high columns, offers views of Rainbow Bridge. Designed with the theme of 'Tokyo Resort', all the rooms - completely renovated in 2009 - are in contemporary, chic tones. For greater comfort levels, there are suites with their own gardens. This is an urban resort hotel with a relaxing, leisurely feel.

■ Price
♦ = ¥ 36,000-62,000
♦♦ = ¥ 42,000-68,000
Suite = ¥ 150,000-400,000
⌂ = ¥ 2,310

Rooms = 435
Suites = 17
Restaurants = 8

TEL. 03–5500–5500
FAX. 03–5500–2525
1-9-1 Daiba, Minato-ku, Tokyo
www.hnt.co.jp

Niwa

                 ♿ ⚫ 🧖 🚴

Opened in 2009, Niwa is next to the Nihon University College of Economics. It was founded as a Japanese-style inn but changed into a more modern lodging hotel over the course of three generations. The bedrooms are decorated with Japanese paper and sliding screens; the carpet is designed to resemble tatami. There is also a lounge and a workout room on the 3rd floor. A 24 hour business corner is available on the 1st floor.

■ Price
† = ¥ 18,900-36,750
†† = ¥ 23,100-40,950
⌂ = ¥ 2,310
Service charge = 10%
Rooms = 238

TEL. 03–3293–0028
FAX. 03–3295–3328
1-1-16 Misakicho, Chiyoda-ku, Tokyo
www.hotelniwa.jp

Okura

The Hotel Okura opened in 1962 and its regal atmosphere has changed little since. Visitors are drawn into the lobby by the all-wood décor and the glow of lantern-like lights suspended from the ceiling. Rooms vary in size, style and the view on offer, but all are comfortable and well equipped. The wine, dining & cigar bar Baron Okura has an impressive wine list. This is a hotel with a proud tradition and impeccable service.

■ Price
♦ = ¥ 36,750-63,000
♦♦ = ¥ 42,000-66,150
Suite = ¥ 94,500-577,500
⌷ = ¥ 1,890
Service charge = 10%

Rooms = 712
Suites = 89
Restaurants = 8

TEL. 03-3582-0111
FAX. 03-3582-3707
2-10-4 Toranomon, Minato-ku, Tokyo
www.hotelokura.co.jp/tokyo

Park

 ♿ ⪕ 🅿 ⇥ 🏂

This hotel, whose interior boasts a modern design, occupies the top floors of the Shiodome Media Tower. The large bedroom windows face Tokyo Tower, Tokyo Bay or Tokyo Station, but those on the Tokyo Tower side enjoy more far-reaching scenery. All rooms, except the suites, have bath and shower modules. The hotel is directly linked to the Shiodome subway station, making it convenient for sightseeing as well as for business use.

■ Price
♦ = ¥ 21,000-37,800
♦♦ = ¥ 26,250-37,800
Suite = ¥ 105,000
⌨ = ¥ 2,310
Service charge = 10%

Rooms = 272
Suites = 1
Restaurants = 2

TEL. 03–6252–1111
FAX. 03–6252–1001
Shiodome Media Tower 25F,
1-7-1 Higashishinbashi,
Minato-ku, Tokyo
www.parkhoteltokyo.com

Park Hyatt

This hotel occupies the 39th to 52nd floors of the high-rise Shinjuku Park Tower, offering panoramic views of the city from the bedrooms; on a clear day Mt. Fuji can be seen from the west. The Club on The Park spa and fitness centre also offers the same spectacular views. Drawings by contemporary artists are on display around the hotel, which was used as the setting for the Sofia Coppola film, Lost in Translation.

■ Price
† = ¥ 69,300-87,780
†† = ¥ 69,300-87,780
Suite = ¥ 167,475-924,000
⊊ = ¥ 2,640

Rooms = 155
Suites = 23
Restaurants = 4

TEL. 03–5322–1234
FAX. 03–5322–1288
3-7-1-2 Nishishinjuku, Shinjuku-ku, Tokyo
www.tokyo.park.hyatt.jp

Royal Park

👨‍🦽 ≤ 🅿 🚫 🧗 🖼 🦽

This hotel is close to Tokyo City Air Terminal and offers regular services to and from Narita and Haneda airports. Bedrooms are on the 6th to 18th floors and have bright walls and chic modern interiors. They have panoramic views and modern extras such as a computer. The private salon, swimming pool, fitness club and meeting rooms are free of charge for those on the Executive Floors. Stroll in the beautiful 5th-floor garden.

■ Price
† = ¥ 27,300-53,550
†† = ¥ 35,700-57,750
Suite = ¥ 89,250-262,500
⌑ = ¥ 1,365
Service charge = 10%

Rooms = 395
Suites = 11
Restaurants = 6

TEL. 03–3667–1111
FAX. 03–3667–1115
2-1-1 Nihonbashikakigaracho,
Chuo-ku, Tokyo
www.rph.co.jp

Royal Park Shiodome Tower

Rooms are varied, ranging from singles to Tower suites, and their décor is modern and simple. Rooms are equipped with personal computers and a Cyber-Concierge; the latter answers queries relating to hotel facilities and delivery services. All rooms have an air cleaning & humidifying system. Ask for a view of Hamarikyu Gardens, Tokyo Tower or the Imperial Palace. The hotel also has a coin laundry for those on longer stays.

■ Price
♦ = ¥ 23,100-69,300
♦♦ = ¥ 25,410-69,300
Suite = ¥ 103,950
⌂ = ¥ 1,501

Rooms = 456
Suites = 2
Restaurants = 3

TEL. 03-6253-1111
FAX. 03-6253-1115
1-6-3 Higashishinbashi,
Minato-ku, Tokyo
www.rps-tower.co.jp

Seiyo Ginza

This 12-storey hotel exudes an air of serenity and comfort. The hotel's aim is to offer high-level hotel services in the ambience of a private residence. In line with this, a tail-coated butler is assigned to each room. Seiyo Ginza was the first hotel in Tokyo to offer this service which, along with a concierge, is available 24 hours a day. Bedrooms are designed in an 18C European style and have spacious bathrooms.

■ Price
♦ = ¥ 63,525-78,540
♦♦ = ¥ 63,525-78,540
Suite = ¥ 92,400-219,450
☲ = ¥ 2,772

Rooms = 51
Suites = 26
Restaurants = 4

TEL. 03–3535–1111
FAX. 03–3535–1110
1-11-2 Ginza, Chuo-ku, Tokyo
www.seiyo-ginza.co.jp

MAP NO. 19/D-2

Shangri-La

Opened in 2009 inside the Marunouchi Trust Tower MAIN and occupying floors 27-37. The west side overlooks the Imperial Palace; the east side, Tokyo Bay. Rooms feature an elegant oriental design. The CHI spa, where the treatments are based on Chinese and Himalayan healing therapy, was the first of its kind in Japan. The lavish facilities and hospitality usher you off into a mystical and graceful land in the heart of the city.

■ Price
= ¥ 73,500-98,700
= ¥ 73,500-105,000
Suite = ¥ 262,500-1,050,000
= ¥ 2,900
Service charge = 10%

Rooms = 194
Suites = 6
Restaurants = 2

TEL. 03-6739-7888
FAX. 03-6739-7889
Marunouchi Trust Tower Main,
1-8-3 Marunouchi, Chiyoda-ku,
Tokyo
www.shangri-la.com/jp

Sheraton Miyako

First opened in 1979 and renamed in 2007. Bedrooms are divided into three types: the bright, standard rooms which are enjoying continued popularity; the premium floors, featuring a tranquil colour scheme, and 'Floor Seven' which fuses Japanese tradition with a modern Western theme. All guest rooms have Sweet Sleeper beds with comfortable mattresses, Egyptian cotton sheets and three types of pillows to choose from.

■ Price
♦ = ¥ 28,350-44,100
♦♦ = ¥ 31,500-74,550
Suite = ¥ 294,000
⌂ = ¥ 2,415
Service charge = 10%

Rooms = 493
Suites = 2
Restaurants = 3

TEL. 03–3447–3111
FAX. 03–3447–3133
1-1-50 Shirokanedai, Minato-ku, Tokyo
www.miyakohotels.ne.jp/tokyo

The Agnes

& **P** ✄ ♿

Based on a warm beige colour scheme, the hotel's accommodation is comfortable and relaxing and most rooms have a balcony. Pleasant staff take care of each guest's needs. The hotel is particularly appreciated by those seeking a peaceful environment. For longer-term guests, there are apartments equipped with a refrigerator, microwave, washing machine, dryer and so on. In the tearoom, enjoy sweets from patisserie Le Coin Vert.

■ Price
🚹 = ¥ 22,000-35,000
🚹🚹 = ¥ 27,000-40,000
Suite = ¥ 50,000-80,000
☕ = ¥ 2,100

Rooms = 51
Suites = 5
Restaurants = 1

TEL. 03-3267-5505
FAX. 03-3267-5513
2-20-1 Kagurazaka, Shinjuku-ku, Tokyo
www.agneshotel.com

The Peninsula

In an enviable position opposite the Imperial Palace Outer Garden and Hibiya Park. The front desk is behind the eye-catching bamboo. Rooms are a 'fusion of Peninsula standard and Japanese culture'. Doors made of horse chestnut, vermillion-lacquered counters and cypress ajiro woven ceilings create a warm feel. The telephone, TV and lights can be operated from the bathtub. Restaurants include the elegant Hei Fung Terrace.

■ Price
♦ = ¥ 69,300-92,400
♦♦ = ¥ 69,300-92,400
Suite = ¥ 115,500-1,732,500
⌂ = ¥ 2,800

Rooms = 267
Suites = 47
Restaurants = 4

TEL. 03–6270–2888
FAX. 03–6270–2000
1-8-1 Yurakucho, Chiyoda-ku, Tokyo
www.tokyo.jp.peninsula.com

The Prince Park Tower

Amid the greenery of Shiba Park is a hotel which stresses the importance of comfort through its relaxation facilities. Its 33 storeys are divided into sections: the Park Floors on the 3rd-18th, the Superior Floors on the 2nd and 19-27th, and Premium Floors on the 29-31st. Personal butler services are available for those staying in any of the comfortable Royal Suites, decorated in British, French, Italian and Japanese styles.

■ Price
♦ = ¥ 34,000-70,000
♦♦ = ¥ 34,000-70,000
Suite = ¥ 104,000-980,000
⌑ = ¥ 3,000

Rooms = 639
Suites = 34
Restaurants = 9

TEL. 03–5400–1111
FAX. 03–5400–1110
4-8-1 Shibakoen, Minato-ku, Tokyo
www.princehotels.co.jp/parktower

The Ritz-Carlton

    ♿ ⟨ ☞ 🅿 ⇎ 🏋 🏞 🆂🅿🅰 ♨

This hotel is in the 53-storey Midtown Tower that soars 248m above the Tokyo Midtown complex. All 248 rooms have a floor space of at least 52m², elegant interior décor and, along with Japanese-inspired Art Deco furniture, they boast large-screen TVs, with a second one in their sleek bathroom. On the 46th floor is a 20m pool, a well-equipped fitness centre and spa. Stunning views take in Mt. Fuji and Tokyo Tower.

■ Price
♦ = ¥ 73,500-89,250
♦♦ = ¥ 78,750-99,750
Suite = ¥ 126,000-2,100,000
☕ = ¥ 2,850
Service charge = 10%

Rooms = 212
Suites = 36
Restaurants = 6

TEL. 03–3423–8000
FAX. 03–3423–8001
Tokyo Midtown, 9-7-1 Akasaka,
Minato-ku, Tokyo
www.ritzcarlton.com/ja/tokyo

The Strings by Intercontinental

Connected by the Skyway pedestrian overpass, this hotel is a two-minute walk from Shinagawa Station's Konan Exit and occupies the 26th to the top floor. Rooms are stylishly decorated in shades of brown and beige and have large windows. Bathrooms feature wood and marble floors. Rooms come in a variety of sizes and facilities include a 24-hour business centre and a fitness centre with the same spectacular views as the bedrooms.

■ Price
♦ = ¥ 31,000-57,000
♦♦ = ¥ 38,000-64,000
Suite = ¥ 162,000-237,000
☕ = ¥ 2,656

Rooms = 199
Suites = 6
Restaurants = 2

TEL. 03–5783–1111
FAX. 03–5783–1112
Shinagawa East One Tower,
2-16-1 Konan, Minato-ku, Tokyo
www.intercontinental-strings.jp

Villa Fontaine Shiodome

Founded in 2004 as a business hotel, it occupies floors 2-10 of the 27-storey Shiodome Sumitomo Building. Calm and stylish colour schemes are used in the bedrooms, which feature spacious bathrooms and plenty of amenities. Computers are available in the first floor business Centre; guests staying in the Premier rooms can borrow computers from the front desk. There is no restaurant, but breakfast is included in the room price.

■ Price
♦ = ¥ 10,000-16,000
♦♦ = ¥ 14,000-18,000
Rooms = 497

TEL. 03–3569–2220
FAX. 03–3569–2111
1-9-2 Higashishinbashi, Minato-ku, Tokyo
www.hvf.jp/shiodome

Westin

♿ ≺ ☞ 🅿 ⚳ ⛷ 🆂🅿🅰 ⛹

This 22-storey building is part of Yebisu Garden Place. Its décor was inspired by early 19C French style and the use of marble fits well with Japanese design elements like prints and folding screens. Choose from two types: Deluxe or Executive Club - those in the latter check in at the exclusive lounge on the 17th floor. Chinese Ryutenmon and Japanese restaurants are on the 2nd; *teppanyaki* and French are on the top floor.

■ Price
♦ = ¥ 65,100-76,650
♦♦ = ¥ 65,100-76,650
Suite = ¥ 157,500-525,000
☕ = ¥ 2,182
Service charge = 10%

Rooms = 418
Suites = 20
Restaurants = 5

TEL. 03–5423–7000
FAX. 03–5423–7600
1-4-1 Mita, Meguro-ku, Tokyo
www.westin-tokyo.co.jp

YOKOHAMA

RESTAURANTS
& HOTELS

RESTAURANTS

STARRED RESTAURANTS

All the restaurants within the Tokyo Yokohama Kamakura Guide have one, two or three Michelin Stars and are our way of highlighting restaurants that offer particularly good food.

When awarding stars there are a number of factors we consider: the quality and freshness of the ingredients, the technical skill and flair that goes into their preparation, the clarity of the flavours, the value for money and, ultimately, the taste. Of equal importance is the ability to produce excellent food not once but time and time again. Our inspectors make as many visits as necessary so that you can be sure of this quality and consistency.

A two or three star restaurant has to offer something very special in its cooking that separates it from the rest. Three stars – our highest award – are given to the very best. Cuisines in any style of restaurant and of any nationality are eligible for a star. The decoration, service and comfort levels have no bearing on the award.

Excellent cuisine, worth a detour.
Skillfully and carefully crafted dishes of outstanding quality.

Chiso Kimura	✕	Japanese	361
Masagosaryo	✕✕	Japanese	363

A very good restaurant in its category.
A place offering cuisine prepared to a consistently high standard.

Aichiya	✕✕✕	Japanese	358
Azabu Nodaiwa	✕✕	Japanese Unagi	359
Chez Naka	✕✕	French	360
Furaikyo	✕	Japanese Soba	362
Mizuki	✕	Japanese	364
Ota Nawanoren	✕✕	Japanese Sukiyaki	365
Rinkaen	✕✕✕	Japanese	366
Shimamura	✕✕	Japanese Unagi	367
Sugai	✕	Japanese	368
Sushi Hachizaemon	✕	Japanese Sushi	369
Sushi Hamada	✕	Japanese Sushi	370
Tenhama	✕✕	Japanese Tempura	371
Tenshichi	✕✕	Japanese Tempura	372
Ukai-tei Azamino	✕✕✕	Japanese Teppanyaki	373

RESTAURANTS BY AREA

AOBA-KU

Chiso Kimura	✿✿	✗	Japanese	361
Furaikyo	✿	✗	Japanese Soba	362
Ukai-tei Azamino	✿	✗✗✗	Japanese Teppanyaki	373

KANAGAWA-KU

Sushi Hachizaemon	✿	✗	Japanese Sushi	369

KOHOKU-KU

Shimamura	✿	✗✗	Japanese Unagi	367

NAKA-KU

Masagosaryo	✿✿	✗✗	Japanese	363
Mizuki	✿	✗	Japanese	364
Ota Nawanoren	✿	✗✗	Japanese Sukiyaki	365
Rinkaen	✿	✗✗✗	Japanese	366
Sugai	✿	✗	Japanese	368
Sushi Hamada	✿	✗	Japanese Sushi	370
Tenhama	✿	✗✗	Japanese Tempura	371
Tenshichi	✿	✗✗	Japanese Tempura	372

NISHI-KU

Aichiya	✿	✗✗✗	Japanese	358
Azabu Nodaiwa	✿	✗✗	Japanese Unagi	359

SAKAE-KU

Chez Naka	✿	✗✗	French	360

RESTAURANTS BY CUISINE TYPE

JAPANESE

Aichiya	❀	𝕏𝕏𝕏	Nishi-ku	358
Chiso Kimura	❀❀	𝕏	Aoba-ku	361
Masagosaryo	❀❀	𝕏𝕏	Naka-ku	363
Mizuki	❀	𝕏	Naka-ku	364
Rinkaen	❀	𝕏𝕏𝕏	Naka-ku	366
Sugai	❀	𝕏	Naka-ku	368

JAPANESE SOBA

Furaikyo	❀	𝕏	Aoba-ku	362

JAPANESE SUKIYAKI

Ota Nawanoren	❀	𝕏𝕏	Naka-ku	365

JAPANESE SUSHI

Sushi Hachizaemon	❀	𝕏	Kanagawa-ku	369
Sushi Hamada	❀	𝕏	Naka-ku	370

JAPANESE TEMPURA

Tenhama	❀	𝕏𝕏	Naka-ku	371
Tenshichi	❀	𝕏𝕏	Naka-ku	372

JAPANESE TEPPANYAKI

Ukai-tei Azamino	❀	𝕏𝕏𝕏	Aoba-ku	373

JAPANESE UNAGI

Azabu Nodaiwa	❀	𝕏𝕏	Nishi-ku	359
Shimamura	❀	𝕏𝕏	Kohoku-ku	367

FRENCH

Chez Naka	❀	𝕏𝕏	Sakae-ku	360

RESTAURANTS SERVING LUNCH AND/ OR DINNER FOR ¥ 5,000 AND LESS

RESTAURANTS OPEN ON SUNDAY

RESTAURANTS WITH PRIVATE ROOMS

Aichiya	❀	𝕏x𝕏	capacity	25	358
Azabu Nodaiwa	❀	𝕏𝕏	capacity	20	359
Masagosaryo	❀❀	𝕏𝕏	capacity	16	363
Mizuki	❀	𝕏	capacity	8	364
Ota Nawanoren	❀	𝕏𝕏	capacity	40	365
Rinkaen	❀	𝕏x𝕏	capacity	20	366
Shimamura	❀	𝕏𝕏	capacity	8	367
Tenshichi	❀	𝕏𝕏	capacity	8	372
Ukai-tei Azamino	❀	𝕏xx𝕏	capacity	16	373

357

Aichiya
あいちや

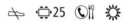

Head west from Yokohama Station and you will come upon this elegant establishment with a serene, timeless atmosphere – one of the few *ryotei* still found in Yokohama. The chef has been showcasing his skills here for over 20 years; his creed is 'everything starts with the ingredients', which are from a Tsukiji wholesaler. He includes one feature dish in the set menus, avoids quirkiness and serves orthodox Japanese cuisine.

■ Opening hours, last orders
Lunch = 11:30-14:00 (L.O.)
Dinner = 17:00-20:00 (L.O.)

■ Annual and weekly closing
Closed late December-early January

■ Price
Lunch = menu   ¥ 5,250-16,800
Dinner = menu   ¥ 10,500-18,900
Service charge = 20% (lunch 10%)

TEL. 045-311-2528
2-17-6 Minamisaiwai, Nishi-ku, Yokohama
www.aichiya.jp/honten

Azabu Nodaiwa
麻布 野田岩

Akio Kanemoto's restaurant shares the same name as his brother's in Tokyo; he prepares the *unagi* earnestly each day so as not to tarnish his brother's name. Rare natural *unagi* is served from April to November and his sauce is slightly lighter than his brother's. The popular set menu is the sweet *unagi* made with *ume*, a rare find in *unagi* restaurants; the rich sourness and natural sweetness is the result of much trial and error.

■ Opening hours, last orders
Lunch = 11:30-14:00 (L.O.)
Dinner = 17:00-20:30 (L.O.)

■ Annual and weekly closing
Closed mid-August, late
December-early January and
Sunday

■ Prices
Lunch = set   ¥ 8,190-11,550
    à la carte   ¥ 2,310-10,000
Dinner = set   ¥ 8,190-11,550
    à la carte   ¥ 2,310-10,000
Service charge = 10%

TEL. 045–320–3224
2-13-9 Kitasaiwai, Nishi-ku,
Yokohama

Chez Naka

The spotless interior of this small restaurant on Kanjo Route 3, with its antique furnishings, radiates warmth. Food is traditionally prepared and every effort made to ensure that flavours are just right – pineapple purée is added to the sauce to give the duck a refreshing taste; portions are kept to a reasonable size. The chef provides courteous service; credit cards can only be used for meals totalling 10,000 yen or more.

■ Opening hours, last orders
Lunch = 11:30-14:00 (L.O.)
Dinner = 18:00-21:00 (L.O.)

■ Annual and weekly closing
Closed late August-early September, late December-early January, Wednesday except Public Holidays and Thursday following a Public Holiday

■ Prices
Lunch = set ¥ 2,500-10,000
à la carte ¥ 8,500-9,500
Dinner = set Mon.-Fri. ¥ 4,200-10,000
set Sat.,Sun ¥ 5,800-10,000
à la carte ¥ 8,500-9,500
Service charge = 10% (dinner)

TEL. 045–891–6701
1-21-16 Koyamadai, Sakae-ku, Yokohama
http://cheznaka.easy-magic.com

Chiso Kimura
馳走 きむら

The monthly set menus are the draw here. The owner-chef goes to the market each day to pick out ingredients and exercises creativity with their textures and tastes. He handles everything himself, so be prepared to wait, although his politeness will leave an impression. With garnishing that includes flowers, the colours are also appealing. Care has also been taken with the serving dishes and interior to highlight the seasons.

■ Opening hours, last orders
Lunch = 11:30-15:00 L.O.14:00
except Saturday
Dinner = 18:00-22:00 L.O.20:00

■ Annual and weekly closing
Closed Golden week, mid-August,
late December-early January and
Monday

■ Prices
Lunch = set ¥ 2,800-9,000
Dinner = set ¥ 6,000-9,000

TEL. 045–901–2606
5-14-1 Utsukushigaoka, Aoba-ku,
Yokohama

Furaikyo
風來蕎

After originally aspiring to be a film director, the owner-chef decided to change course and direct a *soba* restaurant instead. The *seiro soba* is ground with a millstone and cut into thin noodles that are supple and sweet. Smooth, deep-tasting hand-ground *soba* is only served on Saturdays and holidays; the sharp sauce goes well with *sobayu* and has the delicate aroma of bonito. We recommend the *sobagaki-zenzai* if you like sweets.

■ Opening hours, last orders
Lunch = 11:30-15:00 (L.O.)
Dinner = 18:00-20:30 (L.O.)

■ Annual and weekly closing
Closed early January, mid-August, Wednesday and 3rd Tuesday of each month

■ Prices
Lunch = set		¥ 3,500
	à la carte	¥ 2,000-5,000
Dinner = set		¥ 3,500-5,000
	à la carte	¥ 2,000-5,000

TEL. 045–904–8345
4-19-19 Utsukushigaoka, Aoba-ku, Yokohama
www.soba-furaikyo.com

Masagosaryo
真砂茶寮

Built in the style of a tea-ceremony house but surrounded by modern buildings. The owner-chef serves two types of cuisine: *Kaiseki ryori* is artfully arranged, evokes the seasons and draws out natural flavours without excess seasoning; *Enseki* ryori is for family milestone celebrations. The sea bream *shiogamayaki* served on a large plate with *sekihan* is particularly popular. Lunch bookings must be made at least a day in advance.

■ Opening hours, last orders
Lunch = 11:30-14:30
Dinner = 17:30-23:00

■ Annual and weekly closing
Closed mid-August and late
December-early January

■ Prices
Lunch = set   ¥ 5,800-15,000
Dinner = set   ¥ 7,800-15,000
Service charge = 10%

TEL. 045-663-6692
2-16 Masagocho, Naka-ku,
Yokohama
www.masago.jp

Mizuki
瑞木

Light spills out from the latticework that decorates the front of this restaurant. The main attraction on the menu is seafood caught off the Miura Peninsula; the owner-chef goes to the port himself to check the quality. There are also many familiar dishes like *dashimaki tamago* and *ohitashi* and at the end comes *takikomi-gohan*. The owner-chef does everything himself, so patience is required. Holiday closings are irregular.

■ Opening hours, last orders
Dinner = 17:30-23:00 L.O.22:30

■ Annual and weekly closing
Closed mid-August, late
December-early January and
Sunday

■ Prices
Dinner = set ¥ 6,300-10,500
à la carte 5,500-8,000
Service charge = 5% (private room
10%)

TEL. 045-663-8483
5-63 Sumiyoshicho, Naka-ku,
Yokohama
www.geocities.jp/kannai_wasyoku_
mizuki

Ota Nawanoren
太田なわのれん

Using a shallow iron pan, the founder came up with beef dishes that were steamed instead of grilled and opened the first *gyunabe* restaurant in 1868. Today, customers are treated to *kaiseki* style cuisine centred around *gyunabe*. The *butsugiri gyunabe* speciality features cubed pieces of beef boiled in Edo *amamiso*. The *tokusen* beef requires reservations at least the day before. With only 4 tables in a *tatami* room, book early.

■ Opening hours, last orders
Lunch = Sat., Sun. and Public Holidays
12:00-15:00 L.O.14:00
Dinner = 17:00-22:00 L.O.21:00
Sat., Sun. and Public Holidays
17:00-21:00 L.O.20:00

■ Annual and weekly closing
Closed mid-August, late
December-early January, Monday
and 3rd Sunday of each month

■ Prices
Lunch = set   ¥ 7,870-15,750
         à la carte ¥ 10,000-14,000
Dinner = set   ¥ 9,450-15,750
          à la carte ¥ 10,000-14,000
Service charge = 10%

TEL. 045-261-0636
1-15 Sueyoshicho, Naka-ku,
Yokohama
www.ohtanawanoren.jp

Rinkaen
隣花苑

This Ashikaga era country house was relocated by Sankeien founder Sankei Hara; enjoy home-style, straightforward cooking, in a nostalgic setting. First comes several small dishes including seasonal vegetables with sesame dressing and *nuta*. Sankei *soba*, included in every set menu, is famous as the dish served by Sankei at tea gatherings. Ask for the room facing the garden but check in advance about a possible room charge.

■ Opening hours, last orders
12:00-21:00 L.O.18:00

■ Annual and weekly closing
Closed late December-early
January, August and Wednesday

■ Prices
Lunch = set   ¥ 3,675-18,900
Dinner = set   ¥ 10,500-18,900
Private room fee = ¥ 5,250-10,500/h
Service charge = 10%

TEL. 045-621-0318
52-1 Honmokusannotani, Naka-ku,
Yokohama
www.rinkaen.jp

Shimamura
しま村

An inner garden and bamboo trees fuse Japanese sensibilities into the modern, concrete building. The restaurant is run by an *unagi* wholesale company, so both natural and reared *unagi* are selected. The speciality is *ukama*: first it is served as-is, then seasoned, then in *chazuke* and finally with grated yams. Natural *unagi* is available from May to early December. The 2nd floor has a private room with *horigotatsu*-style seating.

■ Opening hours, last orders
Lunch = 11:00-15:00 L.O.14:00
Dinner = 17:00-21:30 L.O.20:00
Sat. and Sun. 11:00-21:30 L.O.20:00

■ Annual and weekly closing
Closed 31 December, 1 January,
Wednesday except Public Holidays
and Thursday following a Public
Holiday

■ Prices
Lunch = set   ¥ 3,780-15,750
          à la carte   ¥ 5,500-10,000
Dinner = set   ¥ 5,565-15,750
          à la carte   ¥ 5,500-10,000
Service charge = 10% (tatami room)

TEL. 045-549-0880
3-4-11 Takatahigashi, Kohoku-ku,
Yokohama
www.simatan.co.jp/shop

Sugai
菅井

Enjoy traditional Japanese cuisine such as the generous appetiser and the tuna *tsukuri* with young green onions, plus a range of dishes with that little bit extra. Just one monthly changing set menu is offered. *Nabe ryori* is served all year, with *shabu-shabu*, loaded with *kinome*. The aroma on the counter grill whets the appetite and at the end comes *takikomi-gohan*. This is a *kaiseki*-style restaurant, but comfortably relaxed.

■ Opening hours, last orders
Lunch = 12:00-15:00 L.O.12:00
Dinner = 18:00-22:30 L.O.20:30

■ Annual and weekly closing
Closed late December-early
January and Wednesday

■ Prices
Lunch = set   ¥ 5,250
Dinner = set   ¥ 10,500
Service charge = 10% (dinner)

TEL. 045–664–2885
5-69 Otamachi, Naka-ku,
Yokohama

Sushi Hachizaemon
すし 八左ェ門

An out-of-the-way restaurant run by the owner-chef alone on the 3rd floor of an ivy-clad commercial building, unadorned by signs. He has the spirit of a true artisan and is very friendly. Because the items are specially selected to go with the rice flavoured with matured red vinegar, there is not a wide selection, but this is one of the things he is particular about. Just leave it all up to him and enjoy the items of the day.

■ Opening hours, last orders
Dinner = 18:00-23:00

■ Annual and weekly closing
Closed Golden week, mid-August, late December-early January and Monday

■ Prices
Dinner = set   ¥ 15,000
Service charge = 10%

TEL. 045-433-3154
Nisshin Building Shinkoyasu 3F, 1-8-3 Shinkoyasu, Kanagawa-ku, Yokohama

MAP NO. 41/C,D-2

Sushi Hamada
鮨 はま田

The owner-chef's restaurant is in Kannai, but he is more committed to *Edomae* sushi than anyone else around. While valuing traditional techniques, he does try new ideas. Focusing on hand-rolled sushi means the selection of seafood is not especially large; he goes to Tsukiji himself to gather the ingredients. The rice is cooked in batches so that it can be served freshly made and is marked by the taste of sake lees vinegar.

■ Opening hours, last orders
Dinner = 17:00-22:00 L.O.20:30

■ Annual and weekly closing
Closed Golden week, mid-August,
late December-early January,
Sunday and Public Holidays

■ Prices
 Dinner = set   ¥ 15,750-21,000

TEL. 045–211–2187
2-21-2 Otamachi, Naka-ku,
Yokohama

Tenhama
天濱

The owner-chef has been honing his skills for over 30 years. He and his wife run the place alone, so proceed into the *tatami* room and announce the reservation name. First comes the fried head and legs, then the body of a lobster straight from the tank, followed by white-fleshed fish, vegetables, *anago* with green tea salt and grated radish, and honey-braised Japanese apricots. The *tencha* is garnished with lime and wasabi.

■ Opening hours, last orders
Dinner = 17:30-21:30 L.O.20:30

■ Prices
Dinner = set   ¥ 10,500-12,600

■ Annual and weekly closing
Closed mid-August, late
December-early January, Sunday
and Public Holidays

TEL. 045-662-6660
4-48 Otamachi, Naka-ku,
Yokohama

Tenshichi
天七

The Port of Yokohama is admittedly close, but it is still unusual to see a chef wearing a beret modelled on a sailor's cap. The oil is a mix of refined sugar and roasted sesame oil. The whiting backbone is eaten with curry salt, and the *anago*, sprinkled with green tea salt, is garnished with radish and lemon; low-salt *umeboshi* and fruit tempura provide variety. We recommend the *tendon* with mild sauce made with crystal sugar.

■ Opening hours, last orders
Lunch = 11:30-15:00 L.O.14:00
Dinner = 17:00-23:00 L.O.22:00

■ Annual and weekly closing
Closed mid-August, late
December-early January and
Sunday

■ Prices
Lunch = set   ¥ 3,800-5,800
Dinner = set   ¥ 8,000-15,000
Service charge = 10%

TEL. 045-681-3376
1-4 Sumiyoshicho, Naka-ku,
Yokohama

Ukai-tei Azamino

Found in an elegant hillside building, this restaurant is enveloped in a resort-like atmosphere and has the feel of an undersea world. French techniques have been incorporated to create an original style. Specialities are rock salt steamed abalone and Ukai beef. At the end comes *somen*, garlic rice with a burnt soy sauce aroma and other eclectic dishes. The private room, for parties of 4 or more, is ideal for special occasions.

■ Opening hours, last orders
Lunch = 12:00-15:00 (L.O.)
Dinner = 15:00-23:00 L.O.21:00

■ Annual and weekly closing
Closed 29 December-2 January

■ Prices
Lunch = set　　　　¥ 5,250-9,450
　　　à la carte ¥ 12,000-15,000
Dinner = set　　　¥ 9,450-18,900
　　　à la carte ¥ 12,000-15,000
Service charge = 10%

TEL. 045-910-5252
2-14-3 Azaminominami, Aoba-ku,
Yokohama
www.ukai.co.jp/azamino

HOTELS

HOTELS BY ORDER OF COMFORT

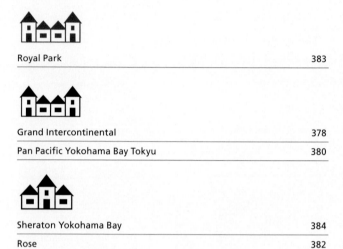

Grand Intercontinental

The building resembles a wind-filled yacht sail and the inside, including the spacious lobby, has a relaxing air. Bedrooms feature light-toned interiors and wicker furniture for a resort-like feel. The Harbour Suite, found at the nose of the V-shaped building, has a bathroom overlooking the harbour. The black, grey and white coloured simple, modern rooms are also suited for business use. Have breakfast facing the ocean.

■ Prices
† = ¥ 50,000-120,000
†† = ¥ 52,000-120,000
Suite = ¥ 120,000-610,000
☑ = ¥ 3,234

Rooms = 555
Suites = 39
Restaurants = 6

TEL. 045–223–2222
FAX. 045-221-0650
1-1-1 Minatomirai, Nishi-ku,
Yokohama
www.interconti.co.jp/yokohama

New Grand

Located in front of Yamashita Park, this hotel has been welcoming celebrities from all over the world since 1927. It consists of a main building and a 17-storey tower added in 1991. For an exotic feel, we recommend the Deluxe Twin or larger rooms in the main building. The atmosphere is reminiscent of bygone days, especially in the elegant bar. The impeccable service is just what one would expect from such an established hotel.

■ Prices
♦ = ¥ 13,860-43,890
♦♦ = ¥ 38,115-49,665
Suite = ¥ 92,400-346,500
☕ = ¥ 2,888

Rooms = 237
Suites = 12
Restaurants = 4

TEL. 045–681–1841
FAX. 045-681-1895
10 Yamashitacho, Naka-ku,
Yokohama
www.hotel-newgrand.co.jp

Pan Pacific Yokohama Bay Tokyu

Your eyes will be drawn to the painting stretching from the pillars to the ceiling. The rooms feature simple interiors and bathrooms have shower booths; reserve a room with a balcony, where the salty breeze makes you forget the everyday. The Pacific Floors (23-25) offer extra services such as an exclusive butler and breakfast in the lounge. Other facilities include a salon and Japanese, Western and Chinese restaurants.

■ Prices
♦ = ¥ 42,000-105,000
♦♦ = ¥ 42,000-105,000
Suite = ¥ 125,000-710,000
⊑ = ¥ 3,003

Rooms = 454
Suites = 26
Restaurants = 4

TEL. 045–682–2222
FAX. 045-682-2223
2-3-7 Minatomirai, Nishi-ku,
Yokohama
http://pphy.co.jp

Richmond

Offering comfort and convenience, this 201-room hotel was opened in 2003 on Bashamichi—which connects Minatomirai-odori with Kannai Station—within walking distance from China Town and Minato Mirai. Situated near JR and subway stations, it is also convenient for business use. The rooms are spacious: single rooms are 18m²; twins 28m². All rooms come with new air purifiers, large flat-screen TVs and negative ion hair dryers.

■ Prices
♦ = ¥ 8,400-26,000
♦♦ = ¥ 12,600-36,000
⇔ = ¥ 1,000

Rooms = 201
Restaurants = 2

TEL. 045–228–6655
FAX. 045-228-6355
5-59 Sumiyoshicho, Naka-ku,
Yokohama
www.richmondhotel.jp/yokohama

Rose

Located near Choyo-mon and the largest hotel in China Town. Guest rooms are spacious, with even the smallest being 26.5m²; beds come in semi-double to king sizes. The Deluxe floor features a tranquil atmosphere, having been created by renowned Hong Kong designer, John Chan. It is close to the popular tourist spots and within walking distance of Yamashita Park, Minatomirai and Yokohama Park, home of Yokohama Stadium.

■ Prices
♦ = ¥ 27,000-41,000
♦♦ = ¥ 32,000-41,000
Suite = ¥ 80,000-90,000
⌂ = ¥ 2,651

Rooms = 174
Suites = 4
Restaurants = 2

TEL. 045–681–3311
FAX. 045-681-5082
77 Yamashitacho, Naka-ku, Yokohama
www.rosehotelyokohama.com

Royal Park

Equipped for a variety of needs, this hotel is located in Landmark Tower, the symbol of Minatomirai. The front desk is on the 1st floor; bedrooms are on the 52nd floor and above. The rooms are comfortable and decorated in calm colours, with the exception of the 60th floor, with its modern décor and vivid colours. The large windows provide superb vistas. Breakfast is served on the top floor, 277 metres above ground.

■ Prices
♦ = ¥ 34,650-60,900
♦♦ = ¥ 39,900-66,150
Suite = ¥ 105,000-525,000
⌴ = ¥ 2,940
Service = 10%

Rooms = 583
Suites = 20
Restaurants = 6

TEL. 045–221–1111
FAX. 045-224-5153
2-2-1-3 Minatomirai, Nishi-ku,
Yokohama
www.yrph.com

Sheraton Yokohama Bay

  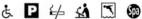

Found just 3 minutes from the West Exit of Yokohama Station, this hotel is also close to department stores, and its lobby is always lively. The wooden furniture of the elegant guest rooms provides a natural feel, while the black veneer adds a modern touch. The express video check-out is a convenient facility. The 'Towers' floors (26th and 27th) offer even higher levels of service. The fitness room has an indoor pool and sauna.

■ Prices
♦ = ¥ 26,000-58,000
♦♦ = ¥ 36,000-63,000
Suite = ¥ 150,000-250,000
⌑ = ¥ 2,800

Rooms = 396
Suites = 2
Restaurants = 5

TEL. 045–411–1111
FAX. 045-411-1343
1-3-23 Kitasaiwai, Nishi-ku,
Yokohama
www.yokohamabay-sheraton.
co.jp

KAMAKURA

RESTAURANTS
& HOTELS

RESTAURANTS

STARRED RESTAURANTS

All the restaurants within the Tokyo Yokohama Kamakura Guide have one, two or three Michelin Stars and are our way of highlighting restaurants that offer particularly good food.

When awarding stars there are a number of factors we consider: the quality and freshness of the ingredients, the technical skill and flair that goes into their preparation, the clarity of the flavours, the value for money and, ultimately, the taste. Of equal importance is the ability to produce excellent food not once but time and time again. Our inspectors make as many visits as necessary so that you can be sure of this quality and consistency.

A two or three star restaurant has to offer something very special in its cooking that separates it from the rest. Three stars – our highest award – are given to the very best. Cuisines in any style of restaurant and of any nationality are eligible for a star. The decoration, service and comfort levels have no bearing on the award.

A very good restaurant in its category.
A place offering cuisine prepared to a consistently high standard.

Bonzo	✗	Japanese Soba	394
En	✗	Japanese	395
Hachinoki Kitakamakura	✗✗	Japanese Shojin	396
Izumi	✗	Japanese Sushi	397
Kamakurayama	✗✗✗	Japanese Beef Specialities	398
Michel Nakajima	✗	French	399
Ren	✗	Japanese	400
Tamoto	✗	Japanese	401
Tsuruya	✗	Japanese Unagi	402
Yonekura	✗	Japanese	403

RESTAURANTS SERVING LUNCH AND/OR DINNER FOR ¥ 5,000 AND LESS

RESTAURANTS OPEN
ON SUNDAY

Bonzo
梵蔵

The thin *nihachi* and *juwari* noodles prepared by this young owner-chef are smooth and firm. First, try the *juwari* as-is to enjoy the fragrance, then add salt to savour the sweetness and finally, dip it in the seasoned sauce; last comes rich *sobayu*. Drinking snacks are also good, like *ayu-miso*, *goma-dofu* and *tamago-yaki*. If there are a few in your party, we also recommend the *kamoyaki*. Reservations are only accepted for dinner.

■ Opening hours, last orders
Lunch = 11:30-14:30 (L.O.)
Dinner = Fri.-Mon. 18:00-21:00
L.O.20:30

■ Annual and weekly closing
Closed early January, mid-August
and Thursday

■ Prices
Lunch = à la carte   ¥ 1,200-2,500
Dinner = set   ¥ 3,000-5,000
         à la carte   ¥ 2,000-3,500

TEL. 0467-73-7315
3-17-33 Zaimokuza, Kamakura
http://bonzo-kamakura.com

En
円

From a window seat on the second floor, one can enjoy the view of the Byakurochi pond in front of Engaku-ji Temple. The simple arrangements accentuate the inherent appeal of the ingredients, and unusual combinations bring out flavours; try the *hiryuzu* and eggplant *takiawase* with bamboo shoots. Also good is grilled trout with *kinome* vinegar. The focus is on set menus, but à la carte dishes are also available at dinner.

■ Opening hours, last orders
Lunch = 11:30-14:00 (L.O.)
Dinner = 17:00-19:30 (L.O.)

■ Annual and weekly closing
Closed mid-August, late December-early January and Monday

■ Prices
Lunch = set   ¥ 3,675-8,400
Dinner = set   ¥ 5,250-10,500
            à la carte   ¥ 3,000-6,000

TEL.0467-23-6232
Kosen 2F, 501 Yamanouchi, Kamakura
www.kitakamakura-en.com

Hachinoki Kitakamakura
鉢の木 北鎌倉

Opened in 1979 as somewhere to enjoy Buddhist cuisine in a *kaiseki* format, it uses only vegetables, including soybeans and seaweed. The turnip in winter, *kintoki* carrot and deep-fried tofu *takiawase* are brilliantly coloured; their flavours enhanced by stock. The speciality is the *Enmei Fukusa*: 7 kinds of fruits and vegetables fried in *yuba*. During hydrangea season, pure white tofu is garnished with vegetable-coloured gelatine.

■ Opening hours, last orders
Lunch = 11:30-14:30 (L.O.)
Sat. and Sun. 11:00-15:00 (L.O.)
Dinner = 17:00-19:00 (L.O.)

■ Annual and weekly closing
Closed early September, late
December-early January and
Wednesday

■ Prices
Lunch = set   ¥ 2,625-7,350
Dinner = set   ¥ 5,250-10,500
Private room fee = 10%
Service charge = 10%

TEL.0467–23–3722
350 Yamanouchi, Kamakura
www.hachinoki.co.jp

Izumi
以ず美

The *uni* is eaten with salt to bring out its refined sweetness. The sushi rice has a mild taste and several types of vinegar are used with the various items; bamboo shoot rice balls are aromatic; squid is cut in a wave-like shape. Enjoy chatting with the owner over his *Edomae* sushi made in the traditional way, but with a twist. For weekend lunches, it is best to arrive by noon. Every detail speaks of the owner-chef's taste.

■ Opening hours, last orders
Lunch = Sat. and Sun. 12:00-14:00
Dinner = 18:00-22:00 L.O.20:00

■ Annual and weekly closing
Closed late January-early
February and Wednesday

■ Prices
Lunch = set   ¥ 15,000-20,000
Dinner = set   ¥ 15,000-20,000

TEL.0467-22-3737
2-17-18 Hase, Kamakura

Kamakurayama
鎌倉山

🏮 🚫 **P** 🖥100 ☎🍴 ☀

Founded in 1970, this restaurant has an elegant atmosphere that fuses Japanese and Western sensibilities; its tables are decorated with orchids. Well-aged meat, selected for its marbling and taste, is cooked tender. It is then sliced in front of the customer, revealing its beautiful red colour. There are two types of sauce: consommé based and soy sauce with garlic. Dessert is served in the courtyard when the weather allows.

■ Opening hours, last orders
Lunch = 11:30-15:00 L.O.13:30
Dinner = 17:00-22:00 L.O.20:00

■ Annual and weekly closing
Closed late December-early January

■ Prices
Lunch = set	¥ 6,300-12,600
à la carte	¥ 20,000-25,000
Dinner = set	¥ 10,500-36,750
à la carte	¥ 20,000-25,000
Private room fee =	¥ 10,500-31,500
Service charge = 12%	

TEL.0467–31–5454
3-11-1 Kamakurayama, Kamakura
www.roastbeef.jp/ho.html

Michel Nakajima

  LUNCH **P**

The name comes from the owner-chef's nickname from his time in Europe. Local ingredients are used to accent the vivid and sometimes playful arrangements. The scallop, shrimp and cucumber dish, set in a mosaic pattern, provides a variety of textures. Also worth mentioning is the unobtrusive way his wife interacts with the customers. This is a welcoming and affordable restaurant, a bracing 30-minute walk from Kamakura Station.

■ Opening hours, last orders
Lunch = 12:00-14:00 (L.O.)
Sat. and Sun. 12:00-13:30 (L.O.)
Dinner = 18:00-20:00 (L.O.)

■ Annual and weekly closing
Closed late August-early
September, late December-early
January and Monday

■ Prices
Lunch = set   ¥ 2,650-5,250
Dinner = set   ¥ 5,250
Service charge = 10% (lunch=5%)

TEL.0467-32-5478
643 Tokiwa, Kamakura
www18.ocn.ne.jp/~m.naka

Ren
連

The owner-chef has put together a menu of seafood and local vegetables and works on adapting to the times – he does not step out of the bounds of tradition, but does incorporate modern touches, such as a plate of banana peppers. The handmade soba and desserts are prepared by his wife; sake is served in cups made by her father. The menu is reasonably priced and it is easier getting reservations for dinner than it is for lunch.

■ Opening hours, last orders
Lunch = 11:30-15:30 L.O.14:00
Dinner = 17:30-22:00 L.O.20:00

■ Annual and weekly closing
Closed Golden week, mid-August, late December-early January, Monday and 3rd Tuesday of each month

■ Prices
Lunch = set   ¥ 2,100-3,990
Dinner = set   ¥ 3,990-7,350

TEL.0467-32-6730
155-1 Tokiwa, Kamakura

Tamoto
田茂戸

Adhering to the basics of Japanese cuisine, the food occasionally pushes boundaries but is never eccentric. There is much creativity, like pigs' feet and ginger, tapioca *manju* with crab meat, and duck wrapped in bamboo; the fried greenling and spring cabbage with micro tomatoes is a perfect fit for the elegant plate. The blend of modern exterior, warm bark interior, food, service and price might well turn you into a regular.

■ Opening hours, last orders
Lunch = 11:30-14:30 L.O.13:30
Dinner = 17:00-22:00 L.O.21:00

■ Annual and weekly closing
Closed mid-August, late
December-early January and
Monday

■ Prices
Lunch = set   ¥ 3,800-6,800
Dinner = set   ¥ 6,800
    à la carte   ¥ 6,000-8,000

TEL.0467-24-0283
8-25 Sakanoshita, Kamakura

Tsuruya
つるや

Opened in 1929 and has welcomed famous literary men of Kamakura like Yasunari Kawabata and Masaaki Tachihara. Preparation begins once an order is taken, so the wait is about 40 minutes. Open the Kamakura-style tiered box to reveal the fatty *unagi*, cooked over a charcoal flame. The moderately sweet sauce, fluffy *unagi* and tasty rice come together in complete harmony. Delivery is available, but it is best right off the grill.

■ Opening hours, last orders
11:30-19:00 (L.O.)

■ Annual and weekly closing
Closed 1 January, 4 days in
February, September, November
and Tuesday except Public
Holidays

■ Prices
à la carte   ¥ 2,500-4,500

TEL.0467-22-0727
3-3-27 Yuigahama, Kamakura

Yonekura
米倉

Near the main gate of Zuisenji Temple; look for the maple tree and bamboo fence to find it. Carefully prepared *hassun* is garnished with a seasonal flower; on certain days in spring comes unforgettable soup with fluffy *shinjo* in *katsuo*-flavoured stock. The set menus are marked by variety, like stone-cooked meat, fermented seafood or handmade *soba*. Creative sweets are another treat. There are just 2 tables for 4, so book early.

■ Opening hours, last orders
Lunch = 11:30-14:30
Dinner = 17:00-21:00

■ Prices
Lunch = set   ¥ 5,250-10,500
Dinner = set   ¥ 6,300-15,750

TEL.0467-25-2395
728-20 Nikaido, Kamakura

HOTELS

Park

Standing beside Route 134, all rooms at this 3-storey resort hotel—most of them twins—offer an ocean view, along with elegantly designed furniture and plenty of amenities. The Japanese-style rooms are best for families; there are also Japanese and Western style banquet halls, and chairs can be provided for the *tatami* rooms. Internet access is available in the lobby. Enjoy the warm hospitality only a small hotel can provide.

■ Prices
♦ = ¥ 25,410-51,975
♦♦ = ¥ 25,410-51,975
Suite = ¥ 57,750-69,300
⌂ = ¥ 2,310

Rooms = 44
Suites = 2
Restaurants = 2

TEL. 0467-25-5121
FAX. 0467-25-3778
33-6 Sakanoshita, Kamakura
www.kamakuraparkhotel.co.jp

Prince

This hotel stands on the slope of a small hill. All rooms overlook Shichirigahama, and Mt. Fuji can be seen from some of them on a clear day. The interior décor is simple and rooms have small verandas. Internet is available for an extra charge. One enjoys breakfast on the 2nd floor, gazing out at the horizon. The chapel is popular for weddings, thanks also to the views. A shuttle bus is available from Shichirigahama Station.

■ Prices
♦ = ¥ 32,400-48,600
♦♦ = ¥ 32,400-48,600
Suite = ¥ 92,400-115,500
☕ = ¥ 2,200
Rooms = 94
Suites = 1
Restaurants = 2

TEL. 0467–32–1111
FAX. 0467-32-9290
1-2-18 Shichirigahamahigashi, Kamakura
www.princehotels.co.jp/kamakura

MAPS

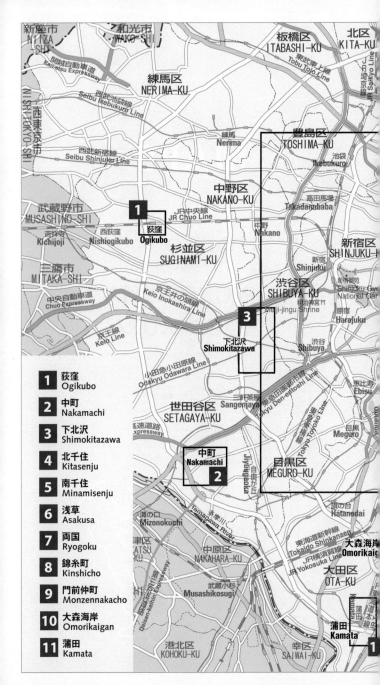

1	荻窪 Ogikubo
2	中町 Nakamachi
3	下北沢 Shimokitazawa
4	北千住 Kitasenju
5	南千住 Minamisenju
6	浅草 Asakusa
7	両国 Ryogoku
8	錦糸町 Kinshicho
9	門前仲町 Monzennakacho
10	大森海岸 Omorikaigan
11	蒲田 Kamata

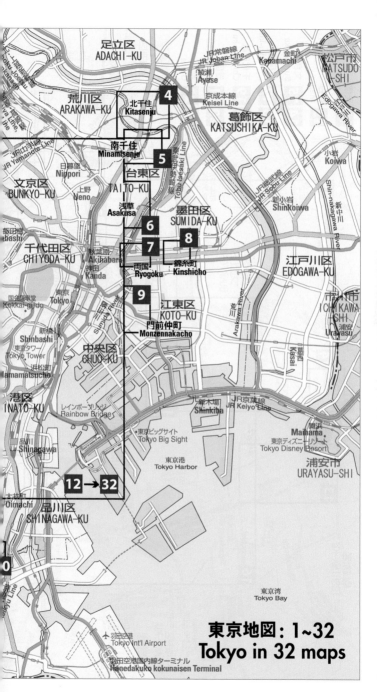

東京地図：1~32
Tokyo in 32 maps

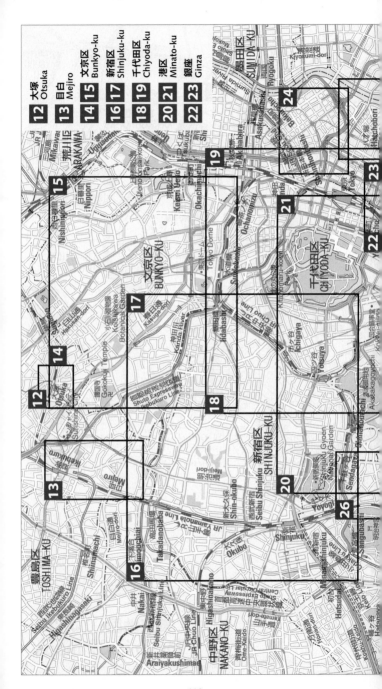

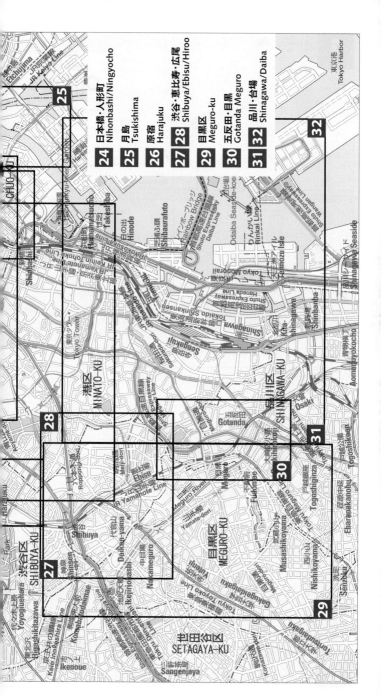

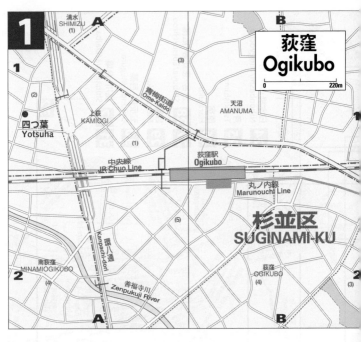

1

A

B

荻窪
Ogikubo

0   220m

1

(3)

(2)

天沼
AMANUMA

青梅街道
Ome-Kaido

四つ葉
Yotsuha

上荻
KAMIOGI

(1)

中央線
JR Chuo Line

荻窪駅
Ogikubo

丸ノ内線
Marunouchi Line

(5)

杉並区
SUGINAMI-KU

南荻窪
MINAMIOGIKUBO

(4)

環八通
Kampachi-dori

荻窪
OGIKUBO
(4)

(3)

善福寺川
Zenpukuji River

A

B

2

玉川台
TAMAGAWADAI
(1)

A

(8)

B

(6)

玉川通
Tamagawa-dori

用賀
YOGA

(7)

深沢
FUKASAWA

(3)

駒沢公園通
Komazawa-koen-dori

砧中仲町通
Yoganakamachi-dori

(5)

1

鮨 嘉瑞
Sushi Kazui ●

駒沢通
Komazawa-dori

世田谷区
SETAGAYA-KU

(4)

(2)

(4)

(5)

瀬田
SETA

環八通
Kampachi-dori

中町
NAKAMACHI

谷沢川
Yazawagawa River

(8)

(1)

上野毛
KAMINOGE

上野毛通
Kaminoge-dori

東急大井町線
Tokyu Oimachi Line

(1)

上野毛駅
Kaminoge

五島美術館
Museum
of Art (3)

(2)

(3)

2

A

B

中町
Nakamachi

0   360m

渋谷区
SHIBUYA-KU

A

笹塚駅
Sasazuka

B

甲州街道
Koshu-kaido

京王線
Keio Line

代田橋駅
Daitabashi

1

(2)

(1)

井ノ頭通
Inokashira-dori

(5)

太原
OHARA

(4)

羽根木
HANEGI

(1)

北沢
KITAZAWA

(3)

与志福
Yoshifuku ●

東北沢駅
Higashikitazawa

1

(6)

小田急小田原線
Odakyu Odawara Line

新代田駅
Shindaita

2

下北沢駅
Shimokitazawa

(2)

(1)

2

環七通
Kannana-dori

(5)

京王井の頭線
Keio Inokashira Line

池ノ上駅
Ikenoue

(4)

世田谷区
SETAGAYA-KU

(2)

世田谷代田駅
Setagayadaita

代田
DAITA

(5)

(2)

鮨 福元
Sushi Fukumoto ●

代沢
DAIZAWA

(1)

3

(3)

北沢川緑道
Kitazawagawa Ryokudo

池尻
IKEJIRI

(4)

(4)

下北沢
Shimokitazawa

0   300m

三宿
MISHUKU
(2)

太子堂
TAISHI
(3)

A

B

4

千住柳町
SENJUYANAGICHO

千住寿町
SENJUKOTOBUICHO

(4)

A

千住桜木
SENJUSAKURAGI

千住龍田町
SENJUTATSUTACHO

(3)

バードコート
Bird Court

B

461

千住中居町
SENJUNAKAICHO

(2)

千住
SENJU

千住旭町
SENJUASAHICHO

**足立区
ADACHI-KU**

(3)

千住宮元町
SENJUMIYAMOTOCHO

(1)

日ノ出町
HINODECHO

北千住
Kitasenju

ヤナギハラ
YANAGIHARA

1

千代田線
Chiyoda Line (2)

千住仲町
SENJUNAKACHO

千住東
SENJUAZUMA

(2)

千住緑町
SENJUMIDORICHO

墨堤通
Bokutei-dori

(1)

461

京成本線
Kelsei Line

(1)

千住河原町
SENJUKAWARACHO

(1)

千住関屋町
SENJUSEKIYACHO

千住大橋駅
Senjuohashi

2

千住橋戸町
SENJUHASHIDOCHO

隅田川
Sumida River

北千住
Kitasenju

0 _____ 440m

**荒川区
ARAKAWA-KU**

A

B

隅田川
Sumida River

**荒川区
ARAKAWA-KU**

A

(6)

1

千住間道
Senju-kando

(5)

(4)

円通寺
Entsuji Temple

(1)

都電荒川線
Toden Arakawa Line

日光街道
Nikko-kaido

464

南千住
MINAMISENJU

南千住
MINAMISENJU

三ノ輪橋
Minowabashi

2

尾花
Obana

2

東日暮里
HIGASHI
NIPPORI

(1)

三ノ輪
Minowa

日比谷線
Hibiya Line

(2)

明治通
Meiji-dori

**台東区
TAITO-KU**

306

A

5

南千住
Minamisenju

0 _____ 320m

B

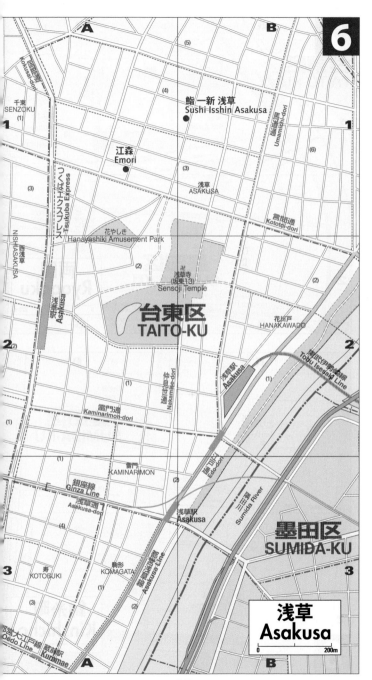

A   B

(5)

(4)

千束
SENZOKU
(1)

1

鮨一新 浅草
Sushi Isshin Asakusa

雷門通
Umamichi-dori

1

(6)

江森
Emori

(3)

国際通
Kokusai-dori

つくばエクスプレス
Tsukuba Express

浅草
ASAKUSA

言問通
Kototoi-dori

花やしき
Hanayashiki Amusement Park

(2)

浅草寺
(坂東13)
Sensoji Temple

(2)

NISHI-ASAKUSA
西浅草

地下鉄浅草
Asakusa

台東区
TAITO-KU

花川戸
HANAKAWADO

2

(2)

浅草駅
Asakusa

(1)

東武伊勢崎線
Tobu Isesaki Line

2

(1)

浅草寺通
Nakamise-dori

雷門通
Kaminarimon-dori

(1)

(1)

雷門
KAMINARIMON

(2)

江戸通
Edo-dori

銀座線
Ginza Line

浅草通
Asakusa-dori

(4)

浅草駅
Asakusa

三田川
Sumida River

墨田区
SUMIDA-KU

寿
KOTOBUKI

駒形
KOMAGATA

(1)

都営浅草線
Asakusa Line

3

(3)

(2)

浅草
Asakusa

0   200m

都営大江戸線
Oedo Line

蔵前駅
Kuramae

A   B

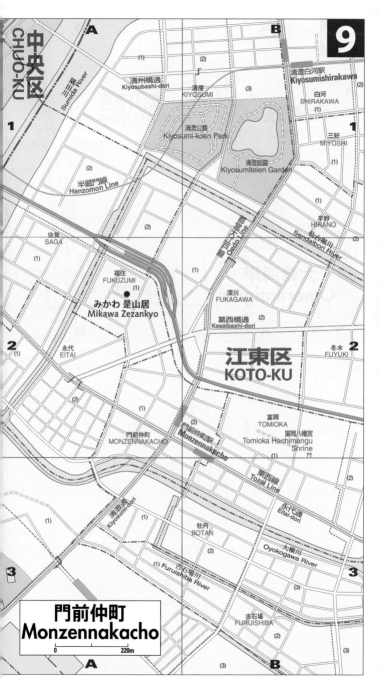

中央区
CHUO-KU

清州橋通
Kiyosubashi-dori

清澄
KIYOSUMI

清澄白河駅
Kiyosumishirakawa

白河
SHIRAKAWA

(3)

三田線
Sumida River

(1)

(2)

清澄公園
Kiyosumi-koen Park

(2)

三好
MIYOSHI

1

1

半蔵門線
Hanzomon Line

清澄庭園
Kiyosumiteien Garden

(1)

平野
HIRANO

佐賀
SAGA

(2)

都営大江戸線
Oedo Line

仙台堀川
Sendaibori River

(1)

福住
FUKUZUMI

(1)

深川
FUKAGAWA

● みかわ 是山居
Mikawa Zezankyo

葛西橋通
Kasaibashi-dori

(2)

2

永代
EITAI

(1)

江東区
KOTO-KU

冬木
FUYUKI

2

(2)

(1)

富岡
TOMIOKA

門前仲町
MONZENNAKACHO

門前仲町駅
Monzennakacho

富岡八幡宮
Tomioka Hachimangu
Shrine

(1)

東西線
Tozai Line

清澄通
Kiyosumi-dori

(1)

永代通
Eitai-dori

(1)

牡丹
BOTAN

大横川
Oyokogawa River

3

(1)

(2)

3

古石場川
Furuishiba River

古石場
FURUISHIBA

(2)

門前仲町
Monzennakacho

0   220m

(2)

(3)

(3)

A

B

A

B

(1)

大森西
OMORINISHI
(7)

川
Nomikawa River

1

西蒲田
NISHIKAMATA

(1)

(5)

(4)

蒲田
KAMATA

(3)

● 初音鮨
Hatsunezushi

(6)

(7)

蒲田
Kamata

東急池上線
Tokyu Ikegami Line

2

東急多摩川線
Tokyu Tamagawa Line

(8)

(5)

大田区
OTA-KU

(4)

環八通
Kanpachi-dori

新蒲田
SHINKAMATA

(1)

蒲田本町
KAMATAHONCHO

(1)

(2)

森ケ崎通
Keikyu Line

第一京浜
Daiichi Keihin

京浜東北線
JR Tokaido Line JR Keihin Tohoku Line

3

西六郷
NISHIROKUGO

南蒲田
MINAMIKAMATA
(2)

蒲田
Kamata

0 ————— 220m

仲六郷
NAKAROKUGO

(1)

東六郷
HIGASHIROKUGO
(1)

A

B

421

池袋
IKEBUKURO
(2)

東池袋
HIGASHIIKEBUKURO
(1)

(3)

(3)

(1)

丸ノ内線
Marunouchi Line

1

西池袋
NISHIIKEBUKURO

西武池袋
Seibu Ikebukuro

有楽町線
Yurakucho Line

(4)

本立寺卍
Honryuji Temple

(2)

明治通
Meiji-dori

JR山手線
JR Yamanote Line

西武池袋線
Seibu Ikebukuro Line

JR埼京線
JR Saikyo Line

(2)

南池袋
MINAMIIKEBUKURO

(3)

2

(3)

副都心線
Fukutoshin Line

豊島区
TOSHIMA-KU

(2)

和幸
Wako

鬼子母神堂
Kishibojindo Temple
卍

(4)

目白
Mejiro

目白
MEJIRO

目白通
Mejiro-dori

(3)

都電荒川線
Zoshigaya

鬼子母神前
Kishibojin-mae

雑司が谷
ZOSHIGAYA
(2)

(2)

(1)

学習院大
Gakushuin Univ.
(1)

3

都電荒川線
Toden Arakawa Line

(2)

高田
TAKADA
(1)

目白
Mejiro

0 ———— 220m

A

(3)

学習院下
Gakushuinshita

B

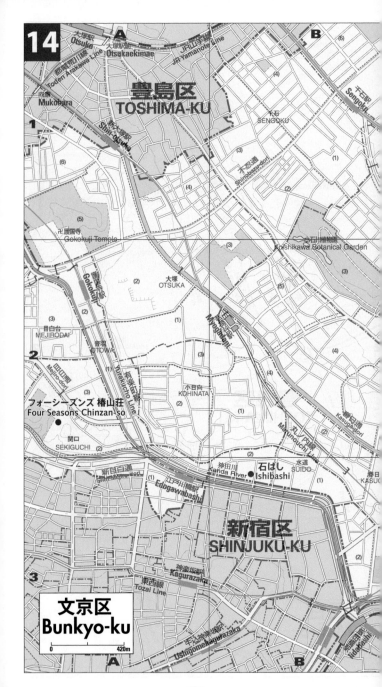

大塚駅前 Otsuka
大塚駅前 Otsukaekimae
JR山手線 JR Yamanote Line
都電荒川線 Toden Arakawa Line
向原 Mukohara

豊島区
TOSHIMA-KU

千石 SENGOKU
千石駅 Sengoku...

(6)

(1)

不忍通 Shinobazu-dori

小石川植物園
Koishikawa Botanical Garden

卍護国寺
Gokokuji Temple

地下鉄有楽町線 Gokoku..

大塚 OTSUKA

茗荷谷駅 Myogadani

目白台 MEJIRODAI

音羽 OTOWA

有楽町線 Yurakucho Line

目白通 Mejiro-dori

小日向 KOHINATA

春日通 Kasuga-dori

フォーシーズンズ 椿山荘
Four Seasons Chinzan-so

丸ノ内線 Marunouchi Line

関口 SEKIGUCHI

神田川 Kanda River
石ばし Ishibashi

水道 SUIDO

新目白通 Shin-Mejiro-dori

江戸川橋駅 Edogawabashi

春日 KASUG...

新宿区
SHINJUKU-KU

神楽坂駅 Kagurazaka

東西線 Tozai Line

文京区
Bunkyo-ku

0 ——— 420m

牛込神楽坂駅 Ushigomekagurazaka

飯田橋 Iidabashi

C (4) D
(5) (4) 千駄木通
Shinobazu-dori 新日暮里
Shin-nippori

南北線
Namboku Line
(2) (3) 一二三庵
Hifumian

本駒込
ONKOMAGOME (5) 千駄木
SENDAGI 日暮里
Nippori

本駒込駅
Hongkomagome 1

三田線
Mita Line 千駄木駅
Sendagi 台東区
TAITO-KU

(5)
白山通
Hakusan (2)
向丘
MUKOGAOKA (1) (2) 千代田線
Chiyoda Line
根津
NEZU 根津駅
Nezu

白山
HAKUSAN
東大前
Todai-mae (1) 弥生
YAYOI (2)

(1)
西片
NISHIKATA (1) (2) 2

(1)
(6) 本郷通
Hongo-dori 東京大
Tokyo Univ 不忍池
Shinobazuonoike
Pond.

小石川
KOISHIKAWA
春日通
Kasuga (5)
本郷
HONGO (7)

(2) 後楽園駅
Korakuen
(4)
本郷
HONGO (4) シンスケ
Shinsuke くろぎ
Kurogi
江知勝
Echikatsu
湯島天神
Yushimatenjin
Shrine

後楽園
Korakuen
都営大江戸線
Oedo Line 本郷三丁目駅
Hongosanchome (1) (3) 湯島
Yushima

後楽
ORAKU (1) 湯島
YUSHIMA 3

水道橋駅
Suidobashi (1) 神田川
Kanda River (1) 御茶ノ水駅
Ochanomizu

千代田区
CHIYODA-KU C JR中央線
JR Chuo Line D

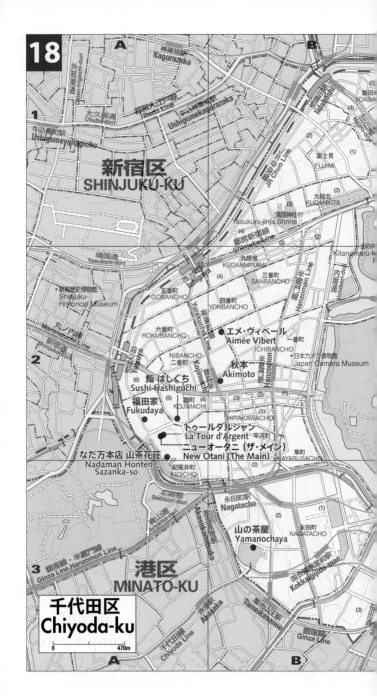

A   B

神楽坂駅
Kagurazaka

外苑東通
Gaien-higashi-dori

大江戸線
Oedo Line

牛込神楽坂
Ushigomekagurazaka

大久保通
Okubo-dori

1

牛込柳町駅
Ushigomeyanagicho

飯田橋
IIDABA

(3)

(4)

JR中央線
JR Chuo Line

飯田橋駅
Iidabashi

(4)

富士見
FUJIMI

(1)

新宿区
SHINJUKU-KU

新宿歴史博物館
Shinjuku-
Historical Museum

九段北
KUDANKITA

(2)

(3)

靖国神社
Yasukuni-jinja Shrine

都営新宿線
Shinjuku-Line

北の丸
Kitanomaru-k

靖国通
Yasukuni-dori

九段南
KUDANMINAMI

市ヶ谷
Ichigaya

三番町
SANBANCHO

半蔵門線 Hanzomon Line

内堀通 Uchibori-dori

五番町
GOBANCHO

四番町
YONBANCHO

丸ノ内線
Marunouchi Line

六番町
ROKUBANCHO

有楽町線
Yurakucho Line

エメ・ヴィベール
Aimée Vibert

一番町
ICHIBANCHO

日本カメラ博物館
Japan Camera Museum

新宿通
Shinjuku-dori

二番町
NIBANCHO

秋本
Akimoto

半蔵門線 Hanzomon

2

(6) 鮨 はしぐち
Sushi-Hashiguchi

麹町 (4)
KOJIMACHI

(5)

(1)

福田家
Fukudaya

平河町
HIRAKAWACHO

トゥールダルジャン
La'Tour d'Argent

平河町

ニューオータニ（ザ・メイン）
New Otani (The Main)

なだ万本店 山茶花荘
Nadaman Honten
Sazanka-so

紀尾井町
KIOICHO

隼町
HAYABUSACHO

(2)

外堀通
Sotobori-dori

永田町駅
Nagatacho

永田町
NAGATACHO

青山通 Aoyama-dori

赤坂見附
Akasaka-mitsuke

(2)

(1)

山の茶屋
Yamanochaya

永田町
NAGATACHO

国会議事堂前駅
Kokkaigijido-mae

3

銀座線・半蔵門線
Ginza Line, Hanzomon Line

港区
MINATO-KU

溜池山王駅
Tameikesanno

赤坂
Akasaka

溜池山王
Tameikesanno

(3)

千代田区
Chiyoda-ku

千代田線
Chiyoda Line

銀座線
Ginza Line

0   470m

A   B

文京区
BUNKYO-KU

神田川
Kanda River

水道橋駅
Suidobashi

(3)

三崎町
MISAKICHO

西神田
NISHIKANDA

(2)

神田神保町
KANDAJINBOCHO

蘭奢待
Ranjatai

神保町駅
Jinbocho

(1)

一ツ橋
HITOTSUBASHI

KANDANISHIKICHO

科学技術館
Science Museum

北の丸公園
TANOMARUKOEN

竹橋駅
Takebashi

東京国立近代美術館
National Museum
of Modern Art Tokyo

皇居東御苑
Kokyo-higashi-gyoen Park

千代田区
CHIYODA-KU

千代田
CHIYODA

オーグードゥジュール ヌーヴェルエール
Au Goût du Jour Nouvelle Ère

皇居外苑
KOKYOGAIEN

グリル うかい
Grill Ukai

皇居前広場
Kokyo-mae-hiroba
Park

ザ・ペニンシュラ
The Peninsula

ベイフンテラス
Hei Fung Terrace

日比谷公園
HIBIYAKOEN

日比谷公園
Hibiya-koen Park

レ セゾン
Les Saisons

帝国
Imperial

庭
Niwa

御茶ノ水駅
Ochanomizu

鍛冶町
SARUGAKUCHO

神田駿河台
KANDASURUGADAI

神田淡路町
KANDA
WAJICHO

新御茶ノ水
Shin-ochanomizu

傳
Den

神田小川町
KANDAOGAWAMACHI

小川町
Ogawamachi

淡路町
AwajiCho

神田多町
KANDA
TACHO

神田美土代町
KANDAMITOSHIROCHO

神田錦町
KANDANISHIKICHO

内神田
UCHIKANDA

大手町
OTEMACHI

大手町駅
Otemachi

丸ノ内
Marunouchi

MARUNOUCHI

東京駅
Tokyo

モナリザ 丸の内
Monnalisa Marunouchi

招福楼
Shofukuro

フォーシーズンズ 丸の内
Four Seasons Marunouchi

有楽町
YURAKU-
CHO

有楽町駅
Yurakucho

銀座一丁目
Ginzaitchome

Ginza

中央区
CHUO-KU

いじ橋
Ishibashi

外神田
SOTOKANDA

秋葉原駅
Akihabara

神田須田町
KANDASUDACHO

岩本町
Iwamotocho

神田紺屋町
KANDAKON-YACHO

新日本橋
Shin-nimbashi

三越前
Mitsukoshi-mae

メトロポリタン 丸の内
Metropolitan Marunouchi

シャングリ・ラ
Shangri-La

新富町
Shintomicho

東銀座駅
Higashiginza

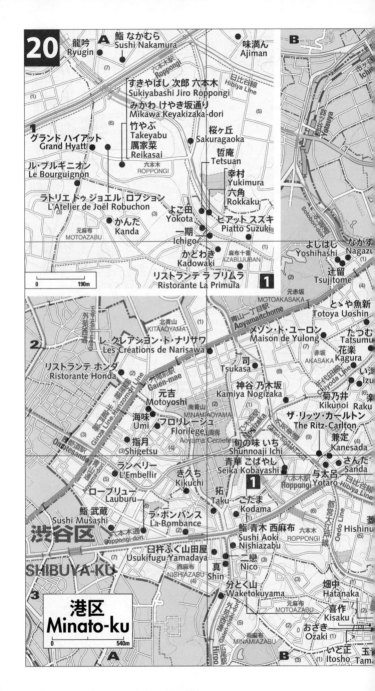

20

龍吟
Ryugin

鮨 なかむら
Sushi Nakamura

味満ん
Ajiman

B

六本木
Roppongi

日比谷線
Hibiya Line

すきやばし 次郎 六本木
Sukiyabashi Jiro Roppongi

みかわ けやき坂通り
Mikawa Keyakizaka-dori

1

グランド ハイアット
Grand Hyatt

竹やぶ
Takeyabu

厲家菜
Reikasai

桜ヶ丘
Sakuragaoka

哲庵
Tetsuan

ル・ブルギニオン
Le Bourguignon

六本木
ROPPONGI

幸村
Yukimura

ラトリエ ドゥ ジョエル ロブション
L'Atelier de Joël Robuchon

かんだ
Kanda

よこ田
Yokota

六角
Rokkaku

元麻布
MOTOAZABU

一期
Ichigo

ピアット スズキ
Piatto Suzuki

よしはし
Yoshihashi

なかず
Nagazu

かどわき
Kadowaki

麻布十番
AZABUJUBAN

辻留
Tsujitome

0 ——— 190m

リストランテ ラ プリムラ
Ristorante La Primula

1

元赤坂
MOTOAKASAKA

とゃ魚新
Totoya Uoshin

北青山
KITAAOYAMA

青山一丁目駅
Aoyama-itchome

メゾン・ド・ユーロン
Maison de Yulong

たつむ
Tatsumu

2

レ・クレアシオン・ド・ナリサワ
Les Créations de Narisawa

外苑東通り
Gaien-Higashi-dori

赤坂
AKASAKA

花楽
Kagura

リストランテ ホンダ
Ristorante Honda

外苑前駅
Gaien-mae

司
Tsukasa

い
Izu

銀座線・半蔵門線
Ginza Line, Hanzomon Line

元吉
Motoyoshi

南青山
MINAMIAOYAMA

神谷 乃木坂
Kamiya Nogizaka

千代田線
Chiyoda Line

菊乃井
Kikunoi Raku

海味
Umi

フロリレージュ
Florilege

青山霊園
Aoyama Cemetery

ザ・リッツ・カールトン
The Ritz-Carlton

表参道駅
Omotesando

指月
Shigetsu

旬の味 いち
Shunnoaji Ichi

兼定
Kanesada

ランベリー
L'Embellir

きくち
Kikuchi

青華 こばやし
Seika Kobayashi

与太呂
Yotaro

さんだ
Sanda

ローブリュー
Lauburu

拓
Taku

六本木駅
Roppongi

日比谷線
Hibiya Line

鮨 武蔵
Sushi Musashi

こだま
Kodama

1

渋谷区

ラ・ボンバンス
La-Bombance

鮨 青木 西麻布
Sushi Aoki
Nishiazabu

六本木
ROPPONGI

都営大江戸線
Oedo Line

麦
Hishinu

六本木通り
Roppongi-dori

臼杵ふく 山田屋
Usukifugu Yamadaya

二懸
Nico

SHIBUYA-KU

西麻布
NISHIAZABU

真
Shin

畑中
Hatanaka

3

港区
Minato-ku

分とく山
Waketokuyama

元麻布
MOTOAZABU

喜作
Kisaku

外苑西通り
Gaien-Nishi-dori

南麻布
MINAMIAZABU

おざき
Ozaki

0 ——— 540m

広尾
Hiroo

いど正
Itosho

玉
Tam

A

B

430

千代田区
CHIYODA-KU

日本カメラ博物館
Japan Camera Museum

外堀通り
Sotobori-dori

銀座線
Ginza Line

西新橋
NISHISHINBASHI (2)

(1) 笹田
Sasada

ほそ川
Hosokawa

ひろ作
Hirosaku

しみづ
Shimizu
(3)

新橋
SHINBASHI

(4)

ロイヤルパーク汐留タワー
Royal Park
Shiodome Tower

チャイナブルー
China Blue
ゴードン・ラムゼイ
Gordon Ramsay

1

鮎正
Ayumasa

タテル ヨシノ 汐留
Tateru Yoshino
Shiodome

鳥皮
Aragawa

パーク
Park

コンラッド
Conrad

ヴィラ フォンテーヌ 汐留
Villa Fontaine
Shiodome

新橋
HIGASHI-
SHINBASHI

(6)

御成門
Onarimon

(1)

芝大門
SHIBADAIMON

芝公園
SHIBAKOEN

タテル ヨシノ 芝
Tateru Yoshino Shiba

浜離宮庭園
Hamarikyu-teien
Garden

汐留
Shiodome
River

海岸
KAIGAN

0 ────── 190m

日比谷公園
Hibiya-koen Park

霞ヶ関
Kasumigaseki

日比谷
Hibiya

銀座
Ginza

花梨
Karin

ピエール・ガニェール
Pierre Gagnaire

虎ノ門
Toranomon

と村
Tomura

東銀座駅
Higashiginza

2

帰燕
Kien

鮨 さいとう
Sushi Saito

虎ノ門
TORANOMON (2)

ANA インターコンチネンタル
ANA Intercontinental
(1)

六本木一丁目
Roppongiitchome

オークラ
Okura
(4)

愛宕
ATAGO

西新橋
NISHISHINBASHI

中央区
CHUO-KU

醍醐
Daigo

東新橋
HIGASHISHINBASHI

(6)

麻布台
AZABUDAI

野田岩
Nodaiwa

芝公園
SHIBAKOEN

浜離宮庭園
Hamarikyu-teien Garden

麻布狸穴町
BUMAMIANACHO

汐留
Shiodome
River

赤羽橋
Akabanebashi

増上寺
Zojoji Temple

クレッセント
Crescent

芝大門
SHIBADAIMON

浜松町
HAMAMATSU-
CHO

東麻布
HIGASHIAZABU

海岸
KAIGAN

2

竹芝
Takeshiba

3

万歴龍呼堂
Banrekiryukodo

中国飯店 富麗華 (1)
hugoku Hanten Fureika

三田
MITA

C

芝
SHIBA

インターコンチネンタル東京ベイ
Intercontinental
Tokyo Bay

D

芝浦
SHIBAURA

431

日比谷濠
Hibiyabori Moat

有楽町駅
Yurakucho

1

千代田区
CHIYODA-KU

日比谷公園
Hibiya-koen Park

都営三田線
Mita Line

地下鉄千代田線
Chiyoda Line

日比谷駅
Hibiya

有楽町駅
Yurakucho

東海道新幹線
Tokaido Shinkansen

丸ノ内線
Marunouchi Line

日比谷通り
Hibiya-dori

アルジェント As
Argento Asc

バードランド
Bird Land

銀座駅
Ginza

すきやばし 次郎 本店
Sukiyabashi Jiro Honten

銀座駅
Ginza

寿司幸本店
Sushiko Honten

鮨 いわ
Sushi Iwa

ル・シズィエム・サンス・ドゥ・オエノン
Le 6eme Sens d'Oenon

あさぎ
Asagi

近藤
Kondo

(5)

七丁目 京星
7chome Kyoboshi

喰切り 江ぐち
Kuikiri Eguchi

三亀
Sankame

(6)

鮨 青木 銀座
Sushi Aoki Ginza

2

JR東海道本線・新幹線・横須賀線
JR Tokaido Line

JR京浜東北線
JR Keihin Tohoku Line

JR山手線
JR Yamanote Line

とよだ
Toyoda

馳走 啐啄
Chiso Sottaku

銀座
GINZA

さわ田
Sawada

すしおおの
Sushi Ohno

小十
Koju

(7)

ラ トゥール
La Tour

鮨 一新 銀座
Sushi Isshin Ginza

ふぐ福
Fugu Fu

よねむら
Yonemura

青空
Harutaka

銀座線
Ginza Line

六覺燈
Rokukaku-tei

浅草線
Asakusa

未能一
Minoichi

室井
Muroi

福樹
Fukuju

ファロ
Faro

かつぜん
Katsuzen

くわ野
Kuwano

鮨 水谷
Sushi Mizutani

鮨 かねさか
Sushi Kanesaka

有季銚
Yukicho

山路
Yamaji

外堀通り
Sotobori-dori

新橋駅
Shinbashi

三井ガーデン 銀座
Mitsui Garden Ginza

やま
Yam

浅草線・銀座線
Asakusa

新橋駅
Shinbashi

3

港区
MINATO-KU

竹葉亭 本店
Chikuyo-tei Honten

哥利Gori

都営大江戸線
Oedo Line

新橋駅
Shinbashi

銀座
Ginza

0 ———— 160m

八重洲
YAESU

Kyobashi 京橋駅

深町
Fukamachi

京橋
KYOBASHI

(1)

23

高速都心環状
Shuto-dori

(2)

JR京葉線
JR Keiyo Line

鍛冶橋通り
Kajibashi-dori

宝町駅
Takaracho

(2)

(3)

1

Ginza-itchome
銀座一丁目駅

ドン・ナチュール
Dons de la Nature

八丁堀
HATCHOBORI

(3)

イコニック
Iconic

西洋 銀座
Seiyo Ginza

(4)

アロマフレスカ
Aroma-Frèsca

すし屋 真魚
Sushiya Mao

ー
hiichi

B
ri

ベージュ アラン・デュカス
Beige Alain Ducasse

(1)

新富
SHINTOMI

(2)

(1)

うち山
Uchiyama

有楽町線
Yurakucho Line

(3)

昭和通り
Showa-dori

タテル ヨシノ 銀座
ateru Yoshino Ginza

中央区
CHUO-KU

新富町駅
Shintomicho

2

(4)

晴海通り
Harumi-dori

東銀座駅
Higashiginza

(1)

新大橋通り
Shin-Ohashi-dori

あら輝
Araki

東銀座駅
Higashiginza

三ツ田
Mitsuta

(2)

うかい亭 銀座
Ukai-tei Ginza

植むら 本店
Uemura Honten

築地
TSUKIJI

やまもと
Yamamoto

築地駅
Tsukiji

(3)

日比谷線
Hibiya Line

清壽
Seiju

3

(7)

(4)

(5)

築地市場駅
Tsukijishijo

C

D

(6)

24 千代田区
CHIYODA-KU

0 ——— 320m

日本橋小伝馬町
NIHONBASHI-
KODENMACHO

馬喰横山駅
Bakuroyokoyama

JR総武線
JR Sobu Line

日本橋大伝馬町
NIHONBASHI-
ODENMACHO

銀座線 Ginza Line

でん茂
Tenmo

日本橋本町
NIHONBASHI-HONCHO

小伝馬町駅
Kodenmacho

センス
Sense

櫻川
Sakuragawa

日比谷線 Hibiya Line

日本橋堀留町
NIHONBASHI-
HORIDOMECHO

濱田家
Hamadaya

浜町公園
Hamacho
koen Pa

日本橋浜町
NIHONBASHIHAM

シグネチャー
Signature

タパス モラキュラーバー
Tapas Molecular Bar

むとう
Muto

日本橋室町
NIHONBASHI-
MUROMACHI

日本橋小舟町
NIHONBASHI-
KOBUNACHO

人形町駅
Ningyocho

中央区
CHUO-K

マンダリン オリエンタル
Mandarin Oriental

半蔵門線
Hanzomon Line

日山
Hiyama

日本橋人形町
NIHONBASHI-
NINGYOCHO

三越前駅
Mitsukoshi-mae

都営浅草線
Asakusa Line

新大橋通り
Shin-ohashi-dori

日本橋駅
Nihonbashi

サンパウ
Sant Pau

日本橋
NIHONBASHI

日本橋小網町
NIHONBASHI-KOAMICHO

ロイヤルパーク
Royal Park

日本橋兜町
NIHONBASHI-
KABUTOCHO

日本橋蛎殻町
NIHONBASHI-
KAKIGARACHO

日本橋
Nihonbashi

永代通り
Eitai-dori

東西線
Tozai Line

日本橋茅場町
NIHONBASHI-
KAYABACHO

茅場町駅
Kayabache

NIHONBASHI
HAKOZAKIC

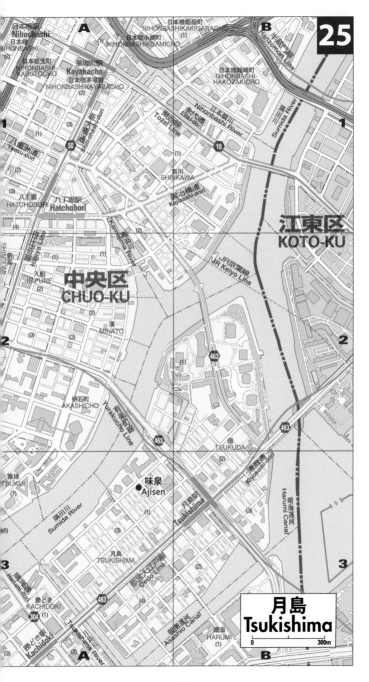

日本橋駅
Nihonbashi
日本橋
(HONBASHI)

A

日本橋馬喰町
NIHONBASHIKAKIGARACHO

日本橋小網町
NIHONBASHIKOAMICHO

B

半蔵門線
Hanzomon Line

日本橋兜町
NIHONBASHI
KABUTOCHO

茅場町駅
Kayabacho

日本橋箱崎町
NIHONBASHI-
HAKOZAKICHO

日本橋茅場町
NIHONBASHIKAYABACHO

日本橋川
Nihonbashi
River

茅場橋
Eitai-dori

隅田川
Sumida River

1

50

新川橋
新川通り
Total Line
Shinbashi-dori

新川
SHINKAWA

1

八丁堀駅
八丁堀
HATCHOBORI

八丁堀駅
Hatchobori

鍛冶橋通り
Kajibashi-dori

10

江東区
KOTO-KU

SHINTOMI

亀島川
Kameijima River

亀島川
Kameijima River

入船
IRIFUNE

JR京葉線
JR Keiyo Line

中央区
CHUO-KU

湊
MINATO

2

463

2

明石町
AKASHICHO

有楽町線
Yurakucho Line

築地
TSUKIJI

463

佃
TSUKUDA

味泉
Ajisen

月島駅
Tsukishima

清澄通り
Kiyosumi-dori

晴海運河
Harumi Canal

隅田川
Sumida River

月島
TSUKISHIMA

都営大江戸線
Oedo Line

3

勝どき
KACHIDOKI

Harumidori

463

3

304

勝どき駅
Kachidoki

佃島運河
Asashio Canal

晴海
HARUMI

月島運河
Tsukishima River

A

B

月島
Tsukishima

0   300m

A　中央線 JR Chuo Line
B　千駄ヶ谷駅 Sendagaya

代々木 YOYOGI (1)

都営大江戸線 Oedo Line

新宿区 SHINJUKU-KU

(5)

(6)

(4)

副都心線 Fukutoshin Line

千駄ヶ谷 SENDAGAYA

(1)

1

明治神宮 Meiji-jingu Shrine

(3)

(2)

代々木神園町 YOYOGI-KAMIZONOCHO

副都心線 Fukutoshin Line

外苑西通り Gaien-nishi-dori

樋口 Higuchi
(2)

凛 Ichirin

東郷神社 Togo-jinja Shrine

レストラン アイ Restaurant I
(1)

えさき Esaki

2

原宿 Harajuku

渋谷区 SHIBUYA-KU

(3)

赤簑亭 Sekiho-tei

明治神宮前〈原宿〉駅 Meijijingumae〈Harajuku〉

神宮前 JINGUMAE

重よし Shigeyoshi

JR山手線、JR埼京線 JR Yamanote Line, JR Saikyo Line

(4)

うかい亭 表参道 Ukai-tei Omotesando

千代田線 Chiyoda Line

明治通り Meiji-dori

表参道 Omotesando

銀座線・半蔵門線 Ginza Line, Hanzomon Line

青山通り Aoyama-dori

表参道駅 Omotesando

3

(6)

(5)

港区 MINATO-KU

B

原宿 Harajuku

0　250m

A　渋谷 SHIBUYA (1)

437

神山町
KAMIYAMACHO **A**

神南
JINNAN
(1)

神宮前
JINGUMAE
(6)

神宮前
JINGUMAE
(5)

B

副都心線
Fukutoshin Line

宇田川町
UDAGAWACHO

戸栗美術館
• Toguri Museum of Art

青山通
Aoyama-dori

● シェ・松尾
Chez Matsuo
(1)

松濤
SHOTO

渋谷駅
Shibuya

渋谷
SHIBU

1

京王井の頭線
Keio Inokashira Line

神泉駅
Shinsen

道玄坂
DOGENZAKA
(1)

円山町
MARUYAMACHO

神泉町
SHINSENCHO

東急田園都市線
Tokyu Den-entoshi Line

セルリアンタワー東急
Cerulean Tower Tokyu

明治通
Meiji-dori

桜丘町
SAKURAGAOKACHO

玉川通
Tamagawa-dori

南平台町
NANPEIDAICHO

レザンファン ギャテ
Les Enfants Gâtés

鶯谷町
UGUISUDANICHO

東急東横線
Tokyu Toyoko Line

旧山手通
Kyu-Yamate-dori

鉢山町
HACHIYAMACHO

2

猿楽町
SARUGAKUCHO

メゾン ポール・ボキューズ
Maison Paul Bocuse

代官山町
DAIKAN-YAMACHO

ル・ジュー・ドゥ・ラシエット
Le Jeu de l'Assiette
(2)

リストランテ Aso
Ristorante Aso

恵比寿西
EBISUNISI

山手通
Yamate-dori

目黒川
Meguro River

パッション
Pachon

代官山駅
Daikan-Yama

モナリザ 恵比寿
Monnalisa Ebis
(1)

駒沢通
Komazawa-dori

目黒区
MEGURO-KU

中目黒駅
Nakameguro

(3)

3

渋谷・恵比寿・広尾
Shibuya/Ebisu/Hiroo

0   300m

A   **B**

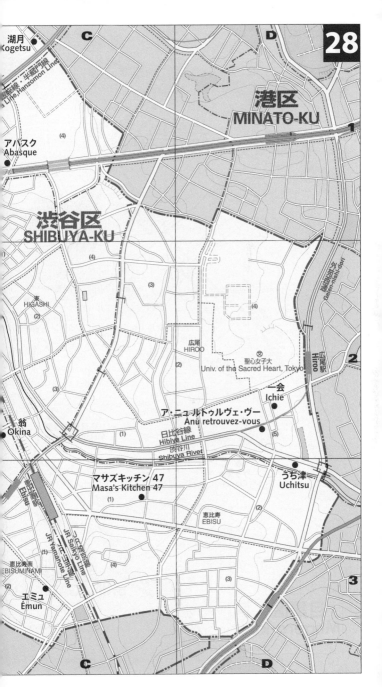

湖月
Kogetsu

半蔵門線 Line, Hanzomon Line

港区
MINATO-KU

アバスク
Abasque

(4)

渋谷区
SHIBUYA-KU

(4)

(3)

(4)

東
HIGASHI
(2)

広尾
HIROO

(3)

(2)

聖心女子大
Univ. of the Sacred Heart, Tokyo

Gaien-nishi-dori

広尾駅
Hiroo

一会
Ichie

翁
Okina

ア・ニュルトゥルヴェ・ヴー
Anu retrouvez-vous

(1)

(5)

日比谷線
Hibiya Line

渋谷川
Shibuya River

マサズキッチン 47
Masa's Kitchen 47

(1)

うち津
Uchitsu

Ebisu

恵比寿
EBISU

(2)

JR Saikyo Line

JR Yamanote Line

(4)

恵比寿南
EBISUMINAMI
(2)

(3)

エミユ
Émun
(2)

29

港区
MINATO-KU

A　　　　　　　B

駒場東大前駅
Komabatodai-mae

京王井の頭線
Keio Inokashira Line

駒場
KOMABA (1)

神泉駅
Shinsen

渋谷
Shibuya

半蔵門線
Hanzomon Line

銀座線
Ginza Line

渋谷区
SHIBUYA-KU

1

大橋
OHASHI

東急田園都市線
Tokyu Den-entoshi Line

玉川通り
Tamagawa-dori

青葉台
AOBADAI

池尻大橋駅
Ikejiriohashi

JR山手線
JR Yamanote Line

東山
HIGASHIYAMA

代官山
Daikan-yama

日比谷線
Hibiya Line

渋谷川
Shibuya River

1

上目黒
KAMIMEGURO

東急東横線
Tokyu Toyoko Line

中目黒駅
Nakameguro-dori

中目黒
NAKAMEGURO

ヒロミチ
Hiromichi

龍天門
Ryutenmon

イカロ
Icaro

祐天寺駅
YUTENJI

祐天寺
YUTENJI

ジョエル・ロブション
Joël Robuchon

ラ ターブル ドゥ ジョエル・ロブション
La Table de Joël Robuchon

三田 MITA

ウェスティン
Westin

2

五本木
(GOHONGI)

駒沢通り
Komazawa-dori

目黒川
Meguro River

目黒
MEGURO

目黒
Meguro

2

中町
NAKACHO

中町
NAKACHO

目黒雅叙園
Meguro Gajoen

学芸大学駅
Gakugeidaigaku

すずき
Suzuki

鷹番
TAKABAN

クラスカ
Claska

目黒通り
Meguro-dori

下目黒
SHIMOMEGURO

不動前駅
Fudomae

東急目黒線
Tokyu Meguro Line

目黒本町
MEGUROHONCHO

碑文谷
HIMON-YA

3

武蔵小山駅
Musashikoyama

品川区
SHINAGAWA-KU

3

中原街道
Nakaharakaido

洗足駅
SENZOKU

玉川
TAMACHI

西小山駅
Nishikoyama

戸越銀座駅
Togoshiginza

目黒区
Meguro-ku

0　　　　　650m

A

東急池上線
Tokyu Ikegami Line

B

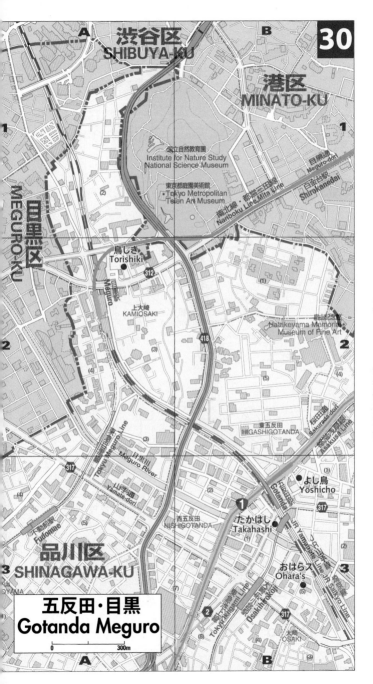

30

渋谷区
SHIBUYA-KU

港区
MINATO-KU

目黒区
MEGURO-KU

国立自然教育園
Institute for Nature Study
National Science Museum

東京都庭園美術館
Tokyo Metropolitan
Teien Art Museum

目黒駅
Meguro-eki

目黒通り
Meguro-dori

白金台駅
Shirokanedai

南北線・都営三田線
Nanboku Line, Mita Line

鳥しき
Torishiki

目黒川
Meguro

上大崎
KAMIOSAKI

畠山記念館
Hatakeyama Memorial
Museum of Fine Art

桜田通り
Sakurada-dori

浅草線
Asakusa Line

東五反田
HIGASHIGOTANDA

目黒川
Meguro River

東急目黒線
Tokyu Meguro Line

山手通り
Yamate-dori

よし鳥
Yoshicho

不動前駅
Fudomae

西五反田
NISHIGOTANDA

五反田駅
Gotanda

JR山手線
JR Yamanote Line

たかはし
Takahashi

品川区
SHINAGAWA-KU

おはらス
Ohara's

JR山手線・JR埼京線
JR Yamanote Line, JR Saikyo Line

五反田・目黒
Gotanda Meguro

東急池上線
Tokyu Ikegami Line

大崎駅
Osaki-eki

大崎
OSAKI

0   300m

441

西麻布 Nishi-dori
Gaien-nishi-dori
六本木 ROPPONGI
麻布狸穴町 AZABUMAMIANACHO
芝公園 SHIBAKOEN

西麻布 NISHIAZABU
麻布永坂町 AZABUNAGASAKACHO 麻布台 AZABUDAI
増上寺 Zojoji Temple
ザ・プリンス パークタワー The Prince Park Tower

たじま Tajima
麻布十番 AZABUJUBAN
東麻布 HIGASHIAZABU
大江戸線 Oedo Line 都営大江戸線

元麻布 MOTOAZABU
赤羽橋 Akabanebashi

ひらまつ Hiramatsu
広尾駅 Hiroo
広尾 Hiroo
日比谷線 Hibiya Line

カーザ ヴィニタリア Casa Vinitalia
港区 MINATO-KU

南麻布 MINAMIAZABU
南北線 Namboku Line
慶應義塾大 Keio Univ.
ばさら Basara

青草窠 Seisoka
明治通 Meiji-dori

三合菴 Sangoan
渋谷川 Shibuya River
鮨 いまむら Sushi Imamura
桃の木 Momonoki

三田 MITA
JR山手線 JR Yokosuka Line
田町 Tamachi

堀兼 Horikane
白金 SHIROKANE
白金桜田通 Shirokadedehamawa

カンテサンス Quintessence
目黒通 Meguro-dori

劉安 Ryuan
白金台 SHIROKANEDAI

シェラトン都 Sheraton Miyako
仙台坂 Sennakuji

三友居 Sanyukyo
高輪 TAKANAWA
JR東海道線 JR Tokaido Line
東海道新幹線 Tokaido Shinkansen

白金台駅 Shirokanedai

畠山記念館 Hatakeyama Memorial Museum of Fine Art
品川 Shinagawa
港南 KONAN

桜田通 Sakurada-dori
高輪台 Takanawadai
都営浅草線 Asakusa Line

ストリングス インターコンチネンタル The Strings by Intercontinental

品川区 SHINAGAWA-KU
北品川駅 Kitashinagawa

目黒川 Meguro River
京浜急行 Keihin Line
山手通 Yamate-dori

品川・台場 Shinagawa/ Daiba

0 ——— 585m

渋谷区 SHIBUYA-KU

A B

1

2

3

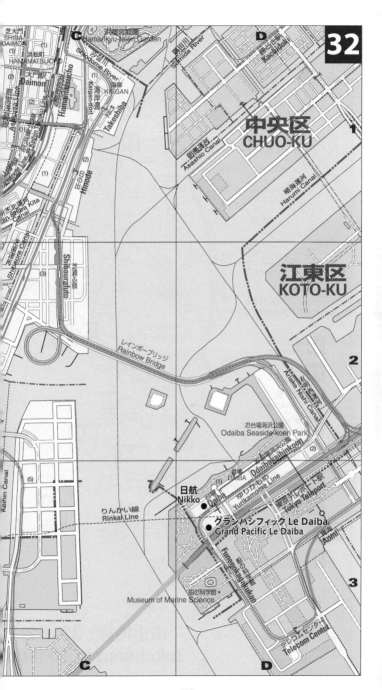

芝大門
SHIBA
DAIMON
(1)
浜松町
HAMAMATSUCHO

C 浜離宮庭園
Hama-kyu-Teien Garden

汐留川
Shiodome River

隅田川
Sumida River

勝どき
Kachidoki

D

(1)
浜松町
(1)

(2)
大門駅
Daimon

海岸通
KAIGAN

海岸通
KAIGAN

中央区
CHUO-KU

1

浜松町
Hamamatsucho

竹芝
Takeshiba

朝潮運河
Asashio Canal

晴海運河
Harumi Canal

芝浦北運河
Jin Shiba Kita
Canal

日の出
Hinode

(2)

(3)

N芝浦ふ頭
Shibaurafuto

レインボーブリッジ
Rainbow Bridge

江東区
KOTO-KU

芝浦西運河
Shibaura Canal

(3)

有明西運河
Ariake Nishi Canal

2

お台場海浜公園
Odaiba Seaside-koen Park

お台場海浜公園
Odaibakaihinkoen

台場
DAIBA

(1)

ゆりかもめ
Yurikamome Line

(2)

東京テレポート駅
Tokyo Teleport

運河通
Keihin Canal

(5)

りんかい線
Rinkai Line

台場
Daiba

日航
Nikko ●

グランパシフィック Le Daiba
Grand Pacific Le Daiba ●

青海
Aomi

船の科学館
Funenokagakukan

3

船の科学館 ●
Museum of Marine Science

テレコムセンター
Telecom Center

C

D

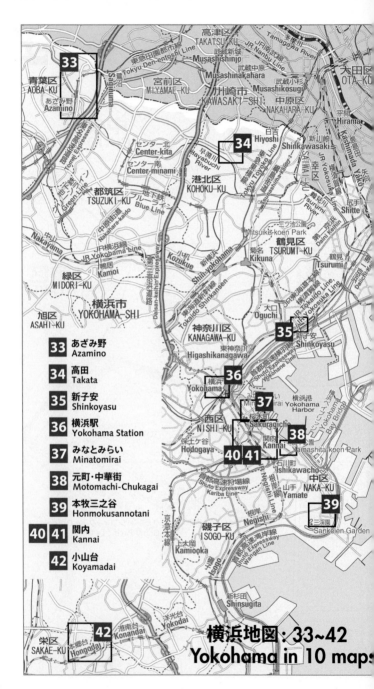

横浜地図：33〜42
Yokohama in 10 maps

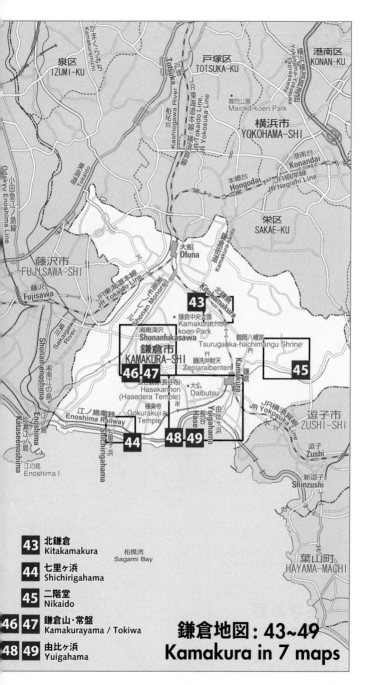

鎌倉地図: 43~49
Kamakura in 7 maps

43 北鎌倉
Kitakamakura

44 七里ヶ浜
Shichirigahama

45 二階堂
Nikaido

46 47 鎌倉山・常盤
Kamakurayama / Tokiwa

48 49 由比ヶ浜
Yuigahama

445

A(3)

B

(4)
風來蕎
Furaikyo

(2)

美しが丘公園
Utsukushigaoka-koen Park

(1)
美しが丘
UTSUKUSHIGAOKA

青葉区
AOBA-KU

(4)

(5)

たまプラーザ駅
Tama Plaza

(3)

1

元石川町
MOTOISHIKAWACHO

2

(4)

(2)

(2)

新石川
SHIN-ISHIKAWA

13

東急田園都市線
Tokyu Den-entoshi Line

(1)

あざみ野
AZAMINO

馳走 きむら
Chiso Kimura

あざみ野駅
Azamino

(1)

早渕川
Hayabuchi River

3

(2)

地下鉄ブルーライン
Blue Line

うかい亭 あざみ野
Ukai-tei Azamino

あざみ野南
AZAMINOMINAMI

(1)

荏田町
EDACHO

246

あざみ野
Azamino

0 ———— 160m

A

B

港北区
KOHOKU-KU

高田西
TAKATANISHI

(3)

A

B

(6)

(3)

(3)

106

(2)

日吉本町
HIYOSHIHONCHO

(5)

1

(2)

高田駅
Takata

しま村
Shimamura

(1)

高田東
TAKATAHIGASHI

地下鉄グリーンライン
Green Line

102

(4)

2

(4)

高田
Takata

0   200m

(1)

早渕川
Hayabuchi River

(2)

新吉田東
N-YOSHIDAHIGASHI

A

綱島西
TSUNASHIMANISHI

(5)

B

A

神奈川区
KANAGAWA-KU

B

子安台
KOMASUDAI

(1)

京浜
Daini Keihin

新子安
SHINKOYASU

(1)

江町公園
hb-koen
Park

八左ェ門
Hachizaemon

JR東海道線・横須賀線 JR Tokaido Line·JR Yokosuka Line
JR京浜東北線 JR Keihin Tohoku Line

京急本線
Keikyu Line

入江
RIE

(1)

1

新子安駅
Shinkoyasu

京急新子安
Keikyu Shinkoyasu

15

(3)

2

新子安
Shinkoyasu

0   140m

子安通
KOYASUDORI

京浜
Daiichi Keihin

守屋町
MORIYACHO

(3)

B

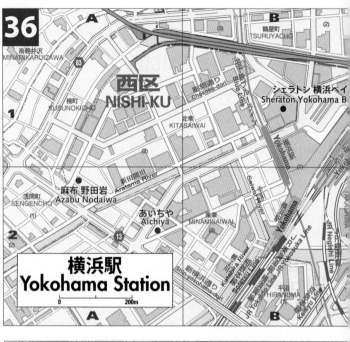

36

南軽井沢
MINAMIKARUIZAWA

西区
NISHI-KU

楠町
KUSUNOKICHO

北幸
KITASAIWAI

鶴屋町
TSURUYACHO

彫刻通り
Choko-dori

シェラトン 横浜ベイ
Sheraton Yokohama B

新田間川
Aratama River

麻布 野田岩
Azabu Nodaiwa

浅間町
SENGENCHO

あいちや
Aichiya

南幸
MINAMISAIWAI

西平沼橋
Saiwai River

JR東海道線 JR横須賀線 JDC
JR Tokaido Line JR Yokosuka Line

JR根岸線
JR Negishi Line

帷子川
Katabira River

相鉄線
Sotetsu Line

新横浜通り
Shoko-yokohama-dori

平沼
HIRANUMA

京急線
Keikyu Line

横浜駅
Yokohama Station

0   200m

37

西区
NISHI-KU

横浜高速鉄道みなとみらい線
Yokohama Minatomirai Line

臨港パーク
Rinko Park

パシフィコ横浜
Pacifico Yokohama

いちょう通り
Icho-dori

みなとみらい
MINATOMIRAI

国際大通り
Kokusai-odori

みなとみらい大通り
Minatomirai-odori

グランド インターコンチネンタル
Grand Intercontinental

横浜美術館
Yokohama Museum of Art

クイーンズスクエア横浜
Queen's Square Yokohama

パンパシフィック 横浜ベイ 東急
Pan Pacific Yokohama Bay Tokyu

みなとみらい大通り
Minatomirai-odori

けやき通り
Keyaki-dori

ランドマークプラザ
Landmark Plaza

ロイヤルパーク
Royal Park

さくら通り
Sakura-dori

よこはまコスモワールド
Yokohama Cosmoworld

新港パー
Shinko Pa

中区
NAKA-KU

JR根岸線
JR Negishi Line

日本丸
Nipponmaru

みなとみらい
Minatomirai

0   160m

448

38

ニューグランド
New Grand ●

横浜港
Yokohama Harbor

B

A

山下公園
Yamashita-koen Park

82

ローズ
Rose ●

横浜マリンタワー
Yokohama Marine Tower ●

中区
NAKA-KU

横浜高速鉄道みなとみらい線
Yokohama Minatomirai Line

山下町
YAMASHITACHO

元町・中華街駅
Motomachi-Chukagai

元町・中華街
Motomachi-Chukagai

0　　　　140m

元町
MOTOMACHI

山手町
YAMATECHO

港の見える丘公園
Minatomieru-
Oka-koen Park

1

2

A

B

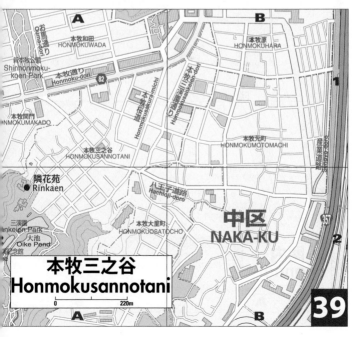

A

B

お馬通り
Omamichi

本牧和田
HONMOKUWADA

本牧原
HONMOKUHARA

新本牧公園
Shinnonmoku-
koen Park

本牧通り
Honmoku-dori

82

本牧間門
NMOKUMAKADO

本牧元町
HONMOKUMOTOMACHI

本
牧
間
門
通
り
Honmokumakadomon-michi

大
鳥
中
学
校
通
り
Honmokusakaekecho-dori

産
業
道
路
Sangyo-doro

本牧三之谷
HONMOKUSANNOTANI

隣花苑
Rinkaen ●

八王子道路
Hachioji-doro

三溪園
Sankeien Park

大池
Oike Pond

念館

本牧大里町
HONMOKUOSATOCHO

中区
NAKA-KU

357

1

2

本牧三之谷
Honmokusannotani

0　　　　220m

A

B

39

449

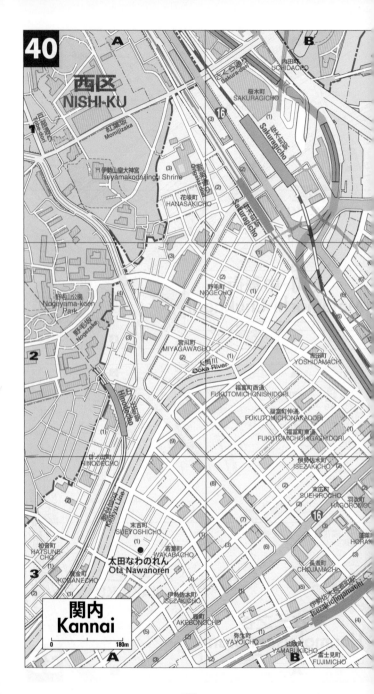

西区
NISHI-KU

内田町
UCHIDACHO

山路通り
Tobe-dori

紅葉坂
Momijizaka

桜木町
SAKURAGICHO

さくら通り
Sakura-dori

伊勢山皇大神宮
Iseyamakodaijingu Shrine

桜木町
Sakuragicho

花咲町
HANASAKICHO

桜木町
Sakuragicho

野毛山公園
Nogeyama-koen
Park

野毛町
NOGECHO

野手坂
Nogezaka

宮川町
MIYAGAWACHO

吉田町
YOSHIDAMACHI

大岡川
Ooka River

日ノ出町
Hinodecho

福富町西通
FUKUTOMICHONISHIDORI

福富町仲通
FUKUTOMICHONAKADORI

福富町東通
FUKUTOMICHOHIGASHIDORI

伊勢佐木町
ISEZAKICHO

末広町
SUEHIROCHO

羽衣町
HAGOROMOCHO

日ノ出町
HINODECHO

京急本線
Keikyu Line

末吉町
SUEYOSHICHO

蓬莱町
HORAI

初音町
HATSUNE-CHO

若葉町
WAKABACHO

太田なわのれん
Ota Nawanoren

黄金町
KOGANECHO

長者町
CHOJAMACHI

伊勢佐木町
ISEZAKICHO

伊勢佐木長者町
Isezakichojamachi

曙町
AKEBONOCHO

弥生町
YAYOICHO

山吹町
YAMABUKICHO

富士見町
FUJIMICHO

関内
Kannai

0   180m

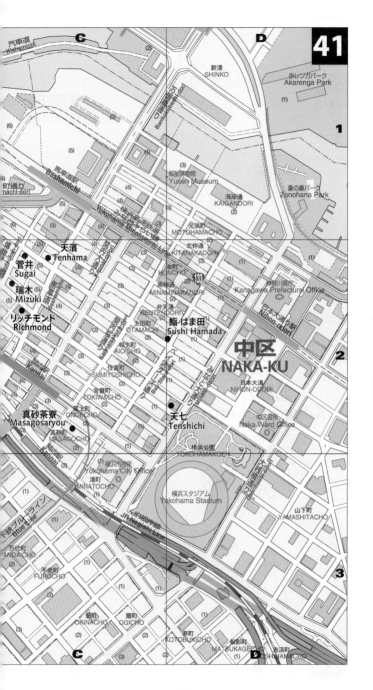

汽車道
Kishamichi

C

D

新港
SHINKO

赤レンガパーク
Akarenga Park

(1)

1

郵船博物館
Yusen Museum

海岸通
KAIGANDORI

象の鼻パーク
Zonohana Park

馬車道通り
Bashamichi

田町通り
nachi-dori

横浜みなとみらい線
Yokohama Minatomirai Line

元浜町
MOTOHAMACHO

天濱
Tenhama

北仲通
KITANAKADORI

菅井
Sugai

本町
HONCHO

133

神奈川県庁
Kanagawa Prefectural Office

瑞木
Mizuki

南仲通
MINAMINAKADORI

弁天通
BENTENDORI

日本大通り
Nihon-odori

リッチモンド
Richmond

太田町
OTAMACHI

鮨 はま田
Sushi Hamada

相生町
AIOICHO

中区
NAKA-KU

住吉町
SUMIYOSHICHO

関内通
Kannai-dori

日本大通
NIHON-ODORI

常盤町
TOKIWACHO

真砂茶寮
Masagosaryou

尾上町
ONOECHO

天七
Tenshichi

中区役所
Naka Ward Office

真砂町
MASAGOCHO

横浜公園
YOKOHAMAKOEN

横浜市役所
Yokohama City Office

港町
MINATOCHO

横浜スタジアム
Yokohama Stadium

山下町
YAMASHITACHO

横浜ブルーライン
Blue Line

JR根岸線
JR Negishi Line

万代町
ANDAICHO

不老町
FUROCHO

3

翁町
OKINACHO

扇町
OGICHO

寿町
KOTOBUKICHO

松影町
MATSUKAGECHO

吉浜町
YOSHIHAMACHO

C

D

A

B

シェ・ナカ
Chez Naka (1)

小山台
KOYAMADAI

港南区
KONAN-KU

本郷台
HONGODAI

(4)

1
(4)

栄区
SAKAE-KU

鍛冶ケ谷町
KAJIGAYACHO

(2)

小菅ケ谷
KOSUGAYA

鎌倉街道
Kamakura-Kaido

21

(1)

元大
MOTOOHA

(3)

2

JR根岸線
JR Negishi Line

(1)

小山台
Koyamadai

鍛冶ケ谷
(2)
KAJIGAYA

0   360m

柏陽
HAKUYO

(2)

本郷台駅
Hongodai
(1)

地球市民かながわプラザ（あーすぷらざ）
Kanagawa Plaza for Global Citizenship
(Earth Plaza)

A

B

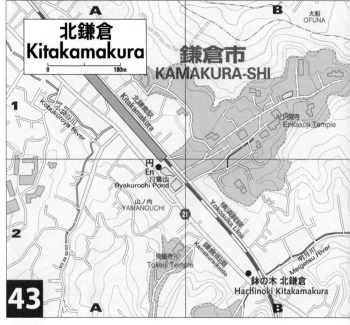

A

B

大船
OFUNA

北鎌倉
Kitakamakura

0   180m

鎌倉市
KAMAKURA-SHI

小袋谷川
Kobukuroya River

北鎌倉駅
Kitakamakura

1

円覚寺
Enkakuji Temple

円
En
白鷺池
Byakurochi Pond

山ノ内
YAMANOUCHI

横須賀線
Yokosuka Line

21

鎌倉街道
Kamakura-Kaido

明月川
Meigetsu River

浄智寺
Takeiji Temple

2

鉢の木 北鎌倉
Hachinoki Kitakamakura

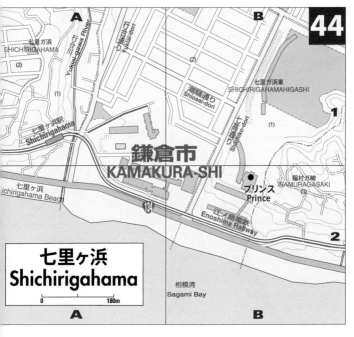

44

七里ガ浜
SHICHIRIGAHAMA
(2)

行合川
Yukaigawa River

由比ガ浜
Yukai-dori

(2)

潮騒通り
Shiosai-dori

七里ガ浜東
SHICHIRIGAHAMAHIGASHI

1

七里ガ浜駅
Shichirigahama

(1)

(1)

鎌倉市
KAMAKURA-SHI

由比ヶ浜通り
Shichito-dori

プリンス
Prince

稲村ガ崎
INAMURAGASAKI
(3)

七里ヶ浜
ichirigahama Beach

184

江ノ島電鉄
Enoshima Railway

2

七里ヶ浜
Shichirigahama
0 ——— 180m

相模湾
Sagami Bay

A B

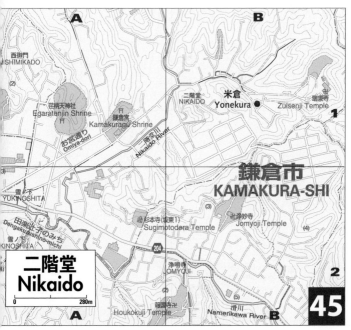

西御門
NISHIMIKADO
(2)

荏柄天神社
Egaratenjin Shrine

鎌倉宮
Kamakuragu Shrine

二階堂
NIKAIDO

米倉
Yonekura

瑞泉寺
Zuisenji Temple

1

お宮通り
Omiya-dori

二階堂川
Nikaido River

鎌倉市
KAMAKURA-SHI

(3)

雪ノ下
YUKINOSHITA

杉本寺(東東1)
Sugimotodera Temple

浄妙寺
Jomyoji Temple
(4)

田楽辻子のみち
Dengakuzushino-michi

雪ノ下
KINOSHITA

204

浄明寺
JOMYOJI

2

二階堂
Nikaido
0 ——— 280m

(5)

報国寺
Houkokuji Temple

滑川
Namerikawa River

B

45

453

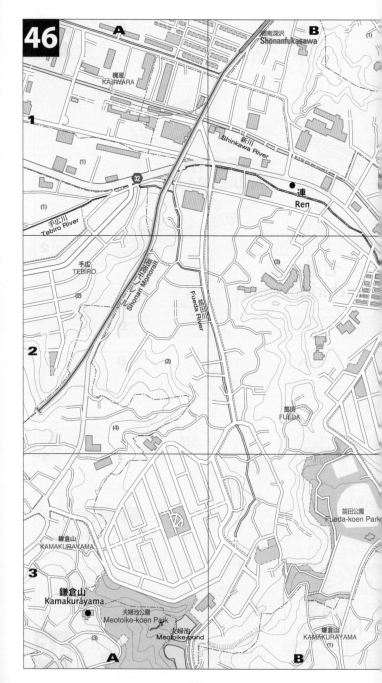

A

B

湘南深沢
Shonanfukasawa

(1)

梶原
KAJIWARA

1

新川
Shinkawa River

(1)

32

連
Ren

(1)

手広川
Tebiro River

(1)

手広
TEBIRO

(3)

(2)

湘南モノレール
Shonan Monorail

笛田川
Fueda River

2

(2)

(4)

笛田
FUEDA

笛田公園
Fueda-koen Park

鎌倉山
KAMAKURAYAMA

3

鎌倉山
Kamakurayama

夫婦池公園
Meotoike-koen Park

夫婦池
Meotoike-pond

鎌倉山
KAMAKURAYAMA

(3)

(1)

A

B

鎌倉中央公園
Kamakurachuo-koen Park
山崎
YAMASAKI

(3)

寺分
TERABUN

(3)

1

(1)

(2)

梶原
KAJIWARA

(4)

2

常盤
TOKIWA

鎌倉市
KAMAKURA-SHI

(4)

32

ミッシェル ナカジマ
Michel Nakajima

市役所通
Shiyakusho-dori

3

鎌倉山・常盤
Kamakurayama/Tokiwa

0　　　170m

(5)

大塚川
Otsukagawa River

(4)

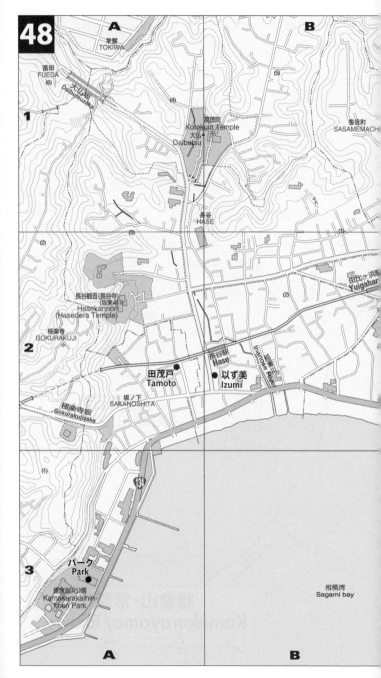

常盤
TOKIWA

A

B

笛田
FUEDA (6)

大仏坂
Daibutsuzaka

(5)

1

(4)

高徳院
Kotokuin Temple
大仏・
Daibutsu

番匠町
SASAMEMACH

長谷
HASE

(3)

(2)

(1)

(2)

2

長谷観音(長谷寺)
(坂東4)卍
Hasekannon
(Hasedera Temple)

田比ヶ浜駅
Yuigahar

極楽寺
GOKURAKUJI

(2)

長谷駅
Hase

稲瀬川
Inase River

田茂戸
Tamoto ●

● 以ず美
Izumi

極楽寺坂
Gokurakujizaka

坂ノ下
SAKANOSHITA

(1)

134

3

パーク
Park ●

鎌倉海浜公園
Kamakurakaihin-
koen Park

相模湾
Sagami bay

A

B

佐助
SASUKE
(1)

御成町
ONARIMACHI

鎌倉駅
Kamakura

小町
KOMACHI

小町大路
Komachioji

本覚寺
Hongakuji Temple

(1)

(1)

大町
OMACHI

御成通
Onari-dori

滑川(座禅川)
Nameri-gawa
Wakamiyaoji

滑川
Namerikawa River

311

横須賀線
Yokosuka Line

つるや
Tsuruya

和田塚駅
Wadazuka

江ノ島電鉄
Enoshima Railway

(2)

由比ガ浜
YUIGAHAMA

(2)

(1)

(3)

鎌倉市
KAMAKURA-SHI

2

(3)

(2)

鎌倉海浜公園
Kamakurakaihin-koen Park

(4)

(3)

由比ヶ浜
Yuigahama Beach

(5)

材木座
ZAIMOKUZA

梵蔵
Bonzo

(4)

134

3

(6)

由比ヶ浜
Yuigahama

0   220m

C

D

GLOSSARY

ainame : greenling
akami : red flesh fish
akaza ebi : Japanese lobster
akazu : red vinegar made from sake lees
ajiro : a woven or plaited wicker mat
amamiso : sweet miso
anago : conger eel
A-sai : a Chinese leafy green
awabi : abalone
ayu : sweetfish
bancha : Green tea harvested from the second flush of sencha
bincho : high-grade charcoal
bozushi : sushi pressed in a box rather than by hand
chakaiseki : tea ceremony cuisine
chameshi : rice cooked with tea
chanoyu : tea ceremony
chawanmushi : savoury egg custard
chazuke : rice with green tea poured over it
chiai : Fish flesh that is red with blood
chimaki-zushi : sushi wrapped in bamboo leaves
chirashi-zushi : a bowl of sushi rice with toppings
chirinabe : for fugu hotpot (boiled water with dried kelp where fugu is cooked
then eaten with ponzu sauce)
chu-toro : the moderately fatty, sweet flesh of tuna
daidai : an Asian variety of bitter orange
dashimaki tamago=dashimaki : soup stock-flavoured thick Japanese
omelette roll
dou ban jiang : broad bean chilli paste Chinese seasoning
ebi-imo : Kyoto yam
ebi-shinjo : shrimp dumplings
edomae : Tokyo-style
enseki ryori : banquet cuisine
eringi : king oyster mushrooms
fugu : puffer fish
fu ru : Chinese fermented tofu
goma-dofu : sesame tofu
gyunabe : beef hotpot
hanasansho : Japanese pepper flowers
hamo : pike conger
hamo zukushi : pike conger set meal
harakami : the upper belly of raw tuna
hassun : appetiser plate
honesenbei : deep-fried or dried fish bones
hinoki : Japanese cypress
hiryuzu : deep-fried tofu mixed with thinly sliced vegetables
horigotatsu-style : low seating at a covered table placed over a sunken
area in the floor
hotate-shinjo : scallop dumplings
ichiyaboshi : fish salted and dried overnight
ikebana : flower arrangement

itawasa : slices of white fish paste served with horseradish and soy sauce
izakaya : Japanese-style pub
jakomeshi : rice with dried fish-fry
junsai : watershield
juwari soba : 100% buckwheat noodles
kabayaki : eel broiled and basted with a sweet sauce
kabuki : Japanese classical theatre
kaiseki : traditional multi-course Japanese meal
kaiseki ryori : traditional multi-course Japanese meal
kaki soba : soba with oysters
kamoyaki : grilled duck
kamonasu : a Kyoto variety of eggplant
kanpo : Chinese herbal medicine
kanpyo : dried gourd strips
kappo : counter style restaurant serving traditional Japanese cuisine
kara-age : soy sauce-marinated fried meat, usually chicken
karasumi : salted and dried grey mullet roe
katsuo : bonito
katsuo-bushi : dried bonito flakes
kiku-zukuri : paper thin centre cuts arranged in the shape of a
            chrysanthemum accompanied by skin and tailfin centrepiece
kimono : traditional Japanese clothing
kinmedai : golden-eye snapper
kinome : young Japanese pepper leaves
kobujime : fish pressed between two sheets of kelp
koi-no-arai : carp sashimi served with a vinegar miso sauce
kombu : kelp
kombujime : fish pressed between two sheets of kelp
konnyaku : solidified jelly made from the rhizome of devil's tongue
koto-negi : a variety of green onion
kudzu : a type of vine
kuroge wagyu : a breed of cattle called Japanese Black
kuromitsu : brown sugar syrup
kushikatsu : Japanese-style deep-fried kebab
kuzukiri : kudzu starch noodles
Kyogen : a form of traditional Japanese theatre
kyo-ninjin : Kyoto carrot
Kyo-ryori : Kyoto cuisine
makiebi : small Japanese tiger prawn
manju : steamed yeast bun with filling
Mapo tofu : Sichuan-style bean curd
maruage-dofu : deep-fried tofu
masu : trout
matcha : powdered green tea
matsubagani : snow crab
matsutake : mushroom
megochi : big-eyed flathead
mirin : a type of sweet sake used in cooking
misansho : Japanese pepper made from immature seeds,
            giving it a stronger taste and smell
miso : soybean paste
mizore-nabu : hotpot with grated radish
mizudako : North Pacific giant octopus
mizunasu : a juicy eggplant (lit. 'water eggplant')
momiji oroshi : grated daikon radish and red chilli peppers
mukozuke : starter dish forming part of the kaiseki
myoga : Japanese ginger

nabe ryori : hotpot cuisine
nama-fu : wheat gluten
name-fu shigureni : wheat gluten and ginger marinated in sweet soy
sauce to be eaten with plain rice
nameko : a variety of mushroom
nanbanni : sweet and sour sauce
negima : dishes based on spring onions and tuna
nianago : simmered conger eel
nidako : simmered octopus
nigiri : sushi
nigari : bittern
nihachi soba : noodles made from 80% buckwheat and 20% flour
nihamaguri : simmered clams
nikiri : condensed soy sauce
nikogori : jellied fish or meat broth
nitsume : soy syrup
nodoguro : rosy sea perch
noh : traditional Japanese chanted drama
nuta : salad seasoned with vinegar and miso
oba : perilla leaf
ochazuke-style : cooking style in which green tea is poured over a rice dish
oden : various ingredients stewed in a thin soy soup
ohitashi : boiled Japanese greens
okara : bean curd lees
okimari : set meal
omakase : set menu with daily changing dishes
ontama soborodon : rice with hot spring eggs and minced meat
oshizushi : sushi rice and other ingredients pressed in a box or mould
o-toro : the more fatty, melt-in-the-mouth flesh of tuna
ponzu : Japanese sauce made primarily of soy sauce and citrus juice
ryori : cooking
ryotei : traditional Japanese restaurant
saimaki ebi : young Japanese tiger prawns
samatsu : mushroom that appears in the rainy season (around April to June)
before the start of the matsutake; aroma not as strong as the latter.
samue : monk's working clothes
samurai : warrior
sanma : Pacific saury
sansho : Japanese pepper
sashimi : sliced raw fish
satsuma age : a fried fish cake
sekihan : sticky rice steamed with azuki beans
seiro : basket used for steaming food
setoro : fatty back flesh of tuna
shabu-shabu : thinly sliced meat or vegetable boiled by dipping it in hot
kombu broth or water, and then in sauce
shamisen : three-stringed Japanese guitar
shiitake : mushroom
shiogamayaki : salt-baked fish or meat
shioyaki : salt-grilled fish or meat
shiraae : salad with mashed tofu dressing
shirako : milt
shirayaki : broiled unseasoned fillet
shiro tora-fugu : white tiger pufferfish
shochu : Japanese liquor similar to vodka
Shojin : Buddhist vegetarian (dishes)
shungiku : chrysanthemum garland

shuto : salted and fermented bonito gut
soba : buckwheat noodles
sobagaki : lumps made by adding hot water to buckwheat flour
sobayu : hot water in which soba has been boiled
somen : thin, white noodles made from wheat flour
sudachi : Japanese citrus fruit
sukiya : tea-ceremony room
sukiyaki : a hot pot dish with thin slices of beef and various vegetables,
        usually cooked at the table.
suppon : soft-shelled turtle
suppon-mushi : soft savoury egg custard
surinagashi : pureed soup made from various vegetables
tai : species of reddish-brown Pacific sea bream
tai-meshi : slices of raw sea bream over steaming hot rice
Tai-no matsukawa-zukuri : snapper 'pine bark' sashimi
takiawase : a medley of vegetables and fish, meat or tofu, simmered separately
takikomi-gohan : a rice dish seasoned with soy sauce and boiled
           with various ingredients
tamago-yaki : Japanese rolled omelette
tatami : Japanese straw floor coverings
teishoku : set meal
tempura : fish and vegetables deep-fried in a light batter
tencha : rice in a green tea broth with tempura
tendon : tempura served over a bowl of rice
tentsuyu : Japanese tempura dipping sauce
teppanyaki : cuisine prepared on a hot steel plate in the centre of the table
tofu-dengaku : tofu with sweet miso sauce
tonburi : a type of edible seed, sometimes called 'mountain caviar'
tonkatsu : pork cutlet
tora fugu : tiger pufferfish
torisashi : chicken sashimi
tsukeyaki : broiling with soy
tsukuri : decoratively arranged sashimi
udon : a type of thick wheat-flour noodle
umaki : Japanese style omelette with eel
ume : Japanese apricot
unagi : eel
unaju : broiled eel served over rice in a lacquered box
uni : sea urchin
usucha : thin tea
uzaku : eel and vegetables with vinegar sauce
wabi-sabi : a Japanese concept of finding beauty in the transient
warabimochi : bracken-starch dumpling
waridashi : seasoned stock
warishita : stock mixed with soy sauce, mirin and sugar
wasabi : Japanese horseradish
wasabi-yaki : chicken skewer with wasabi on top
watari-gani : blue crab
yakitori : chicken pieces grilled on a skewer
yoshoku : Western-influenced cooking
yuba : bean curd skin
yuzu : Japanese citrus fruit
zuke-maguro : soy marinated tuna
zarudofu-zaru tofu : tofu served on a bamboo draining basket
           with a dipping sauce on the side
zenmai : Japanese royal fern
zosui : risotto-like rice soup made from pre-cooked rice and water

PICTURE COPYRIGHT

Michelin, 64 – Aimée Vibert, 65 – Michelin, 66 – Michelin, 67 – Ànu retrourvez-vous, 69 – Aragawa, Michelin, 70 – Michelin, 71 – Argento Aso, Michelin, 72 – Michelin, 73 – Michelin, 74 – Michelin, 75 – Michelin, 76 – Michelin, 77 – Basara, Michelin, 78 – Beige Alain Ducasse, Michelin, 79 – Michelin, 80 – Michelin, 81 – Michelin, 82 – Chez Matsuo, 83 – Michelin, 84 – China Blue, 85 – Michelin, 86 – Chugoku Hanten Fureika, Michelin, 87 – Michelin, 88 – Cuisine[s] Michel Troisgros, 89 – Michelin, 90 – Michelin, 91 – Michelin, 92 – Michelin, 93 – Michelin, 94 – Michelin, 95 – Michelin, 96 – Faro, 97 – Florilège, Michelin, 98 – Michelin, 99 – Michelin, 100 – Fukudaya, Michelin, 101 – Michelin, 102 – Gordon Ramsay, 103 – Goriot, 104 – Grill Ukai, Michelin, 105 – Hamadaya, 106 – Michelin, 107 – Michelin, 108 – Michelin, 109 – Hei Fung Terrace, 110 – Hifumian, 111 – Michelin, 112 – Hiramatsu, 113 – Hiromichi, Michelin, 114 – Michelin, 115 – Hishinuma, Michelin, 116 – Michelin, 117 – Michelin, 118 – Michelin, 119 – Michelin, 120 – Michelin, 122 – Michelin, 123 – Michelin, 124 – Michelin, 125 – Iconic, 126 – Michelin, 127 – Michelin, 128 – Michelin, 130 – Michelin, 131 – Izumi, 132 – Joël Robuchon, 133 – Michelin, 134 – Michelin, 135 – Kamiya Nogizaka, 136 – Michelin, 137 – ANA Intercontinental, 139 – Michelin, 140 – Michelin, 141 – Michelin, 142 – Michelin, 143 – Michelin, 144 – Michelin, 145 – Michelin, 146 – Michelin, 147 – Michelin, 148 – Michelin, 149 – Kuikiri Eguchi, 150 – Michelin, 151 – Michelin, 152 – Michelin, 153 – Michelin, 154 – Michelin, 155 – La Table de Joël Robuchon, 156 – L'Atelier de Joël Robuchon, 157 – Michelin, 158 – La Tour d'Argent, 159 – Michelin, 160 – Michelin, 161 – Le Jeu de l'Assiette, Michelin, 162 – Michelin, 163 – L'Embellir, Michelin, 164 – Le Pergolèse, 165 – Les Créations de Narisawa, Michelin, 166 – Les Enfants Gâtés, Michelin, 167 – Le 6eme Sens d'Oenon, 168 – Les Saisons, 169 – Lugdunum Bouchon Lyonnais, 170 – Maison de Yulong, 171 – Maison Paul Bocuse, 172 – Michelin, 173 – Masa's Kitchen 47, 174 – Michelin, 175 – Michelin, 178 – Michelin, 179 – Michelin, 180 – Monnalisa Ebisu, Michelin, 181 – Monnalisa Marunouchi, 182 – Michelin, 184 – Muto, 185 – Nadaman Honten Sazanak-so, Michelin, 187 – Nagazumi, 188 – Nakajima, Michelin, 189 – Michelin, 190 – Nodaiwa, Michelin, 191 – Ogasawara Hakushaku-tei, 193 – Michelin, 194 – Michelin, 195 – Michelin, 196 – Pachon, 197 – Michelin, 198 – ANA Intercontinental, 199 – Michelin, 200 – Michelin, 201 – Ranjatai, 202 – Reikasai, Michelin, 203 – Michelin, 204 – Restaurant-I, 205 – Ristorante Aso, 206 – Michelin, 207 – Michelin, 208 – Michelin, 209 – Michelin, 210 – Ryuan, Michelin, 211 – Ryugin, 212 – Ryutenmon, 213 – Sakuragaoka, Michelin, 214 – Michelin, 215 – Michelin, 216 – Sangoan, 217 – Michelin, 218 – Sant Pau, 219 – Michelin, 220 – Michelin, 221 – Michelin, 222 – Seiju, Michelin, 223 – Seika Kobayashi, Michelin,

Manufacture française des pneumatiques Michelin
Société en commandite par actions au capital de 304 000 000 EUR
Place des Carmes-Déchaux – 63000 Clermont-Ferrand (France)
R.C.S. Clermont-Fd B 855 200 507

Made in Japan

Published in 2010

Although the information in this guide was believed by the authors
and publisher to be accurate and current at the time of publication,
they cannot accept responsibility for any inconvenience, loss, or
injury sustained by any person relying on information or advice
contained in this guide. Things change over time and travellers
should take steps to verify and confirm information, especially time
sensitive information related to prices, hours of operation, and
availability.

E-mail: nmt.michelinguide@jp.michelin.com
Maps: 2010 Cartographic data Shobunsha / Michelin
Publication design: Kan Akita & Akita Design Kan Inc. Tokyo, Japan

Pre-Press: Nord Compo, Villeneuve-d'Ascq, France
Printing and Binding: Toppan, Tokyo, Japan